Cultural Diversity and Social Discontent

Anthropological Studies on Contemporary India

R.S. Khare

Sage Publications
NEW DELHI • THOUSAND OAKS • LONDON

First published in 1998 by
Sage Publications India Pvt Ltd
M–32 Market, Greater Kailash–I
New Delhi–110 048

Sage Publications Inc
2455 Teller Road
Thousand Oaks, California 91320

Sage Publications Ltd
6 Bonhill Street
London EC2A 4PU

Published by Tejeshwar Singh for Sage Publications India Pvt Ltd, phototypeset by Line Arts, Pondicherry and printed at Chaman Enterprises, Delhi.

Library of Congress Cataloging-in-Publication Data
Khare, R.S. (Ravindra S.)
    Cultural diversity and social discontent: anthropological studies on contemporary India / R.S. Khare.
        p.   cm.   (cloth: alk. paper) (pbk.: alk.paper)
    Includes bibliographical references and index.
    1. Ethnology—India—Uttar Pradesh. 2. Uttar Pradesh (India)—Social conditions. 3. Ethnology—India. 4. India—Social conditions.
    I. Title.
    GN635.I4K48   306'.09542—dc21   1998   98–11303

ISBN: 0–7619–9250–2 (US-hb)   0–7619–9278–2 (US-pb)
       81–7036–707–7 (India-hb)   81–7036–737–9 (India-pb)

Sage Production Team: Jaya Chowdhury, N.K. Negi and Santosh Rawat

Cultural Diversity
and
Social Discontent

◄ India's 50th year of Independence ►

...sarvabhutahiteū ratāḥ

(The Gita, XII, 4)

pokhra khoday kavan phal, more sahab
ganvan piyey jura pani, tabai phal hoiyhain

(From an Avadhi folk song)

The self-hood of Indians is so capacious, so elastic, that it accommodates 1 billion kinds of difference.

(Salman Rushdie, *Time*, 11 August 1997, pp. 18–20).

Contents

Acknowledgments

At the center of this book stand the people I had the privilege to know and study during my several field trips in the Lucknow–Kanpur region in India, during the last 15 years. This was also the period when perhaps some of the most socially significant post-independence events occurred as caste disputes, regional politics, industrial disasters, religious nationalism and state power contended against one another. Simultaneously, anthropology engaged in a critical evaluation of its own dominant assumptions about the non-Western cultural other. All these strands intertwined as I started to work on the book in the spring of 1990, when I was a visiting fellow of the Commonwealth Center for Literary and Cultural Change at the University of Virginia. The four themes that increasingly claimed my attention over time were: daily lives of 'ordinary' Indians drawn from discordant castes and communities, the challenged (and challenging) contemporary Hindu world, the role of the modern Indian nation-state, and recent anthropological/sociological analyses of contemporary India. Between 1990 and 1997, my academic colleagues, students and friends in Charlottesville, and at the universities of London, Oxford, Toronto, Wisconsin–Madison, Uppsala (Sweden), Lucknow, Harvard, Delhi, Berlin, and Heidelberg heard me present aspects of the studies collected in this volume.

Complementing (and even superseding) my debts to professional colleagues are those that I accumulated as I studied the people of my own culture and cultural region in Uttar Pradesh for many years. I thus feel obligated to acknowledge them in appropriate Indian cultural terms. Foremost, I pay respect to those elders who, representing several major religious and caste groups, became, over time, my 'field guides' (even gurus), genuine critics, collaborators, skeptic observers, unhesitating helpers, and friends in the Lucknow–Kanpur region. If my firm anchor and intellectual challenger for various upper-caste Hindu issues was Pandit D.S. Misra and a cluster of residents at Khurshed Bagh in Lucknow, I also had the privilege of critical collaboration and discussion, during the 1990s, from several Dalit leaders, particularly Shri Chedi Lal Sathi, Shri Badlu Ram Rasik, Shri Darapuri and Shri Bhagwan Das (New Delhi). Included in this group are also my 'field assistants', who actively helped me by discussing issues and selecting sites of work. In this regard I am particularly indebted to Pradeep Kumar, Miss U. Bajpai, B. Prasad, and Miss Ratna for their support during the last several years. They maintained close contact with me as my long-term collaborators in the field. They veritably became my 'eyes' and 'ears' in absentia, responding to my numerous queries while also collecting documentary data and nurturing my old contacts and scouting out new ones.

The crucial role of this circle of collaborators remains incomplete and rootless until I also refer to that even more significant layer of 'ordinary' Indians, representing local religious and social diversity, who most often gave me their unreserved and sustained cooperation. Most others are recognized in my accounts by context. Although too many to list here individually, and while already contextually recognized in my accounts, I must record my special debt of gratitude to all these men and women (of different religions, castes, occupations, and economic positions) in the Indian way—by recognizing their relationship to me by age, gender, and self-image. To those older to me (whether men, women, upper castes or Dalits), I express my respectful gratitude for freely sharing their knowledge, learning, and life experiences, alongside personal concerns, anxieties, and self-doubts. Those of my age similarly earn my profound thanks as they generously contributed their time, effort, and criticism while organizing different 'discussion groups'. The younger ones, deferential yet forthright, helped me see the world from their location and viewpoint. In retrospect, I am particularly beholden to all these 'ordinary' people who, in life, showed how they try to maintain and convey their *sense of moral and social balance* under conflict and discord. These people also showed how they normally, often without an explicit idea of nationalism, try to view themselves in local, regional and the larger—Indian—terms.

My many urban Brahman and Dalit discussants, thus, showed much more than a simple polarization, alienation and antagonism. They moved, depending on the context, all over the spectrum of cultural consensus and conflict, and they spurned any simple high and low, center and periphery, or dominant and dependent pigeon holes. To do so today also makes good practical and political sense to both sides. But how this really happens is best shown, as we see in the book, around concrete life situations on the one hand, and in the way 'facts', 'data', 'people', 'history', 'religious faith', and social conflict and discontent are *contextually* interrelated and approached, on the other. This underlying practical and cultural sensibility is ethnographically precious to capture, since it perhaps best shows those elusive yet vital (and often sociologically underreported) 'connecting switches' and cultural sensibilities that still shape pan-Indian culture and communication. But such discussions would have been impossible in the field without an open, keen, and honest discussion by upper castes and Dalits themselves, including their certainties, claims, self-doubts, and sorrows.

My 'field community' thus figures in my acknowledgments in yet another way. It grapples with the perpetually unfinished issue of 'unity-in-diversity', especially as India celebrates its 50th anniversary of independence. For, in a critical scholarly view, the overall contemporary Indian picture cannot but reflect increasing cultural waywardness, social discord and discontent, and political instability. Though traditionally age-old, India still remains unsure of itself in many ways, popularly evoking a sense of accomplishment in some areas and concern in many others. This continuing profile and quandary of Indian culture, religion, history, and philosophy prompts (and amply justifies) the book's dedication at the end of this century.

My acknowledgments to specific professional colleagues, friends, and students must open with that obligatory caveat: While

I appreciate the generous comments and suggestions of all those mentioned below (and even those inadvertently omitted), including the anonymous sparing reader. I alone am solely responsible for all the material presented between these covers.

Chapter 1 gained from the comments of the late Richard Burghart, along with those of Professors Karl Potter, Audrey Cantlie, Adrian Mayer, David Parkin, T.N. Madan, N.J. Allen, and the late Edwin Ardener. Chapter 2 was written (and subsequently updated) for the M.N. Srinivas festschrift volume, essentially as a result of my seminars on contemporary anthropological theory at the University of Virginia. Written at the invitation of *Reviews in Anthropology*, Chapter 3 could not have been completed without library and word-processing help from two research assistants at the time, Raphael Alvarado and Bruce Koplin. Chapter 4 was the product of a seminar series on 'Cultural Distance', sponsored by the Commonwealth Center in spring 1990, and it received helpful comments during the seminar from Professors Wendy Doniger, Ashis Nandy, Anthony Easthope, Stephen Bann, and Steven Lukes. Besides Virginia Commonwealth Center's seminar series on 'Remembering and Forgetting' (for Chapter 5), the second part of the book owes most to an international conference on law, justice, and human rights, sponsored by the University of London (Chapter 6), and to the Wissenschaftskolleg (Introduction and Chapters 7 and 8).

While writing, updating, expanding or revising various chapters of this book, I gratefully acknowledge the award of a sesquicentennial research associateship (1993) of the Center for Advanced Studies, University of Virginia; a short-term senior fellowship (1993) of American Institute of Indian Studies; a field research grant (summer 1996) from the Dean, Faculty of Arts and Sciences, University of Virginia; and a fellowship (1996–97) of the Wissenschaftskolleg zu Berlin. I am particularly thankful to Professor Ralph Cohen and Professor Wolf Lepenies, for I could not have opted for a more congenial surrounding for either starting or finishing the volume. While preparing the typescript for publication, I had much needed help from the Bibliothek and Fellow-Sekretariat of the Wissenschaftskolleg. Ms Gesine Bottomley and her efficient staff located or rechecked references on a short notice. Under Ms Christine Arnim's expert coordination, Mitch Cohen read the typescript and Elissa Linke carefully worked through several drafts on the computer (with expert help from Doris Reichel) to produce the final version.

The following sources are acknowledged for giving me permission to republish my articles: for Chapter 1, *Contributions to Indian Sociology* (n.s.) 24: 177–99, 1990; for Chapter 2, *Theory and Method: An Evaluation of the Work of M.N. Srinivas*, edited by A.M. Shah, B.S. Baviskar and E.A. Ramaswamy, pp. 55–78, Sage Publications, New Delhi; for a slightly revised Chapter 3, *Reviews in Anthropology* (in press), Gordon and Breach Publications, Lausanne, Switzerland; for corrected Chapters 4 and 5, *New Literary History: A Journal of Theory and Interpretation*, 23: 1–23, 1992 and 26: 147–68, 1995; and for the expanded and revised Chapter 6, *Changing Concepts of Rights and Justice in India*, edited by Michael Anderson and Sumit Guha, Oxford University Press, Delhi.

Introduction:
Cultural Diversity, Discontent,
and Anthropology

The ruling order, whatever it may be, is repressive: it is the order of domination. Social criticism frequently takes the form of a joke aimed at the ped-
antry of the educated and the ridiculous results of 'good upbringing'. It is an
implicit—and at times explicit—tribute to the wisdom of the ignorant.

Octavio Paz (1982: 19)

I India's Multiplying Others and Anthropology

India, a land of enormous cultural diversity and of the dominant
and the oppressed, continues to test the naiveté of anthropology.[1]
If anthropology studied Indian castes, villages and traditional culture in descriptive, taxonomic and structural–functional terms
during most of this century, then the discipline has recently given
more attention to social conflicts and their cultural consequences,
with more studies of the socially marginal, the contested dominant, and the confronted state. The challenges for anthropology
increase as Indian social reality changes, especially when cultural
certainties are questioned and self-asserting oppressed groups
and violent religious politics unsettle long-standing Indian caste

and customary traditions, on the one hand, and the forces of 'law and order' in the modern state, on the other.

Within such inquiries, contemporary India, historical change, and anthropology face one another, commenting as much on each other as each on their own identity problems. As India presents a complicated cultural otherness to anthropology and history, these modern disciplines, with their distinct modern assumptions and discourse viewpoints, in turn, present otherness to India. To recognize such a cultural dialectic in contemporary India is not only unavoidable, it is also a sound research strategy for developing a fair, interdependent discursive practice. Anthropology already shows such a movement by successively redefining its subject matter in ways that would bring it closer to the world of the people studied, while explicating some implicit assumptions of its own discourse.

Not restricted to proposing parsimonious scientific typologies, holistic functional descriptions, or grand theories for an ordered, certain social reality, anthropologists now seek understanding of a people and culture by pursuing them 'as they are', as they and the anthropologist establish their collaboration under mutual trust and responsibility. Any 'thick' interpretation is thus a product of such responsible collaboration, often reflecting people's (and the anthropologist's) imperfect, conflicted and contested social reality. The descriptions, 'structures', and meanings concern more than symmetrical aesthetic or literary elegance; they concern 'the way things really are' for the people, including counter-meanings. The discipline has indeed moved slowly but surely in such a direction, as even a cursory look at some representative books over time may show.[2] Given global human sharing, anthropology cannot objectivize the people it studies any more. Here its best renewable resources are found in intensive fieldwork and ethnography. They are crucial since they best expose the people's and the ethnographer's worlds in all their strengths as well as weaknesses, uncertainties, dilemmas, and unresolved 'loose ends'.[3]

Ethnography and ethnographers have always retained a higher profile in anthropological research in India for describing and conceptualizing cultural ideas and social processes and explanations during this century. Attention to narratives, dialogues, and human experiences only strengthen their role. They seem to have increasingly better captured Indian society and its culture in their diversity, social texture and openness, in the place of an acquired (and constraining) theoretical stance, terminology and taste. Such a locus also helps keep that general India–West discourse axis generally toned down. As an individual scholar, perhaps Professor M.N. Srinivas has most consistently maintained, over the decades, a well-nuanced ethnographic stance on Indian society and culture. Controlled, understated and observant of what socially endured (and what did not), he characterized the continuing as well as emerging social directions in Indian society, and in sociological studies (on the latter, see Srinivas and Panini 1973; see also Chapter 2).[4] Most recently, he (Srinivas 1996: xi) remarked,

> It is my plea that the movement from studying one's own culture or a niche in it, to studying oneself as an ethnographic field, is a natural one.... 'Sociology of Self' should be a rich field given the diversities and unities which the members of Indian civilization, are heirs to.[5]

My exercises in this book concern an anthropology of contemporary India in the midst of some crucial social changes and in the presence of the quotidian Indian. With the help of interrelated ethnographic research on widely different social groups and their experiences, mostly in Lucknow, a north Indian city, and against the background of a review of some recent anthropological approaches, debates and issues, I explore a series of interdependent issues that the cultural otherness among Indians today produces from within. The issues I focus on center around status and gender inequalities, social violence and suffering, injustice and human rights, and new challenges to Hindu cultural reasoning.

In sociological terms, such multiple Indian others appear within a network of unresolved religious tensions, moral dilemmas, social conflicts and political control and exploitation. They generate and support that distinctly inward-growing (or involuted) cultural otherness that gives today's India a distinct cultural and historical profile. In practice, Indians (i.e., Hindus and all others) in such a self-alienating ethos begin to find even those near and familiar, a little strange. 'We do not know today who to believe. Even our own children sometimes look so unfamiliar.' This was repeatedly the comment of my urban, educated informants, men and women. They thought that the reason for such a condition was selfish competition and conflict for the same practical goals in life (education, work, money, and a secure family). 'Even those close sometimes exude otherness [*parayapan* in Hindi].'[6] And accordingly, they must also be always ready to draw a line ever more clearly around the 'self', 'ours' (*apne*), and 'all the others' (*ajnabi* or *paraye*). Under such thinking, besides hierarchical ranking, various social and psychological borders, fences, boundaries, screens, and 'walls' multiply, and these become more prominent in role and meaning in everyday life. These in turn increase the potential of more conflicts within and between individual persons and communities. Religious traditions either dilute or become rigid to avoid losing uncontested authority, while the modern liberal state seldom delivers as much as it promises. Exposing each other's weaknesses, the two sides confront and conflict, while also seeking compromise if the context is appropriate.

Yet the conflicts alone would give only a one-sided picture of a country like India if the countervailing cultural forces are left out. These concern the ordinary Indian's instinctive tendency to relate the existence of human physical, cultural, and religious diversity at both local and cosmic levels. Those educated, detect here the shaping by some of those inclusive and continuing forces of Indian culture and civilization. Some among them elaborated the ways the civilization secured continuity by 'adapting', 'neutralizing with worship', 'assimilating', or 'ignoring' the opposed or threatening forces. Such a cultural strategy, as my ethnography repeatedly corroborated, is part of people's practical cultural sensibility. They employ it to avoid seeing either too much or too little in power conflicts and resistance (for an initial echo, see Brown 1996: 729–35). Ordinary rural and urban Indians (often called the 'Indian masses'), whose sole interest is daily survival, thus muster a major consensual social presence against extremes and extremists.[7]

Still, however, Indian social conflicts cannot be wished away. The forces of conflict repeatedly seem poised for an ever bigger, more violent showdown. Thus the recent major religious conflicts centered on Sikh extremism, the Amritsar temple assault (1984), and the Ayodhya temple–mosque dispute (1992) should be sufficient to convey how, on any major issue, social divisions, political polarization and religious nationalism line up in India, on the one hand, and how cultural ambiguities, exploitative politics, broken social trust, and moral dilemmas further complicate conflict resolution, on the other. The residual grievance from earlier events often remains a part of people's memory until a similar event occurs once again. Actually, as the tempo of social conflicts accelerates, so does the pace of an Indian's 'temporization' (i.e., mainly equivocation or *tāl-matol* and indecision or *asmanjas*), essentially as a common adaptive social strategy.[8]

The preceding conceptual, evaluative and pragmatic issues variously concern the exercises of this book. Unquestionably, India increasingly reflects—and anthropology correspondingly tries to address—cultural diversity, conflict, and discontent. Thus, in Part I, the four essays situate anthropology as a discipline deeply engaged in and shaped by the diversifying self–other cultural dialectic. India is seen as a land of many castes, religious communities, and politico-economic interests. The locational issues of Indian anthropology and anthropologists are a part of this cultural condition, and it has been a recognized part of disciplinary history, method, writing, and discursive practices in India. But without making it into a full-fledged issue of (or for) 'native' anthropology or the 'native' anthropologist, Indian discussions, as we will discuss later on, have raised the question of how (and how far) the discipline accounts for the practitioner's cultural background, knowledge, and sensibilities.[9] An anthropologist's work and writing reflect his/her identity and cultural placement, maintaining a tension between the discipline's 'local' and 'global' face (Chapter 4). India's diversity and anthropologists' locations are also variously evident as an explicit or implicit thread in the major contributions of the three scholars—M.N. Srinivas, Louis Dumont and McKim Marriott—discussed in the first part of the book.[10]

Part II carries four exercises on contemporary Indians' approaches to increasing social divisions, conflicts, ambiguities, and cultural interpretations. The studies conceptually and ethnographically interrelate the local and the regional to the national. Employing ethnography as a narrative and a writing and discursive strategy, each attempt discusses a specific group of people and/or current social problems, cases or commentaries in order to analyze a distinct social consequence of Indian conflicts. Urban Untouchable women from Lucknow are the concern of the first two attempts, enabling me to see what—and where—they are as women and as Untouchables, and what they are trying to struggle against and achieve. And as all this is recounted, we also get a glimpse of the struggles of a 'historicizing' India, going on at their own selective yet relentless pace. Here, an ethnographer attempts to capture people's experiences and expressions as closely as possible. Neither patronizing, nor apologetic, nor merely a politically correct gesture from a caste Hindu,[11] these exercises try to present them from up close in everyday life and living.

Thus, Chapter 5 shows how personal and social memories, body, sensoria, and self-worth struggle to recompose the Untouchable woman's self for 'a life with self-respect and honor'. Chapter 6 completes the theme as these women strive hard to attain social justice for themselves and their families, from their own men, the community, and the wider society. While the notions of social justice remain bound up with karma and dharma and an unfailing notion of 'divine justice', these women actively seek social justice and fair play every day, either as a matter of daily survival or of new social assertion.

Chapters 7 and 8 discuss Indian social divisiveness and conflicts in two distinct but related social contexts. The first concerns the cultural politics of increasing social violence and 'violence narratives', and the second is about the new moral, cultural, and practical challenges the Dalit, Muslim and modern formulations pose to what I have called 'Hindu cultural reasoning'. If the first exercise (Chapter 7) on 'violence narratives' shows the role the cultural politics of diverse Indian traditions and the modern state today play in worsening gender and communal violence, then the other traces its social consequences further as the minority ideologies and their politics challenge the dominant Hindu reasoning, and as the Hindu, Dalit and Muslim positions betray increasing social mistrust toward one another.

This is related in some ways to the current debate among the political scientists working on the 'governability issue' in India, with a focus on the governing institutions and the elite (Kohli 1990). As Rajni Kothari also recently remarked, here however, the crucial missing piece might still be 'a polity that is socially sensitive and representative to the changing demands from the grassroots...' (Kothari 1996: 4–5). An anthropologist might add to this remark that such a polity means sensitizing the governing institutions and elites to read continually—and correctly—the changing 'pulse' of Indian people along cultural regions and localities. The earlier major leaders did so during the freedom movement. M.K. Gandhi, for instance, observed what a local ethnography still upholds: 'The masses are by no means so foolish, or unintelligent as we sometimes imagine … [and] disastrous results can easily follow a bad, hasty, or what is worse, a selfish lead' (quoted in Bondurant 1971: 171). Jawaharlal Nehru's comment illuminated another side of the same social reality: '[Philosophy as religion] gave them some sense of purpose, and cause and effect, and endowed them with courage to face trial and misfortune and not lose their gaiety and composure' (Nehru 1946: 73–74).[12]

Relatedly, the challenge facing anthropology is to situate and explicate contemporary Indians as more than caste members, since they socially strive in increasingly diverse social, economic and political domains, interrelating multiple local, regional and national issues, interest groups and their networks. We need to know how, for instance, they, as persons, critics and political constituents, locally negotiate and represent such major national or regional issues as the recent Sikh radicalism, Dalit political solidarity, Muslim minority cultural politics, the Ayodhya conflict, and the post-Mandal rise of the Hindu right.[13] At such junctures, ordinary Indians employ some enduring cultural conceptions as operative frames and practical templates for coping with changes and conflicts. As they do so, they also convey what civilization, nation and history mean to them in idea and everyday life. They become vital 'talking' and reference points, where even those who seriously differ find a way to express their discontent and viewpoint.

While I do not regard the cultural resilience of ordinary Indian masses somehow either beyond all historical strife or mysteriously limitless, it is nevertheless a sociological fact, evident in people's mental and pragmatic disposition. Most importantly, it includes a cultural way to look at the issues of power conflicts and social consensus in perspective. In civilizational terms, it is about the Indians' ability to live life with—and without—a Gramsci, a Foucault, a Habermas; and it is about seeing both the range as well as the limits of cultural assimilation.[14] But this still largely unmapped aspect of the ordinary Indian majority must become crucial as Indians entangle themselves more in their own involuted otherness.

II Operating Cultural Frames, Divergence and Practical Templates

Indians display distinct ways by which they, as my Lucknow informants and discussants would say,

> entangle—and disentangle—ourselves when matters of mine-and-thine [apna-paraya] are concerned. When faced with adversity, opposition, or major conflicts, we recognize location, the time [samay or vaqt], and the way this world [duniya] now is. We have to watch where the country is going, and what the rulers and government do. We cannot survive today without such a compass [qutubnuma].

In contemporary India, one could sociologically argue (and ethnographically verify) that most Indians find their cultural 'otherness' and its conflicts often keyed to a practically effective use of such widely recognized cultural conceptions or frames as samay or vaqt (time/s), duniya (world), desh (locality, region, country), and sarkar (ruler, government, provider).[15] Indians (Hindus and non-Hindus) variously employ these to find their bearing within today's society. General and specific, and moving and multivocal, these markers situationally rearrange themselves to help most Indians measure social nearness, distance, opposition, enmity, and estrangement. These concepts, at once popular and reflexive, also connect religious and traditional life with the practical, conflicted, and political. The notions of desh and sarkar are as striking markers of interrelationships of domination and power over time and circumstance as samay or vaqt and duniya are for explicating moral, religious, and practical social constraints, commentary, and criticism.

In contemporary India, this framework of local/global cultural knowledge remains, however, incomplete until complemented by that of practical reasoning, social conflicts and competitive action. Only the two together forge an adequate basis not only 'for facing one's life and its times', but also for recognizing how the samay (social circumstances), desh (locality–region–nation) and sarkars (governments and/or people in power) today bring about significant (and sometimes traumatizing) change for people and community. Under such conditions, localities, regions, and the nation (all variations of *desh*) become issues of major discussion (or dispute) by need, event or circumstance. When people's experiences fall short, speculation, gossip, and imagination fill in to comprehend whatever is happening to the world. The people realize that *sarkars* (governments) and the *desh* (nation) are integral to this new world. And since these would not go away, they must forge a viable practical outlook. The older generation, for instance, may tend to view the *samay–desh–duniya* matters in more moral terms and with self-inspection (and for social honor) than the younger generation, facing social competition and political contest for a better life.

For example, during the open field discussions in the summer of 1993, in Lucknow, a Hindi–Urdu speaking region, Hindus, Muslims, Sikhs, and Dalits routinely employed a cluster of popular expressions to convey a variety of messages and meanings among themselves. I give here only two sets to illustrate the moral and practical underpinning they give to the contemporary Indian's organization and measure of cultural estrangement. One cluster concerns moral issues and the related social world of kinship, lineage, and caste rank, while the other deals with personal effort and achievement. The themes stressed in the first cluster were: (*a*) to remain karma-based while living in a conflicted *vaqt* or time and unreliable *duniya* or world: *apna boya, aap katna* or *apni karni, apni bharni*; (*b*) to watch for one's own honor and insult or gain and loss: *apna uncha-nicha aap dekhna*; and (*c*) to distinguish and protect one's 'own blood': *apna khun* versus *paraya khun, apna-apna, paraya-paraya*, epitomizing the essential principles of social closeness, caste hierarchy and otherness. While facing the practical world of competitive effort, *sarkar*, and economic betterment, some frequent usages were: (*a*) to become economically justly rewarded and independent: *apne pairon par khara hona*; (*b*) to succeed in today's world by being an opportunist, even selfish: *apna ullu sidha karna* or *apna ghar bharna*; (*c*) to indulge in self-promotion and self-praise: *apne muh miyan mittho banna* or *apni toonti aap bajana*; and (*d*) to fight for one's own rights: *apne haq ke liye larna*.

The ordinary Indians engage so routinely in these social exercises to interrelate their moral, practical and political worlds that one tends to overlook the crucial role they play in forging new conceptual and social relations across a wide variety of events, practical struggles, and experiences. Their mine–thine (*mera aur tera*) web, most Indians insist, is also at the heart of the contemporary society, but only in a much more socially aggravated form. It is the veritable prism which reflects (and refracts) numerous gradations of social status, power, and authority and privilege, especially as different communities (Hindu, Sikh, Dalit, Muslim, etc.) claim or dispute legal, economic, political, and religious entitlements.

Here appears immediately the *sarkar* (government) in all its complicated ways of determining who is who, and who shall receive social and economic help. Under such conditions, words and phrases like 'Hindus', 'non-Hindus', 'Hindus and others', or 'Hindu Indians', 'Muslim Indians', 'Dalit Indians', 'ordinary Indians', and 'the Indian', among others, also raise a plethora of serious 'mine–thine' political, historical, religious, caste-hegemonic, and 'national issues'.[16] If these remind to Dalits 'accumulated injustice', then to the Hindu right they are 'social disorder'. Politically, therefore, such demarcations are increasingly more serious now than the largely esoteric and harmless definitional quandaries of an Indologist, a philologist, an ancient Indian historian, or a structural anthropologist used to treating India 'in essence' and 'in totality'.[17]

Throughout this century, similarly, the meanings of such words as 'Indians', 'Hindu', and 'Hindutva' have kept changing. To get a sense of this, one must view the changing reform and protest positions. M.K. Gandhi, as a national reformer, for example, was found exhorting in 1930 that, despite the diverse orthodox religious faiths in India, 'we must be in the Congress Indians first and Indians last' (quoted in Bondurant 1971: 152). Dr B.R. Ambedkar similarly remarked in 1927 that Hindutva belonged 'as much to the untouchable Hindus as to the touchable Hindus. To the growth and glory of this Hindutva, contributions had been made by Untouchables....' (quoted in Keer 1971: 96).[18] During the 1990s, however, 'Hindutva' attracts meanings of upper-caste Hindu religious nationalism (even of fascism for some), while the modern secular left stands at the opposite end. Yet the basic issue of India being the land of both Hindu and non-Hindu communities gets enshrined in the Indian Constitution's opening declaration: 'India, that is, Bharat'.[19]

Thus, beyond academic debate, 'Hindu', and 'Indian', 'Hindustan', 'Bharat', and 'India' today constitute a complex arena of national cultural politics, where religion and modern secularism enter into direct or indirect conflicts and encourage Indians to identify themselves as ethnic or religious communities for a different reason than the government's caste reservation policies. The 'Hindu' and 'non-Hindu' issue is ethnographically unavoidable for this study, since it concerns widely different (including both Brahman and Untouchable) castes, communities and local leaders engaged in politically reidentifying one another in Lucknow, the capital of India's most populous and a political bellwether state, Uttar Pradesh. Overall, the prevailing local cultural politics recognizes that: (*a*) words like 'Hindu thinking' and 'Hindu', 'non-Hindu', and 'Indian' are slowly becoming more politically differentiated by context, but still 'being an Indian' quickly reappears in a shared and resilient cultural sense when the matters of nation and nationalism appear; (*b*) various Hindu, Dalit, and Muslim conflicts in identity and politics reassert themselves during episodes of communal violence, near or distant; and (*c*) those marginal and oppressed (e.g., women and Dalit) now constitute an increasingly persistent moral and political voice demanding social justice and even sharing political power.

Given such a contested situation, I must unequivocally state that my usage of words and phrases like 'Hindu', 'non-Hindu', or 'Hindu and others' is purely nonpolitical. Unless the context specifies some other sense, they are anthropologically descriptive, culturally comparative or civilizationally interpretive markers for me. 'Hindu' is both a sociologically descriptive and analytical category for me, evoking social facts as well as widely-shared contents of cultural knowledge shaped by historical forces, social memory and people's practical sense and commonsense.[20] But when treated as a community and a religion, 'Hindu' is only one of the several groups that comprise India as a contemporary society and a modern nation-state.[21]

With especially strong political currents and sensitivities after the Ayodhya violence, 'Hindu' and 'Muslim' stand for clearly opposed extremes for many in Lucknow. Historically, some argue, the two communities are known to produce confrontational ideological extremes. Thus, if 'Hindu communalism', 'Hindu nationalism' (*Hindu rashtra*), 'Hindu chauvinism', and 'Hindutva' these days quickly flag one extreme, rendering any and all common uses of 'Hindu' intellectually suspect, then the issues and images of 'Islamic fundamentalism', 'revivalism', 'violent extremism', and 'the holy war or *jihad*' are pointed out for the other side.[22] Most everyday religious and social differences, however, still remain outside such extreme positions, and these are the ones (excepting the 1991–92 Ayodhya conflict period) that I observed during my ethnographic fieldwork in Lucknow.

But I had to learn by the late 1970s that some Dalits had to be explicitly asked whether they considered themselves Hindu, Buddhist, or non-Hindu. Whenever I assumed their self-placement, they corrected me, pointing out my naiveté or outdatedness. However, many wanted to remain ambiguous; they sometimes called themselves Hindu and sometimes not.[23] For an ethnographer it was crucial to see (*a*) whether one's political rhetoric and life practices corroborated each other or not, and (*b*) how the informants interpreted such a difference, whether as an act of political *and* social defiance or not. My field notes on Untouchables in Lucknow, accumulated ever since the late 1970s, clearly show their slow (and initially imitative) but sustained effort to distinguish themselves first from Brahmans and later on from all upper-caste Hindus. Similarly, my field visits to Lucknow from the 1970s to the 1990s recorded the increasing political sensitivities among upper-caste Hindus when lower castes and Untouchables were considered. While the term 'Hindu' and 'Indian' remained largely coterminous for upper castes (but with new nationalist commentaries) during the period,[24] Dalit activists and reformists vociferously objected to such assumptions even during the 1970s.

A Lucknow publication, *Dalit Asia Today* (1994), makes further distinctions during the 1990s, arguing that Dalits find their opponents particularly among the Aryans, Brahmans, the twice-born caste Hindus, and caste Hindus. But they also comment on increasing religious and political divisions within their own communities, including Dalit Panthers, neo-Buddhists, Ambedkarite Buddhists, and 'the Dalits forgotten by the Dalit elite'.[25]

To get an idea of the overall social picture of contemporary India, one must multiply such a mosaic of local and regional cultural otherness many times over, within and across the different Indian states and administrative zones. Viewed sociologically, such multi-layered differences, as well as conflicts, serve not only distinct social functions and meanings but they also produce a distinct commentary on the Indian view of social unity and divisions. Thus, some of the social functions of cultural otherness evident among the Dalits in Lucknow were (*a*) to sort out central and peripheral 'mine–thine' differences in social and political terms around major conflicts and political stakes; (*b*) to drop or 'cancel out' the less significant social differences and revive/revise/create those now politically more potent (e.g., the current Dalit movement approaches earlier reformers like Jotiba Phule and other earlier regional reformers in addition to Dr Ambedkar); and (*c*) to seek to magnify social differences from the Hindu majority to help produce greater 'internal' unity and collective social action.

However, while reviewing the disciplinary position of sociology and anthropology vis-à-vis such increasingly involuted Indian cultural otherness, one might argue that as long as the widely different castes and communities continue, despite increasing conflicts, to live their lives with customary and practically expedient social sharing across localities and regions, these disciplines have a socially factual basis for approaching India as a whole, and there is no reason for separate Hindu, Islamic, Sikh or Dalit sociology or 'ethnosociology' to emerge. Of course, one could anthropologically study and explicate the culturally distinct conceptual ideas, assumptions, reasoning patterns, formulations, experiences, and expressions of any of the constituent knowledge systems of India on their own or on comparative grounds.

Let us see how some recent disciplinary discussions and their quandaries relate to the diversifying flux of social forces released by contemporary India.

III Disciplinary Issues and the Anthropologist's Quandaries

Once placed within the disciplinary practices and its evolving discourse, Indian society and culture immediately pose the questions of distinct social events, agents, experiences, and expressions across a wide social time and space. The questions concern what—and how—India recognizes such issues and their interrelationships and what theoretical formulations, relations, and expressions anthropology affords. As a first step, it means explicating the

ways in which events, experiences, and narratives interrelate
across the hidden Indian cognitive, cultural, and social processes,
enabling us to map how, for instance, one group links up locally
with another, and one locality to another until districts, states, and
regions ultimately sketch a sense of the national. And how does
the reverse occur? While other studies have sought to recognize
such interrelationships either by interlinking 'social structures'
(Fuller 1992), or, as with Veena Das (1995: 201), through 're-
narrativization as a means of establishing the continuity of time',
I employ ethnography as a crucial methodological template to
create a dialogue between anthropology and Indian reasoning,
experiences, and expressions across social groups and their time
and space. In my attempt, anthropology first pursues the people's
interlinking conceptual spaces, relations, experiences, and expressions in the background of their own perspectives. It is only
when they seem to exhaust, I conceptualize about some culturally
probable next steps, models, templates, etc. Here ethnography
particularly helps unearth how ordinary people go about interrelating time, events, actors, and space in their way by employing
various devices of communication (including protest, conflict and
violence) at their disposal. Given the major influence of the modern media and ever-expanding modes of electronic communication (from local language newspapers and magazines to domestic
radio and satellite television in even shanties and slums), people
depend on much more than face-to-face contact and 'the message
of the local knowledgeable elder'. Their occasional, informal
'neighborhood conclaves' (*mohalle ki baithak*), and stray gossip
and rumor circuits in a city like Lucknow keep the social and political interest high, churning up new linkages in practical knowledge and ideas as people constantly hear, learn, tell, narrate,
memorize, and retell. Selective reception, routine expressions,
personal biases, and incomplete narration are as integral to these
attempts as are the people's recognition of changing (expanding
or deleting) social networks over time and space. They show
spontaneous creativity, imagination, and 'new' or 'counter-
memories' to cope with the changing world (*badalti duniya*).

To problematize ethnography this way is to locate how people,
as necessary, create empirically supportable interrelations across
time and space among diverse events, agents, experiences, and
accounts. Here also appear the roles of the so-called 'vernacular'

and regional Indian narratives and explanations vis-à-vis national debates and commentaries. Moreover, such accounts make us move closer to everyday Indian society and culture, showing a changing dynamics between the socially dominant, the temporizing cultural middle, and the marginal yet protesting cultural other. An ethnography also helps reveal how people themselves either follow some existing or create new interrelationships, including changing accountability patterns and political meanings among local, regional and national events and their explanations. This way we arrive at a 'thick' cultural description that does not hide people's social conflicts, struggles and doubts, enabling anthropology to relate directly not only to the real everyday world of the people studied, but also to some of its own conceptual, moral and professional quandaries within globalizing forces. Anthropological examples of responsible work and writing get continuously debated, including the earlier accepted views of literary aestheticism and 'scholarly authority' (for two recent perspectives but guided by different scholarly locations, see Geertz 1994; Sahlins 1995).

But the question 'how' anthropology might study an India entangled in its own cultural otherness is related to certain problems in anthropological discourse. Some concern the discipline as a whole while others might be specific to the Indian situation. As in other parts of the world, anthropology and anthropologists, while working in/on India, develop a healthy tension between their Indian findings and global disciplinary debates and perspectives. India, by its sheer population and spatial size, and cultural complexity, historical past, and unresolved conflicts, orchestrates massive social forces both in and against its institutions, offering anthropology a vast ground for new research initiatives and vigorous cultural criticism. Actually, India and anthropology, as earlier leading anthropologists sensed, engage one another in evermore challenging ways.[26] Given the institutionalized teaching, research and professionalization of anthropology/sociology in India during most of this century, the discipline's perspective is increasingly a part of the modern Indian intellectual milieu.

But recent Indian developments make more demands on and raise more issues for anthropology. It must view from up close the institutionalized *and* 'fluid' social conditions, and juxtapose the culturally certain to the uncertain. It must explicate people's moral, political, and practical dilemmas as well. Anthropology must yield not only scholarly but also socially responsible and *just* representations of the people's conditions and concerns under study. If these criteria pull anthropologists toward moral and political value issues, there is increasingly little chance of ignoring them, since the people in India, as elsewhere, today seldom stand socially uninvolved and passive just to remain 'ideal subjects' for anthropological studies. Actually, except in anthropological imagination, they seldom are that way in life. A search only for 'law-like social regularities' for producing 'the authoritative account' is already little more than a romantic anthropological fantasy of a bygone era.

India is currently, as in the past, a battleground of refutation and rejection of assumed traditional regularities. Even customs, over time, test their strengths and they modify or decline in power and influence. Contemporary India betrays contextually eroding or strengthening spheres of diverse Indian traditions where strong interest politics encounters weak and fragmentary 'public culture' and ad hoc state power is surrounded by fragmented, disjointed and uneven forces of modernity. Under such conditions, anthropology must grapple with much more vulnerable and complicated forces of modernity in India, especially since Indian traditions and modern polity today, paradoxically, rely on—yet revile—each other; and as they so combat and collude, they also most often introduce new conflicts for long-standing civilizational forces to somehow reconcile.[27]

The same Indian society thus ends up showing increasing forces for and against social domination, discrimination and oppression, traumatic political and communal violence, and ecological degradation. As all these converge, ever more Indians have stories to tell of social and personal suffering and of the denial of social entitlements and human rights. Anthropology must address two issues interdependently under such conditions, first to study these and second to examine their relationships to anthropologists' work, responsibility, and writing. The last three are increasingly crucial issues since they concern the interrelationships between (*a*) an anthropologist's work and the people's vital interests and safety, including their cultural knowledge; (*b*) the anthropologist's personal and emotional self vis-à-vis his/her professional face and its scholarly and local responsibilities; and (*c*) local and global accountability in anthropological writing and representation. The fact that all anthropological writing and knowledge, even the most abstract, becomes local at some point, today hits home in a new way, especially as the processes of legal and moral accountability simultaneously localize and globalize (see Robertson 1992).[28] The more difficult situations may be when local or national developments directly involve an anthropologist with victims of violence (Veena Das 1990b, 1995; Tambiah 1986).[29] The earlier as well as more recent reviews of anthropology/sociology in India have variously reflected different scholars' cultural assumptions and backgrounds (e.g., for recent accounts, see Madan 1994; Srinivas 1996; for some earlier significant ones, see Dumont 1966; Madan 1966; Yogendra Singh 1986; Srinivas and Panini 1973; and Uberoi 1968).[30]

Related to the preceding discussion, Veena Das (1995: 1–24, 25–54, 197–210) has recently developed within the discipline a discussion of contemporary Indian issues, with several insightful points. Concerned with creating or claiming appropriate conceptual spaces and relations for recent Indian events and experiences within anthropological discourse, she composes a picture of relatable 'critical' Indian events and narratives to pose a crucial anthropological question:[31] 'What mode of being does an anthropologist possess in the contemporary world?' The fact that anthropologists must periodically revisit this issue should suggest how major social changes help the discipline to problematize itself anew. Das' discussion of the 1960s' debate between Louis Dumont and A.K. Saran, for instance, still makes a crucial point in such a context. It helps us evaluate the contemporary anthropological discourse for its accomplishments as well as the continuing dilemmas. In brief, Saran criticized Dumont for imposing external explanations on India's knowledge systems and Dumont responded by raising the specter of 'neo-Hindu "provincial" and backward feelings'. Missing Saran's point altogether, and assigning unqualified supremacy to post-war modern European rationality and universalism, he ended up assigning to Saran's India-centered criticism something fantastic: shadows of fascism. In retrospect, however, one can see that Dumont's response only reflected what was still too painful in the recent European—and his personal—memory, experience and location. Anthropologists also cannot but reflect their own social circumstances. Whatever the part of the globe, anthropologists reflect whatever is ethnically or nationally overwhelming, most traumatizing (see Daniel 1996; Tambiah 1986; 1996). In this sense, all anthropologists are 'native' to a culture (or cultures) they find constituting (or reflecting) them most intimately.[32]

The issue now also variously relates to the anthropological discourse organizing itself around major 'centers', 'zones of particular theoretical influence', and 'peripheries'. Recognizing these as a reality confronting anthropology in India as well, I concur with Das that the prospect of anthropology becoming a 'genuinely multicentered' (i.e., European and/or non-European) discourse is still not on the horizon. But, on the other hand, since some major non-Western centers of anthropological teaching, research, and public knowledge and discourse have already existed for quite some time (e.g., India, Latin America, and Japan), following their own research issues, strategies, new conceptual formulations, and public use, the multicentered (if less reciprocal) approach is de facto here. Its presence is seen in the pages of major journals (e.g., *Current Anthropology, Anthropology Today*, and *Contributions to Indian Sociology*) particularly as regional theoretical and conceptual formulations, irreplaceable in themselves, exchange findings with (and influence) other regions and the disciplinary 'centers'. Anthropological studies in India during this century have already contributed by explicating caste systems, hierarchy, 'fluid' world-views, local politics, and violent conflicts. But evidently such efforts are still far from producing a genuinely interdependent (regional–global) disciplinary paradigm that could replace the current center–periphery model of disciplinary discourse.

Similarly, the controlling disciplinary conceptual language and its assumptions also become increasingly problematized as the regional cultural or 'other' civilizational social forces (e.g., the Indian and Chinese, to name only the two most populous areas on the planet) now *selectively* approve or criticize modern Western ideology and its power structures. India is in the thick of both conflict and selective cooperation with modernity; it intensifies its religious, cultural, and political strife while globalizing its economy.

Though Das and I pursue such issues as we see them from our different locations, she and I seem to converge in studying the sociocultural location of and modern accountability for the victim's 'body', experiences of exploitation, and expressions of pain and suffering, including their limitations. But our significant biographical and social locational differences (age, gender, life course, field experiences, intellection, and personal predilections) yield two different ways and stances for approaching contemporary India. Such differences become crucial, I find, in the way she and I approach the current conflicts within and between a whole spectrum of Indian cultural (traditional, popular, modern Indian intellectual, and public) forces now contending with those of the modern state. Her attempts at creating and claiming new conceptual spaces and relations keep her more deeply anchored in the modernist world and its ideological assumptions and solutions, whereas I find *both* Indian traditional cultural and modern forces corrupted and rife with conflict, injustice, and suffering. Yet I do not think such traditional and modern conflicts, exclusions, and suffering tell the whole Indian story, until the creative tensions these produce from the local to regional and national levels are taken into account for exposing new social differences and demands set against that vast Indian civilizational canvas of cultural resilience, upheld in life by the massive ordinary Indians (Hindus and non-Hindus). Here appear from the grassroots, the issues of moral disquiet and social mistrust as well as a serious local search, with or without the *sarkar's* help, for a life with moral order, social justice, and fairness for oneself and tolerance of those opposed or excluded.

Anthropological discourse in such an inquiry builds primarily on those ethnographically explicated relationships in events, experiences, memories, and expressions that either people themselves consciously or unconsciously pursue in life or occasionally their leaders decipher, articulate, or intuit. Here, the role of modern mass media, transportation and information–communication technology works both ways: it divides as well as unites people, churning up religious and modern democratic and secular forces in different—even contradictory—ways. In this way Indians now embroil themselves in ever new conflicts yet discover new conceptual spaces, presences, and relations across communities, events, experiences and expressions for forging new local, regional, and national interrelationships.

In such a context appeared, for instance, the 1980s televised events of the *Ramayana* and the *Mahabharata*, on the one hand,

and of the rising resistance to Hindu social dominance by those advocating the cause of Dalits, Sikhs, Muslims, tribals, and women, on the other. Such a changed dynamics of social forces may also give us a better sense of what has changed since Dumont tried to package India (a culture and a civilization) within his 'structural analysis' and Saran, in response, had accorded an unquestioned primacy to what he called the 'primordial tradition'. Both, like many others, grabbed only parts of the proverbial elephant.

So we ask (see Chapter 3): Where do we stand today, almost 50 years after Dumont's contributions? The unavoidable answer is an image of India that has broken down the Dumontian ideological opposites (e.g., modernity and traditional ritual power and kingship) in a thousand different ways, up and down an entire society and a nation, seeking, conflating and yet questioning what Dumont had assumed for modernity.[33] Now as the 'many-sided, uncertain Indian self' encounters the ever-multiplying, conflicting other, the traditional and modern forces learn new ways to combat each other, as well as to selectively co-opt, collaborate, and collude for new strategies of both survival and revival. Compared to mid-century India, this picture conveys the message that Indians have vastly complicated both the table and the game that Dumont tried to decipher.

For anthropological studies, such a situation holds both promise and risk. Promise as long as anthropology knows how to satisfactorily translate cultural diversity and its attendant power conflicts into *interdependent* cultural knowledge systems of diverse configuration, the people studied and India as a whole. Interdependent construction of knowledge and its even-handed, persuasive representation are here keys to a unified 'anthropological community' in the future. Risks arise, however, when anthropology remains rigid with its Euro-centered discourse orientation, and treats others' knowledge systems as dependent. Actually, the discipline thereby exposes its own weakness and self-doubt.[34] The issue is pressing for the anthropologists studying countries like India or the US, where 'minorities' already demand specific—Islamic, Dalit, Black, and women's—conceptual orientations, explanations, perspectives and professional platforms.[35] To become genuinely inclusive, on the other hand, ensures a richer, more vibrant anthropological discourse, shaking off the recent sterile debates on its insecurities (see Geertz 1994; Scheper–Hughes 1995: 22–23).[36] The discipline definitely can avoid a debate which, however contextually or personally worthwhile, sinks to obvious, untenable and harmful 'center–periphery' controversies. Ironically, the more committed such debaters become to fight a trench warfare in the name of cultural bias or 'rigorous scholarship', the more tenuous and flimsy their arguments become for anthropology within a 'globalizing' world.[37]

In contrast, meanwhile, contemporary India, not unlike other major societies, engages anthropology in a distinct cluster of social issues. This study deals with five, all interrelated by Indian social contexts, as India oscillates between reading either too much or too little into its own traditional or modern forces. The issues are: current identity problems of the Hindu, the non-Hindu, and the Indian;[38] spreading social and communal violence and the resulting social suffering; miscarried traditional justice and unattended modern injustices; emerging social mistrust among the socially near and the distant; and the changing role of the ordinary Indian and the Indian civilization. These five issues, as the discussions of this book show, today raise debates vertically and horizontally within the entire Indian society, challenging anthropology to account for them within local and Indian cultural and historical terms, while grappling with its own disciplinary quandaries.

IV The Ethnography of Crucial Issues, Multiform Reasoning and Ordinary Indians

A suitably refocused ethnography could perhaps best show how the people have moved focus from the mid-century caste–kinship–village based social forces to many violent social conflicts, moral quandaries, and politically contested cultural identities. The issues of *vaqt* (time/s), *duniya* (world), and *sarkar* (government and power) reappear, but this time distinctly in the way these must grapple with the conditions of 'violence', 'injustice' and 'mistrust'. Once followed ethnographically, they show how they relate to specific events, agents and agencies, and to disputed claims and consequences.[39] This also means, among other things, seeing what engages people everyday, and often why in practical, rational terms. Increasingly practical and this-worldly for social survival, the world of ordinary Indians is about much more than a mechanical revalidation of customs and elders' past experiences, because 'all [i.e., those trusted, nearby and socially distant] now question', as an old Brahman woman had said in Lucknow in 1995, 'what was never questioned before. Some people shout for the timeless [God] Rama, and some against. What a time [has come]. Some kill … for Rama in Ayodhya, while still others burn temples [in retaliation in Bangladesh]. Who do you believe? Who is right, only Rama knows!'

To capture people's social uncertainties, self-doubts, and moral quandaries, ethnography weaves together a variety of expressions—descriptions, narratives, didactic dialogues, cathartic emotional monologues, and self-evasive but highly meaningful deferral or silence. Once mutual trust is established, an ethnographer and a community of people enter into convergent quests and discussions with the help of such 'languages' of dialogue and debate. Soon, ethnography helps reveal how the community-identity categories of 'Hindu', 'non-Hindu' and 'Indian' are substantiated with people's daily experiences of social triumphs, quandaries, mistrust, and tragedies. They tell how, for instance, a Hindu, under certain conditions, might be less than both a Hindu and an Indian; a Dalit, similarly, a Hindu, a non-Hindu and yet an Indian; and a Muslim, a socially participating or withdrawing Indian.

At the height of the Ayodhya temple–mosque conflict, the Hindu, Muslim, and Indian/non-Indian differences came into sharp focus several times in the Lucknow localities under study. The families whose views and experiences were being recorded included several upper castes, Dalits, Sikhs, and Muslims. It was perhaps the only time, some people (Hindus and non-Hindus) said, when they felt so disoriented for a period that they did not know who to trust, who to turn to for guidance, and 'how to identify one's real enemy—within oneself or in a familiar neighborhood'.

Locally, in such situations, only ethnography can reveal how broken social promises, misunderstanding, unjust treatment, and accumulating social exploitation work to sow the seeds of social mistrust between neighbors. The socially dominant, the marginal or the weak, all have a story to tell and an opinion of their own, but all are surrounded by deepening social mistrust between communities.

But, as my ethnography among the upper castes and Untouchables (men and women), Rajasthani women, and the victims of the Bhopal industrial accident showed, the problem of unexpressed social mistrust appeared to take hold among the suppressed, the victims, and the dominant. It lingered with the victors and the vanquished alike. It even corroded the security one's own caste and community gave. Social injustice, exploitation and mistrust therefore tend to link together at both intracaste and intercaste levels these days, posing a difficult practical problem. The more one mistrusts one's neighbors, the more caution and effort even the most routine tasks demand. Deepening mistrust definitely introduces a social cost in all people's lives in a diverse society like India.

The Ayodhya temple–mosque violence occurred in the backdrop of such a slowly-rising mistrust. While some Lucknow Muslims under study (who had relatives in the Ayodhya area) had loudly protested the 'naked injustice (*nanga zulm*) in Ayodhya', others were calmer. They wanted to avoid rash judgments. But if we examine the issue of 'unbearable or naked injustice' (*asahya annyay* or *intiha beinsafi*) in general cultural terms in India, the condition triggers some type of immediate response from all Indians (Hindus and non-Hindus). All major Indian religions oppose such a condition, historically encouraging people to protest, resist or flee such a condition. Today, in addition, those facing outright injustice collectively demonstrate, strike, besiege (or gherao in India), revolt, sabotage, and even terrorize. Indian democracy, despite its imperfections, thus allows diverse avenues of protest, while also creating new conceptual and practical linkages among traditions, politics, power, and the state. Politically and sociologically, contemporary India exhibits what European societies and nations also report.[40]

Reviewing such contemporary Indian developments against the background of what traditional India historically provided, we once again encounter the issue vital to an anthropological inquiry: How is India handling such a divergent range of social forces—from passivity, withdrawal, and non-violence to active social demonstration, subversion and counter-violence? One tactic repeatedly resorted to by my informants consisted of selecting relevant strands from both traditional and modern social spheres to reconstruct a practical, life-guiding cultural keyboard. In a narrative historian's terms, it is to have crucial keys from both the 'exemplary' and 'critical' models of narration (for a dense comparative summary of these narrative frames, see Rüsen 1987: 87–97, 91). The culturally 'timeless' here faces historical struggles, deviations and alterations, threatening the given ideas of continuation; but still there is no victor or vanquished here, since the people themselves want it that way. The culturally given identities are also refuted, attacked or denied, and the past and the present are opened to new judgments, but still only against the seamless backdrop of cosmic moral order.[41] Hence, when viewed from the ordinary Indian's standpoint, experts and intellectuals, guided by their own agendas, tend to read either too much or too little into their customary cultural past, religious ways and real-life struggles, on the one hand, and in their adept uses of modernity, modern power and Indianness, on the other.

Given such a cultural situation, local ethnography, once appropriately designed with people's active participation and support, may help us compose a multilevel and multivocal social picture, in which the ordinary Indian neither gets lost nor becomes so dominant as to reify himself/herself as an analytic template and drown out critical social differences and conflicts. To do so would be counterproductive for my exercise, a pursuit of culturally crucial matrices of social forces, events, agents, and dilemmas in contemporary India.

I attempt such a strategy in Chapters 1 and 8, which approach Indian cultural otherness under a diverse range of social conditions and their explication. While the first chapter proceeds against the background of uncontested traditional Hindu and Indic conceptions and categories,[42] the last chapter accounts for the social challenges now posed to the dominant Hindu cultural reasoning. If the first exercise shows how the four anthropological approaches (structural–functional, structural, ethnosociological, and critical cultural) have tried so far to grapple with India as the cultural other, the second illustrates the conflicts engaging the contestants, the ordinary Indian, and anthropology. Here, the traditional Hindu and the customary Hindu reasoning must squarely face the challenges, denunciations, criticisms, and controls the modern secular temper and nation-state produce on such customary problems as female infanticide, gender discrimination, caste exclusion, communal violence, and the resulting cloud of costly social mistrust.

A comparative, issue-based ethnography of everyday Indian cultural reasoning is thus at the heart of my studies. The social events, examples, struggles, and popular commentaries are contextualized by ethnography to enable us to see better how the ordinary Indian, despite a rising clamor of violent conflicts and the ensuing social debates, peeps through to converse with the Hindu, Dalit, Sikh, Muslim, and other non-Hindu faces. These teeming but mostly silent ordinary Indians are India's 'black box', always crucial but always slippery, readily valorized, and little examined. Since they tend to remain too varied and unpredictable for both modern 'structural' and the conflict theory models of power and domination, they disconcert many an expert ready to represent them, whether Marxist, modern liberal–secularist, postmodern Foucauldian, or subaltern historiographer. Ethnography in such a context can hardly be anything other than modest, given its local emphasis on the world of a few groups and their members. Yet it is possible to track, map, and trace what actually happens (i.e., how people collect information, reason, decide with accountability) when people concretely face a long-standing social problem, violent conflicts, injustice, suffering or challenge to group identity and personal survival. Certain patterns of thinking, reasoning and practical action emerge from such a local scene, open to wider cultural comparison and inference. Given contemporary India's social forces, such a picture can support neither sheer uncritical cultural romanticism nor an utter cultural chaos and annihilation.

In the last half of this century, M.N. Srinivas' work (see Chapter 2) seems to corroborate repeatedly such an ethnographic view of 'culturally resilient' Indians and India. Whether in or out of the changing theoretical fashions of the discipline, his accounts, though more concerned with sociological 'regularities', neither shun nor magnify social, religious and political conflicts. Yet the significance of his works may rest on his style of ethnographic writing and presentation, where, to better reflect everyday India and Indian, his ethnographic descriptions transformed into image and meaning-filled anthropological narration, using 'memory' as a veritable cultural–aesthetic ally as well as criticism. Without any theoretical pretensions, Srinivas' writings intuitively captured early, an India/Indian-suitable mode of ethnographic expression. Similar paths were theoretically articulated in anthropology, literary criticism and history as narratives and narrative time and structures were more closely examined (Rüsen 1987; White 1973).[43]

My ethnography took a similar turn when working with the socially lowest, particularly the silent victims of social exploitation and violence. Such Indians (Hindus and non-Hindus) initially stared at me in the field, trying to find out if I understood what they were telling me. For, thankfully, they refused early to confirm glibly my usual anthropological (institutional–structural–symbolic) view of their life and social relations, to assert what they saw as their social reality. As the fieldwork proceeded, Untouchable or Dalit men and women of Lucknow, juxtaposed to upper-caste Hindus, Sikhs and Muslims, became my paradigmatic cultural compass of today's local Indian society. If they starkly represented social differences, they also intimated sharing in thinking and practical reasoning via their actions, leaving me to reconcile a whole blurred, overlapping spectrum of actions, experiences, and words. I was faced with both ends of the power spectrum, those 'totally oppressed' (i.e., Untouchable women could not, sociologically speaking, dominate any group in turn) and those upper castes who, in most people's view, only (and often unjustly) dominated.

The last four chapters of the book try to present people's distinct strategies for identifying problems, along with narration and explication. Chapter 5 problematizes older Untouchable women's bodies, sensoria, selves, and rational practice as ethnographic templates of social communication. These and the politics of their memories and 'counter-memories' take center stage while the ethnographer consciously decides to get out of the way. Such a strategy proved most rewarding to me personally and professionally over time. The next chapter, exploring young and old urban Untouchable women, focuses on an ethnography of social judgment and judgmatic reasoning as these women experienced, reasoned and narrated their efforts to redress grievances before an employer or the *sarkar*. They variously redeploy the body, self and speech not only to re/claim what they assert is theirs but also to create moral and social room for what they think they are entitled to, and now claim as their social right.

Chapters 7 and 8, discussing the *vaqt*, *desh* and *sarkar* issues while spanning the local to the national (or vice versa), employ ethnography as a contextual and textual interpretive strategy.

Exploratory in character, such 'ethnography' grapples with the challenges educated people (reformers, leaders, journalists, and academics) face and express today as they deal with situations of social conflict, discrimination, suppression, violence, injustice, and cultural uncertainty. Here it is as crucial to 'read' modern experts' critical reasoning and observations ethnographically as of those socially dominant, ordinary, or the victimized and the oppressed. In such ethnography, sufferers, perpetrators, spectators, and local wise men are heard speaking alongside intellectuals, experts, ethnographers, and commentators, but without any one becoming either a passive listener or occupying center stage to the exclusion of others. All stand side-by-side in a circle of sorts. The last chapter completed one such ethnographic journey for me[44] as it re-examined 'Hindu cultural reasoning' while under increasing social and moral challenge (rather than enjoying the assumed traditional dominance), showing how politicized conflicts run out of control and result into calculated violence, increasing social injustice, and a deepening mistrust of the local, the regional, and the global. Obviously, such social situations were not without many difficulties and problems, some foreseeable and others not. Sometimes tensions disrupted or terminated discussions, yet, fortunately, all participating sides eventually returned to resume where they had left off (Chapter 5). Over time, to put it another way, each got sufficiently into—and out of—the other's way for critical discussions to occur. With no anthropological formula for such attempts, it has to be the participants themselves who attempt better strategies at communication. Underlying it all is the 'open' informal Indian popular (and public?) cultural ethos in a large city, where people talk even when differing or quarrelling. As I argue elsewhere (see Chapter 4), the crucial question is one of mutual, 'equipolar' recognition among the participants, including the ethnographer. Conceptually, in such an ethnography, all try to stand 'side by side' in idea, history and practice, rather than only as socially separate and different.[45]

V The Crucial Local Worlds behind the *Sarkar* and the Country

My argument in the exercises assembled here has been that Indian sociology or anthropology must now concern itself with socially *crucial* issues, where personal, community, public, and governmental (*sarkari*) decisions concern matters of secure survival, cultural–religious identity, fairness, and social dignity. Untimely, unfair, wrong, and inappropriate decisions in crucial social issues have a social cost for all—those governing, the reformers/leaders, ordinary people, and the weak. Crucial social issues surrounding the aggrieved, the *sarkar* (government), and the *desh* (locality, region, or the nation) erupt into critical, tell-tale events but gather force from long-standing diverse cultural (traditional/religious/modern) dilemmas, unresolved social conflicts, contradictions, and practical struggles. They range over critical and common events, interweaving local concerns with those regional and national (and vice versa). In contemporary India, in crucial issues also appears the Indian 'government' (i.e., that necessary and sprawling but seldom satisfactory *sarkar* with its intrusive tentacles and forces, representing modernity, 'modern progress', and the secular modern state), locking its horns with people's contentious traditions, religious strife, and life ways.

As a result of British colonial and post-independence confrontations, we already have before us two generations of derivative social formations, for example, distinct Indian communalism and caste and religious factionalism, on the one hand, and more recently religious nationalism, tribal and religious homelands, and 'minority' and women's empowerment, on the other. Together, they intensify 'involuted otherness', in which Indians are increasingly asking themselves such questions as: Who is a Hindu, a Dalit, a non-Hindu, an Indian, etc.? Who contests whose claims? What are *we* today vis-à-vis *them*? Who are our threatening opponents and what are they really up to? And how do we keep them in check?

As a method, interpretive device, and critical vantage point, ethnography helps study these complicated social situations in the ways in which people actually approach and deal with them in local, regional, and national contexts (i.e., all as somehow a part of one's *desh*). If their efforts show incompleteness, cultural biases, anger, frustration, tentativeness, and both reversible and irreversible success, then they also reveal to us their sense of larger cultural sharing under conditions of increasing social otherness and mistrust within caste and communal politics, violent religious conflicts, and social protest against exploitation and injustice. An internally comparative ethnographic stance tries to reveal how antagonistic groups, communities, and perpetrators and victims mend and rediscover conceptual spaces, social communication and limited but effective local interdependence as a matter of everyday social necessity. As they do so with a convergent sense and perceptiveness, they also reveal the other side of social divisions, conflicts, and power politics—a shared (if frayed) tendency to return to long-standing cultural resilience and a shared civilizational background. Here ordinary Indians, illiterate and literate, men and women, and old and young, make their social presence felt. Despite the politics of self-interest and domination (or counter-domination), they show patient endurance under crisis and forbearance under provocation.

An ethnographic study of such conditions of conflict and consensus, I realized, had to pay close and careful attention (*a*) to people's daily social experiences, reasoning patterns, conceptions of time (*samay* or *vaqt*), and its criticisms, and (*b*) to any existing or new paradoxical relationships the local social and religious aspects encountered vis-à-vis the 'government' (*sarkar*, a word used in India in a very inclusive sense as I also do) for local, regional or national reasons. The relationships between the *sarkar* and various religions, sectarian groups and religious organizations are far from simple, since if religions claim protection under secularism, then they (and the *sarkar*) also confront and attack one another when there is conflict. Ethnography helps show how such conflicts get sorted out enough to let social life go on, recording diverse narratives of victims, spectators, listeners, skeptics, and even those disputing the whole story.

A complementing if transient discussion appeared in my ethnography at such points. Some informants introduced local newspaper stories as evidence of 'what goes on today not only in our neighborhood but in Lucknow and its vicinity'. A range of conflicts were thus mentioned and discussed in July 1996: from a disputed shrine in a neighborhood to an unresponsive local trader, labor protest, political leader, and national party politics.[46] Such local urban issues were, however, linked with (*a*) unresponsive or exploitative regional politicians; (*b*) communalism and 'communal chauvinism'; (*c*) Dalit activism; and (*d*) religious revivalism and the dilemmas facing a secular democratic India.[47] However, such linkages were far from academic or speculative, since they also helped my informants recall similar experiences in their own (or their relatives' and friends') lives.

Correspondingly, there appears a flourishing Indian cottage industry of local, regional, and national social commentators, especially as some recent crucial Indian events have overtaken the Indian intelligentia. One need only recall the Indian 'emergency' of the mid-1970s onwards, with the 1980s unfolding the June 1984 Amritsar temple military operation, 1984 Bhopal industrial accident, the 1987 Deorala Sati, the 1989 acceptance of the Mandal Commission Report, and the 1992 Ayodhya temple–mosque dispute. Though these are still historically too close to us for anything other than provisional analysis, my group discussions with some Hindu, Dalit, Muslim, and Sikh informants (latest in 1996 summer) offered some observations about 'what was wrong with the country'. To summarize *their diagnosis* of the current time/s (*vaqt*), the world (*duniya*), the government (*sarkar*), and the country (*desh*): (*a*) The 'ruling minority' and selfish politics, including corruption, have overtaken all these events, and these collusions bleed us and the country. (*b*) These modern times somehow revive all possible social differences and inequalities among people, where unfair means and social oppression go on at the same time as protests and demonstrations against them. (*c*) When an unselfish leader is nowhere to be found, and when people compete in their selfish behavior, modern politics and the state can hardly improve without radical change. (*d*) The society reflects only what its rulers and the ruled are willing to tolerate at any time. (*e*) Today a minority rules and controls, while the majority acts like a minority, and the suppressed minority acts like tomorrow's majority. It is a confused world. All conceal their real motives, shirk responsibility, and blame the other side.

Such a ground-level thumb-nail sketch of contemporary India is revealing both for what it says and how it does so. It shows, for instance, increasing concern for 'what is wrong with India yet not irremediable', rather than a modernist/secularist alarm (and a corresponding cultural deafness from the other side) about the 'semitization' of Hinduism, or the rise of 'fascist' Hindutva.[48]

Simultaneously, Indian social reality is far from the poles of either unchallenged weighty traditions or an unstoppable juggernaut of modernity. Instead, Indians selectively reconstruct—and deconstruct—both in a thousand different ways in accordance with their practical needs and partisan political interests. Protesting Indians (e.g., in the Dalit thought from Jotiba Phule to Ambedkar, to the recent Kanshi Ram–Mayawati Bahujan Samaj political combine) have thus long pursued anti-caste and anti-Manu (and recently anti-Gandhi) cultural politics as a fight against both oppressive traditions and the failing Indian welfare state (see Omvedt 1994; 1995). While within such a frey, Indians not only reposition themselves for practical reasons but also re-imagine their local, regional and national identities, changing themselves—and their *sarkars*.

Not surprisingly, my account ends by reflecting (rather than 'tidying up') all the various loose or entangled ends of the society Indians live in. Imposing 'order' over social reality is not a function of late 20th century anthropology; it describes, narrates, and interprets the way a society is, with its orders, disorders, and loose ends, all in full view. Here anthropology explores the culturally knowable, the little known, the hidden, and the unknown, but it cannot include or exclude by unilateral scholarly authority the concerns a people experience, raise or remain undecided about. Anthropologists (or historians), as products of their own social circumstances and times, carefully strive to describe and account for the times and issues of the people they study, lest there be a temptation to read either too much or too little into the culture or history, and thereby missing, misinterpreting and misrepresenting the cultural other—or oneself. In the ethnography sketched, both sides raise the questions of accountability for each other, and in each other's equal historical presence.

◁ NOTES

1. As in the prevalent Indian usage, 'anthropology', 'sociology' and 'ethnography' in my discussion will be almost synonymous. However, I accord ethnography a distinct methodological and explicatory role, and give 'Indian sociology' a somewhat different emphasis than my colleagues in India. Neither limited to the Dumontian initiative of the same name, nor as eclectic as the new journal series, *Contributions to Indian Sociology*, my usage stresses reciprocal interdependence between Indian and global disciplinary concerns. This starts with field data and experiences and develops into conceptual frameworks, discourse strategies and expressions, and civilizational ideas. Now more than a

century old, and grown beyond its limited colonial beginnings, Indian anthropology or sociology must vigorously interrelate the South Asian peoples' experiences and ideas to the rest of the world. The post-Dumontian studies of Indian society and civilization do not flow only toward the West, but in several directions.

2. Consider, for example, Raymond Firth's book of 1938 was called *Human Types* and subsequently reprinted until the 1950s, while Clyde Kluckhohn (1949) called his book *Mirror for Man* in the 1950s and John Beattie's (1964) textbook became *Other Cultures*. The 1980s widely reflected the disciplinary self-questioning. For example, Johannes Fabian's book became *Time and the Other* (1983) for raising issues about the relationship between anthropology and its study of the cultural other.

3. In such a situation, for example, reading Geertz is useful but as insufficient as reading only good guides, whether on ethnographic imagination and writing, historical ethnography and power, or domination and resistance (e.g., Clifford and Marcus 1986; Comaroff and Comaroff 1992; Geertz 1983; 1994; Ortner 1984; 1995; and Scott 1990). Beyond these, an anthropologist has to find his/her own way when faced with a specific field situation, its chosen critical social issues and their representatives, and available field participants and discussants (rather than what are usually termed 'informants').

4. However, Srinivas and Panini (1973) review developments only up to the early 1970s and they reflect an emphasis on straightforward empirical descriptions and analyses rather than to later narrative and humanistic aspects. Compare Srinivas (1996).

5. Srinivas remarks here on the issues of both 'Indian' (i.e., implicitly Hindu and non-Hindu) unity and disunity. See also Srinivas (1966). For an explanation of my use of 'Indian', 'Hindu' and 'non-Hindu' terms, see Section II.

6. A note on transliteration: the words or phrases or idioms of Hindi, Urdu and even Avadhi Hindi will remain without diacriticals. Only uncommon Sanskrit or Sanskritized words or concepts will have diacritics. This is done to simplify reading and to reflect the ethnographic cultural time and temper of the study.

7. These quotidian Indians are best left without any special technical label, for they are simply much more diverse than the dominant caste Hindu and the Hindu religious right, or the 'lumpen proletariat', the 'subaltern', 'the oppressed Dalit', and 'the suppressed victim'. See Section V.

8. The comment, however, in practice has both a sociological and a moral side to it. I pursue the first where temporization means a non-committal or delayed response which, when used adroitly, becomes a strategy for controlling and dampening a conflict. The government may also resort to it when facing politically sensitive and emotionally charged social situations. In violent events, as a recent Guggenheim Foundation report also remarks, a 'no-response response' might be most prudent (Colvard 1996: 6).

9. As a discipline, anthropology demands a form of re-socialization from its practitioners, with eventual reconstruction of one's world and world-view. How someone goes about doing it from a non-Western world-view is a vital question yet to be explicated. The recent accounts recall a professional life around disciplinary developments. For the story of establishing field-based 'sociology'

in India, see Srinivas (1996: 1–72); and for another professional profile via contemporary anthropologists, see Madan (1994).

10. Besides their outstanding scholarship and insights on India, they have also been, directly or indirectly, a part of my passage into anthropology ever since the late 1950s. Though my studies never stood in a simple confirmatory or contesting relationship to their contributions, I regard an evaluation of their works, as this book shows, central to the current disciplinary history and issues. The discipline has, as yet, neither superseded nor rendered obsolete the issues they raised.

11. To even remotely impute such motives would be perverse. Being a non-resident Indian (caste Hindu) male ethnographer, I could not have done any more or less than what I did between 1974 and the present. I tried to depict Untouchable women as directly and attentively as possible, especially considering that most still remain very aloof and dismissive toward those who, in their own words, 'just come to bother us in this large city for their own selfish goals'. They put off some younger men and women of their own community.

12. Such cultural sensibilities, while local and regional, change sufficiently with time, requiring the governing elite to give attention to such cultural grassroots on a continuing basis. Simultaneously, one should not assume what they know or do not know. For a discussion of the problem of political governance, see Kohli (1990) and for a comment on the same issue, see Kothari (1996: 4–5). On M.K. Gandhi, see Bondurant (1971: 171), and Nehru (1946: 73–74).

13. Sociological and anthropological accounts of such local discussions, spatially proximate or removed, are still very rare. But they must be the backbone of political sociology in India. Similarly, the accounts of communal violence (e.g., Hindu, Sikh or Muslim) need to be followed up as they travel to major localities of the involved communities. For a helpful and perceptive recent anthropological discussion of women victims during the partition, with a reference to other works in progress, see Veena Das (1995), and for the role of the historian's history in making these accessible, see Pandey (1994: 188–221).

14. See Chapter 8. At the civilizational level, India gives us a general view of its enduring cultural conflicts. For instance, in Paz's (1982: 31) perceptive words: 'Inside India, Hinduism and Buddhism were the protagonists of a dialogue. This dialogue was Indian civilization'. Islam's journey in India, however, continues to be a challenge of a different order, showing limitations in assimilation on both sides.

15. Those familiar would readily know that these cultural notions as life-markers have a whole range of denotative and connotative meanings in the Hindi–Urdu (hence Hindu and Muslim) speaking regions of India. However, in cultural conception and practical usage, these may cover much more of India. Thus, the 'time/s' (samay or vaqt) may mean many things: from the present or prevailing life circumstances to good or bad duration, misfortune, injustice, and even the contemporary regional, national and global time and temper. Similarly, desh may refer to different spatial categories, placements, locations and their good, bad, or indifferent, and familiar, unfamiliar or hostile consequences. It is applied as readily to one's indigenous and familiar sociocultural surroundings as to unfamiliar disputed or contested territories, regions,

frontiers, wild spaces, and the modern nation-state. A nationalist is called *desh bhakta.* The *sarkar,* conceptually, intrudes and works through all the three to ostensibly organize, order, control and distribute, under peace, justice and fairness, goods and services to people. In practice, the notion helps capture a whole spectrum of just and unjust influence, dominance, control, power, authority, governance, and order.

16. The cultural otherness that such markers flag is at once sociologically specific and historically related to India's colonial past. For some historical meanings of 'Hindus' and 'Indians' within the 19th century nationalism in Bengal, see Chatterjee (1994: 1–49).

17. Attention to such an issue greatly varies today. Some Indological scholars are more sensitive to such implications than others. A German Indologist and religious historian, Heinrich von Stietencron, for example, devoted a seminar to the issue at the Wissenschaftskolleg zu Berlin in the fall of 1996. But an Indian philosopher, on the other hand, interested in linking Indian philosophy to the living culture continued to equate 'Hindu' with 'Indian' (see Krishna 1991).

18. However, as is well known, Gandhi and Ambedkar increasingly diverged, and Ambedkar identified the Hindu caste order as the root of all social evils. The recent Dalit literature carries the divergence much further. See Anand and Zelliot (1992).

19. To get a sense of the range of recent messages and meanings Hindutva raised in India, see Nandy et al. 1995 (Chapter 3, 56–80). However, only time will tell what will endure after a decade or two of the current politicized uses and meanings of 'Hindu' and 'Hindutva', especially after the Ayodhya temple–mosque violence.

   Similarly, the phrase 'India, that is, Bharat', anthropologically speaking, betrays a long internal civilizational and historical struggle with cultural alterity. On the 19th century Bengali nationalist formulations on India, see Chatterjee (1994: 1–49).

20. For an anthropologically similar but not conceptually identical use of 'Hindu' and 'Hinduism', see Fuller (1992, Chapter 3).

21. By comparison, some 'activist scholars' may take a politically partisan view of the word 'Hindu'. They maintain that 'Hindus' (i.e., those twice-born or *savarna*) are only those that are left after all the non-Hindu Indians have counted themselves out. See Omvedt (1995).

22. In current Indian intellectual circles, the same divide has already produced a wide range of debates. For a recent spirited defense of 'the Hindu position', see Jain (1994: 2, 3, 11, 59–60, 107–8). For an equally spirited opposite Muslim viewpoint by an array of political leaders and newspaper commentators, see the articles or excerpts published together in *Muslim India,* 127, July 1993, including Shahabuddin's (1993: 290–92), who sounds the alarm on the 'massive disenfranchisement of Muslims' by the Sangh Parivar.

23. This is a situation Untouchables in particular face today. Among Untouchables, the first were those who considered themselves 'Hindu' but were anti-caste, and next were those who were converted Buddhists but did not care to protest against being called a Hindu, 'socially exploiting both sides for practical gain'.

24. In the summer of 1996 in Lucknow (while Atal Behari Vajpayee was to be sworn in as Prime Minister), some Hindu nationalists explained to me in detail on what their encompassing political slogan 'Hindu, Hindi and Hindustan' meant.

25. Though the distinction was not very clear, 'Ambedkerite Buddhists' in the Lucknow region seemed to rely less on the leftist Marxist ideology and more on Buddhist religion. The general ethos reflected cultural alienation. Thus a specific issue of *Dalit Asia Today* (1–15 December 1994), for example, discussed such topics as 'Media and the Muslim', 'Law and the Dalit', 'Dalit Bureaucrats a Target of *Savarna* [Twice-Born] Bureaucrats', and 'Bye-Bye Hindu Dharma'.

26. For example, Professor D.N. Majumdar, my teacher of anthropology at Lucknow University, used to say, 'One does not have to go far in search of anthropological issues in India; they are just outside your door.' Claude Lévi–Strauss had characterized India 'as a land of structuralism' in a conversation with me in the fall of 1972 in Paris.

27. The civilization includes both 'Indic' and Indian (syncretic) components. For my conception and use of 'Indic', see Khare (1984). The term 'Indian' refers to a cultural synthesis (with flaws and limitations, of course) between the indigenous Indic and the 'external' (notably Islamic, Christian, etc.) cultures. For another recent piece of writing that problematizes Indian 'civilization' by remarking that Indian nationhood might be built 'on the ruins of one's civilizational selfhood', see Nandy et al. (1995: xi).

28. Anthropologists under such conditions have to recognize the full local, regional, and global implications of their fieldwork and writing, especially since the people may themselves demand accountability in their local terms. All anthropological knowledge, unless solipsistic, concerns and relies on that of cultural others, and hence it is in this sense, as Geertz (1992: 129–35) argues, local, and we might add, with responsibility and credit to local sources of knowledge.

29. Anthropological writing reflecting others' ethnic, national or regional strife is already available, but direct accounts of an anthropologist's (or his/her caste or community's own suffering) still remain perhaps outside the scientific canons of the discipline. Besides Veena Das (1990a, 1995), see, for example, Tambiah (1996).

30. Among those accounts reviewing different conceptual approaches and issues while summarizing the last 50 years of sociological or anthropological developments in India, see Srinivas (1996); Dumont (1966: 17–32); Madan (1966: 9–16; 1994); Srinivas and Panini (1973: 179–215). For raising some early epistemological questions, see Uberoi (1968: 119–23) and Yogendra Singh (1986).

31. Das' study of recent critical Indian events particularly emphasizes the conflict and resistance aspect of Indian social reality on the one side, and the experiential dimension of pain and suffering, on the other. Her levels and languages of articulation emerge from the accounts of specific events, and her analysis runs along the victim–community–nation axis. My studies, in comparison, rest on the moving and changing templates of cultural reasoning and social relations which Indians forge among themselves, often repeatedly. These are deciphered via a series of ethnographic exercises conducted in a major north

Indian city (Lucknow) among ordinary people (including women as victims of violence), local leaders/reformers, and divergent local communities (from Brahmans to Dalits, to Sikhs and Muslims). In dialogue with me and among themselves, these people conversed as they faced their daily life struggles, near and distant crucial social events, including injustice and social mistrust.

32. For a biographic approach to discussing what (or how much) is 'native' in an anthropologist 'belonging to' many cultures, see Narayan (1993: 671–86).

33. However, a distinctly pro-Dumontian interpretation of such events is also feasible, if one were to see all such Indian social strife as a result of the massive ideological conflict that modern Western ideology has instigated for its eventual supremacy. Such a view sees India painfully 'historicize' itself until eventually there is the birth of genuine politico-economic individualism from the ashes of the Indian past and its traditions.

34. But evidence of epistemological openness is still lacking, as the recent reception given to McKim Marriott's 'ethnosociology of India' might have shown. In an Indian commentator's words, 'What unites us, Marriott and his Indian "subjects", is peripheralization: he is on the periphery, metaphorically, and his subjects are on the periphery literally'. See Rajendra Singh (1992: 143–49).

35. However tentative at present, young Dalit social scientists provide us with an example. They not only want to criticize the dominant sociological explanations (e.g., for treating Hindu and Indian as synonymous and for assuming the success of upper-caste Sanskritization), but also want to replace it with their 'correct' sociological formulations. For examples, see Khare (1984).

To maintain a single universal disciplinary ideology on the terms Dumont had assumed and professed in his day, is thus increasingly questioned from the top down and from the bottom up in a country like India. Besides facing the charge of maintaining neo-colonial hegemonic centers of knowledge (where the Anglo-Americans control one world segment while the Germans, French, Dutch, Spanish, etc., control others), anthropological knowledge suffers most whenever the world's peoples and cultures find it one-sided.

For Dumont's position on anthropology as a discipline of modern ideology, see Dumont (1979: 785–817).

36. Readjusting its sights, anthropology today does its best by closely reflecting and responding to the changes it encounters in the societies it studies. However, the debate is far from over, given the reviving 'centers' and evermore critical 'peripheries'. For recent disciplinary discussions facing new questions in a changing world, see Geertz (1994) and Scheper–Hughes (1995: 22–23).

37. The recent debate between Marshall Sahlins and Gananath Obeyesekere on the Hawaiians and Captain Cook might suffice for our purpose. See also Chapter 3 for discussion. The reviews of Sahlins' work and Obeyesekere's critique fell along a rather predictable spectrum of Western/non-Western opinions. See Bernstein (1995).

38. To repeat, I employ 'Hindu', 'non-Hindu' and 'Indian' as anthropologically descriptive cultural terms, rather than as expressions of political dominance or dependence.

39. Ethnography particularly helps explicate a range of local social meanings of 'violence' and 'mistrust' in today's social circumstances. Thus, for the northern urban Hindi–Urdu region I studied, social violence often resulted from

personal or social frustration, and attracted special concern when faced with injustice. In behavior and the language of the learned, it evoked a range of notions, ranging from violation (*atikramaṇ*), fierceness (*ugrata*), and virulence (*prachandata*), to tyranny (*atyachar*). At the other end of the spectrum, in polite company, even mere thoughtlessness (*avichar*) could count as a form of violation. Popularly, violence included any form of ill-treatment (*durvyavhar*), high-handedness (*zabardasti*), apprehension, arrest or seizure (*pakar-dhakar*), and of course fighting and killing (*mar-kat*). Similarly, injustice could be any form of *annyaya* or *beinsafi*, whether it is denying someone his/her due or putting whole ethnic groups through physical confinement, starvation, torture, mass killing, or genocide.

'Social mistrust', a part of the same ethos, is conceptually deeper than occasional distrust or distrust between competitors and political opponents. It refers to that slow but unmistakable transformation which occurs when deep mistrust (*avishvas*) results from dispersed social suspicion (*shak, shanka, sandeh*, or *shubah*). It results in a socially enduring loss of trust (*bharosa na karna*) and faith (*apratiti* or *āsthābīntā*).

40. The subject of resistance and protest movements is vast, with an equally vast research literature. But to get a sense of some distinct directions in a recent European (Italian and German) study, see della Porta (1995); on general comparative comments on India, see Juergensmeyer (1993); and for a general commentary on the politics of violence, see Colvard (1996).

41. Particularly, Rüsen's (1987: 91) table on 'typology' was helpful in comparing historical and anthropological ideas of criticism. Though the two of course converge and help in each other's efforts, one side seldom satisfies the other, since one works with 'documents' and the other with living beings (and their 'records' and 'representations') in all their complexity. Anthropological narration goes wherever people's ideas, memory, narration and history take them to make a sense of their social life and times.

42. At the center is India's 'dual cultural grammar of otherness', first as India discusses its divergent philosophical ideologies about I-ness/otherness, and then again as daily social differences of 'us'/'them', 'like-us/unlike-us', and 'indigenous'/'foreign' (including Indian/Western) test their strengths against one another.

43. See Chapter 4. Narratives and narrative history in the West, imply a whole range of theoretical fields, ideas and meanings. But such intuitive developments in ethnographic writing have their advantages as well as disadvantages. Theoretically unaware of, and thus unencumbered by Western practices, Srinivas' writing does not have to struggle to escape the Western narrative forms to approximate the Indian conditions. Yet more complicated and conflicting Indians and Indian events challenge it to evolve further to capture new and different memories, meanings and messages. Western theorists face the same challenge on their side. For making an early persuasive argument, see White (1973). For further outlining and mapping the comparative theoretical import and reasoning in narrative history, see Rüsen (1987).

44. Put in a personal context, the ethnography presented in the second section of this book took me (a non-resident Indian, an upper-caste Hindu, male ethnographer) on a journey of learning as well as self-discovery. Given my

sheltered childhood, shyness, and extensive religious background, the journey was forced and dramatic at first but increasingly rewarding and 'freeing'
later on. All this happened particularly when Untouchable women, old and
young, repeatedly took me along on their (for me, chastening) journey of
social defiance for daily survival and for an unremitting search for social
honor and justice.

45. These ethnographic accounts (based on Lucknow upper-caste Hindus,
well-known and unknown Dalits, social commentators, and ordinary and
learned Muslims, Rajasthani women, and the Bhopal gas victims) were also
exercises for me on sustaining an *interdependent* discursive 'we-ness' with
those studied, forged around *their* local and wider social concerns. To do so
was to repeatedly encounter the demand (particularly from Dalits, Muslims
and Sikhs) that they would come for a discussion with others 'only under the
conditions of equality, justice and fairness'.

46. A three-day (23, 24, 25 July 1996) random survey of local news stories, for
example, was done in the Lucknow *Pioneer* and its Hindi edition *Swatantra
Bharat*, two daily newspapers.

47. Increasingly diverse commentaries are available on the subject of communal
violence, especially after the 1992 Ayodhya temple–mosque conflict. For a
clear modern, humanist statement 'guiding' post-1992 Indian polity, see
Tarkunde (1993: 312–13). For a review of a range of the recent secular Indian
intellectual's approaches to the same conflict, see Nandy et al. (1995).

48. For references to such positions, see Chapters 7 and 8. For a range of additional citations, see Nandy et al. (1995); and Juergensmyer (1993).

Part I

Disciplinary Issues and Perspectives

1

Indian Sociology and the Cultural Other*

Background

Indian sociology,[1] as discussed in the pages of *Contributions to Indian Sociology* (hereafter *Contributions*), original and new series, raises some unavoidable issues about its own identity as it tackles Western approaches and perspectives on India. The issues of the West's cultural other variously influence the content, form, history, and development of Indian sociology.[2] In the context of major researches conducted since the mid-1950s, Indian sociology, I shall argue, must still more fully investigate the burden of its Western ancestry. Such an examination requires developing more interest in the sociology of knowledge in India, with attention to the roles of Indian cultural logic and reasoning. The whole issue, I argue, demands a closer study of the West as India's 'cultural other' from different Indian cultural vantage points, illustrating Indian sociology's approach to the universal and the relative.

Our discussion of the subject will be informed by cultural critiques of anthropological representation on the one hand, and issues in critical philosophy and hermeneutics, on the other.[3] We

* This article was originally published in *Contributions to Indian Sociology* (n.s.), 1990, 24 (2): 177–99 (Sage Publications, New Delhi).

will purposely take a critical view of modern Western epistemology and its universalist claims, especially when it adopts a rigid position against other civilizations and their rigorous, time-tested epistemologies. Similarly, we suggest that Indian sociology must move beyond its conundrums of status quo—e.g., where the modern, universal West must confront traditional, localized India (for early formulations in *Contributions*, see Dumont 1966; Dumont and Pocock 1957; 1960; Madan 1966).

Indian sociology needs to launch a sustained critical discourse on itself, and on Western thought (for an initial formulation of such a position, see Uberoi 1968; 1978). However, such an exercise demands a better reading of India's own cultural past, and a critical understanding of others' accounts of India over time. Such exercises will also help Indian sociology discover the crucial roles the Indic (i.e., Hindu, Buddhist and Jain) systems of knowledge and interpretation play in constituting Indian reality.

Etymologically, the word 'other', related in Old High German to *andar*, and in Sanskrit to *antara* (*Webster's Dictionary* 1985: 835), refers to relationships of plurality, addition, diversity, opposition, exclusion, and the temporally former. Our usage draws on all these meanings by context, rather than subscribing to a simple opposition between inside and outside. But an India–West sociological comparison must confront a basic issue: Can the social sciences lay claim to genuinely universal truths? Is a 'truly universal social science' not mostly about dominating alternative systems of knowledge; and their truth values? Is it not often the case that rationalists, relativists, and orientalists end up pointing fingers at each other's 'blind spots'? More useful for Indian sociology may therefore be a study of changing historical conditions and relationships between the dominant Western and the subdued non-Western epistemologies. It may focus on the role played by the educated Indian's ambivalent handling of the colonial past and its mechanisms of cultural control via the antagonistic politicization of caste, language, region, and religion. As an 'insider–outsider', and often a jumble of the colonial–nationalist–traditionalist temper, the modern Indian intellectual carries his own blind spots. Retrospectively, Dumont and Pocock may have insufficiently recognized the continuing influence of colonial thinking on Indian studies.[4] Indian sociology must therefore much more carefully reconstruct India's many—familiar and alien— faces from within.[5]

But this requires viewing India neither selectively, nor in ways that stifle Indian sociology. It also means discovering how India develops its 'science of appropriate distinctions'. Such studies can neither be 'reactionary', nor automatically opposed to all that is non-Hindu, Western, modern, and universal. Similarly, 'indigenous' thought has to be neither archaic, parochial, underdeveloped, or incomprehensible. Such labels are often red herrings employed to maintain the unique supremacy of Western intellectual tradition, and to deny the possibility of multiple centers of equally authentic knowledge.[6]

Within the prevailing Western epistemic paradigm, India or any other major non-Western literate tradition can only become a traditional other (as in Dumont's India–West oppositional schemes; see Dumont 1977; 1980); or a significant other (e.g., in Marriott's *plural* cultural or 'ethno' social sciences 'of other lands', providing 'an expanded, multicultural set of sciences' to evolve 'that "*universal* significance and value"'; see Marriott 1989: 3; also Marriott and Inden 1977: 227–38). However, such initiatives help us review the development of Indian sociology for the instructive markers it provides on India's otherness to the West in the pages of *Contributions* (e.g., Ahmad 1972; Bailey 1959; Dumont and Pocock 1957; 1960; Jaer 1987; Kantowsky 1969; Madan 1966; 1981; Saberwal 1983; Uberoi 1968; Venugopal 1986). Though not restricted to the original Dumont–Pocock theoretical program, the overall emphasis in *Contributions* remained on the sociocultural distinctness of India in Western sociological terms. With the review and criticism of Dumont's essentialist–comparativist cultural view of India, Marriott's 'monistic' approach, especially since the 1970s, evolved more rigorous standards for studying India from within.[7]

Let us now consider some general approaches to studying the cultural other.

The Other: Essential or Non-Essential

We face a crucial question: Is the cultural other ultimately dissoluble by an epistemological universalism that modern man and his scholarship produce? Or must it remain a subject of only contextual interpretations? (For a recent but inconclusive round of philosophic discussions, see Larson and Deutsch 1988; for a review and a continuing debate, see Rorty 1989a; 1989b; Taylor 1989.) The Western philosopher's position on such questions remains rather unhelpful. He is either a rigid rational universalist or a relativist. On the other side, Indic philosophical discourses (e.g., the Brahmanic, Buddhist and Jain) differ. Indian sociology therefore might do best to deal with the issue in terms of the 'lived culture', where cultural ideals, social contexts, and historical forces must contend with the cultural other.

However, learned Indic texts remain a part of such inquiry. We cannot deal with the Hindu's otherness without grappling with different notions of self, soul and the universal soul (Potter 1965).[8] For example, the vedantic Hindu treats all forms of otherness (a sign of plurality) as a manifestation of illusion (*māyā* or *prakṛti*). For him, only self (the absolute *ātman*) exists; his ideal is the total dissolution of alienating self (the ground of 'I-ness' and 'I'). Some of his philosophical ways of expressing such an essentialist position are: 'parts are unreal', 'effects pre-exist in cause', and 'difference is non-grasping of similarity'. At the opposite end stand the skeptics (Cārvāka) and Buddhists who see the other as an irreducible part of reality. Here the whole becomes unreal; effects do not pre-exist in cause; and similarity is non-grasping of difference. This non-essentialist position disputes the all-encompassing ideal and its reality.

However, such a story of Indic philosophies remains incomplete until we include those with 'middle positions' (Jains, Mīmāṃsikas), where both self and the other remain real and distinct. Everything is found to be both same and different, and equal and unequal under a philosophy (*anékāntavāda*) which strives to avoid taking either of the two extreme positions. Others color self (as self colors others) moment to moment, but the moment is denied any essentialism of its own. Both self and the other could thus be viewed from endless standpoints, with differing messages and meanings.

For sociological purposes, we may distinguish four general values or 'faces' of otherness: (*a*) the rational other (pursued by modern scientific universalism), (*b*) the critical other (evaluating the modern), (*c*) the contextually relativized (and transforming) other, and (*d*) the unique other (usually discovered via the history of a specific human culture and civilization). We will briefly consider below each of these 'faces' in a schematic form, to help us

better interpret Indian sociology's treatment of the cultural other—
so far.[9]

The rational, scientific approach reduces all forms of cultural
otherness to such scientific universals as causality, impartiality,
symmetry and reflexivity (Hollis 1982: 67–86). The other (or any
non-other universal) cannot have an independent or irreducible
'essence and existence' outside such a rationality. The cultural
other can produce only particular and conditional knowledge. It
is fully 'explained' and best represented by modern canons of
logic and rationality (see Hollis and Lukes 1982).

The second 'face' of the other appears when such a conquest of
modern reason encounters criticism from both within and without
the West, yielding not only to 'postmodern' and 'poststructural'
critiques, but also to debates on the effectiveness of modern reason in today's world (e.g., Clifford 1988; MacIntyre 1981; Overing
1985; Said 1978; 1983). Not merely a secondary, verifying example
within this discourse, the other launches a critical evaluation of
modern universals and their limitations and failures. However,
this position of the cultural other still has to discover ways to avoid
regression into the simple relativism of earlier decades (see Hatch
1983), and it must make sense of its own diversifying critical debates (e.g., Smith 1988).

The third face of the other appears when self, the other, and its
otherness are discovered to be without any ultimate essence.[10]
The 'particular other' and the 'particular universal' can coexist
here but only as conditional products of a multi-sided and ever-
changing human cultural reality. (Compare this with the preceding summary of the Jain and the Mīmāṃsa schools of Indic
philosophies.) Since the claim to an absolute, single universal is
given up as either untenable or impractical, any approach or
methodology that still hopes to reach the unconditional universal
is subjected to criticism. Some dispute the very possibility of
knowing the other.[11]

The fourth face asserts that all cultural otherness is in some
sense unique (and irreducible). It is integral to people's cultural
and moral perceptions of themselves. Though not beyond translation, it can only be incompletely translated, generalized and ap-
propriated by another culture (Overing 1985: 1–28; Parkin 1985:
131–51). India, China, and the West are thus culturally distinct from
each other. However, when deeply probed, they may disclose a

long-standing ground for pursuing convergent (but indepen-
dently-reached) similarities in reasoning and confirming reliable
knowledge (Staal 1988: Introduction).

An anthropological account is likely to pursue, by context, all
the four values of the other. In addition, it develops a distinct
interpretation of otherness as a part of postmodern knowledge,
usually in two phases. In the first phase, the anthropologist uses
the other culture simply as a sounding board for viewing and reviewing his own culture, usually with an uncritical acceptance of
modern epistemology. The second phase criticizes modern epistemology in order to open it to the existence of major alternative
epistemologies. Though rare, such an attempt may still aspire for
some kind of universalization, often by intertwining emic and etic
epistemologies. Marriott's 'construction' of ethnosociology perhaps exemplifies such an effort.

Four Approaches and Their Characteristics

Let us now discuss the other in the context of some major developmental phases of Indian sociology—pre-Dumontian structural–
functional approach, Dumontian 'structural sociology of India',
Marriott's 'ethnosociological' approach, and the recent critical and
interpretive explanations of aspects of Indian society and civilization. These phases implicate the four general values of otherness
as they render India to be the West's cultural-other (or vice versa).

Structural–Functional Approach

As the 19th century Indian cultural renaissance culminated in independence, many prominent West-educated Indians (of whom
Mahatma Gandhi and Jawaharlal Nehru were later examples)
increasingly viewed India in terms of its own cultural history,
disputing or dismissing the colonizer's otherness that the British
introduced in their accounts (for psycho-historical studies of such
19th century conflicts among observers of India, see Chatterjee
1989; Nandy 1980; 1983). Most British writers recorded facts as
they saw them, often for administrative and political goals of the
Raj. Out of such general pools of data developed the 'empirical'
social science field studies of India, especially after the second

world war. They fostered among the researchers a West-inspired 'scientific' intellectual temper, within which anthropologists and sociologists (Indian and foreign) viewed Indian society as an 'object' of study. These researchers mostly mapped, cataloged, classified and evaluated India's basic cultural units (i.e., villages, castes, and tribes) with a studied political purpose. Succeeding them appeared numerous 'village studies' and caste and kinship accounts based on fieldwork, providing a 'scientific' basis for discovering India's 'social reality'. Objectivity here translated as a sort of aloofness (even for those Indian social scientists who studied their own villages or caste groups).[12]

Within this phase of logico-empirical research, India showed two distinct values, first as the 'cultural other' (most and best evident to a foreign scholar), and second as the scientifically produced 'objective other' (subscribed to by both Western and Indian scholars). Objectivity was considered both a necessary and sufficient condition to reach scientific truth, the analyst's ultimate quest.

During this phase, as the anthropologist collected maximum field data on the chosen subject, he consistently tried to remain aloof from the subject, projecting himself as subtly superior and enigmatic. He rarely felt the need to share *his* own field experience with his 'subjects', much less to accord *their* judgments a serious place within his scientific explanations. His informants were almost always passive 'producers of facts' rather than truth-knowing participants. The major analytic reasoning sought, discovered and established in such an approach, rested on the investigator's notions of 'scientific' observations and social science theory. People's own voice and reasoning remained indirect and muted even within careful field reports (e.g., Marriott 1955).

However, some of the best attempts, over time, tried to break away from such constraints. M.N. Srinivas' work, for example, successively expanded the range and connotation of sociological description and characterization in India as it dealt with changing caste groups and villages on the one hand, and as it suggestively depicted the fullness of Indian village life and its cultural sensibilities, on the other (Srinivas 1964; 1976). Adopting the precarious (insider-yet-outsider) stance of a social anthropologist, Srinivas perhaps best exemplified a carefully crafted 'sociological' approach suitable to a newly independent non-Western nation—his own.

Structural Sociology of India

With the rise of structuralism, such Western categories as subject and object, ideology and practice, inside and outside, parts and the whole, and the individual and the collective, acquired center stage, and they yielded, in turn, a West-complementing India. The proposal for pursuing a distinct 'Indian sociology' thus starts, as is well-known, with Louis Dumont's program of studying such binary (logical) oppositions as high and low, purity and pollution, status and power, and hierarchy and holism (formulated after certain classical Hindu notions; see Dumont 1980, especially Postface).

The significance of Dumont's research scheme on India must, however, still be thoroughly investigated for its overall theoretical grounding in certain modern Western social philosophies.[13] First, it remained very close to the 19th century British-and-Brahman-pundit resurrected 'India'. Despite his initial announcements to establish a genuine 'Indian sociology', his 'ideological' approach severely limited his ability to embrace the diversifying, vociferous India of the 20th century. Second, Dumont's sociology instead chose to deal with one social quality (hierarchy) of the Hindu world and its cultural consequences. Third, it kept a glaring distance from the long-recognized and rigorously-worked studies of Indic cultural logic, epistemology and reasoning, available in texts, and often reflected within everyday life. While Marriott's work (1976a; 1989) has dealt with the second issue, the first and third points still need careful study and critique (for another discussion of some of the repercussions of the original Dumontian proposal, see Thapan 1988).

Ideologically contrasted to the historical, egalitarian, and modern West, India provides a perfect counterfoil for Dumont to demarcate the West's own cultural boundaries, and a better self-definition, especially after the trauma of the second world war. Dumont's study of India remained Europe-centered in many ways, and to depict India as the West's 'total' other (in the Maussian sense), he freely equated the Indian caste system with the Hindu world, and the latter with India (for observations on India as the non-European other, and the role of the 'anthropological community' within it, see Dumont 1977; 1986a; and for a review, Khare 1989).

In such a 'structural' view, Dumont found India without true history, genuine secular power, real economic motive, and the enduring moral individual. At the level of ideology, Dumont could not detain himself to deal with complicating alternative Indic models of parts and the whole (e.g., for a summary see Potter 1965: 103; see also Khare 1983a; 1986). He implicitly assumed a confirmation of Durkheimian 'holism' within the vedantic view of 'the one over many', in order to contrast it with modern European individualism. We thus entirely miss in Dumont's work any attention to Indic (or even Brahmanic philosophic and epistemological) 'logics' to explicate the issues of the universal and the particular, or the self and the other.

Dumont's India, as some have commented, may have barely moved beyond the orientalist's notion of the 'dependent other' (see Appadurai 1986 for a reappraisal of Dumont's approach; for crisis in anthropological representation, see Marcus and Fischer 1986). However, Dumont's approach has had a rather persistent and diverse influence on the succeeding sociological studies of India. For example, anthropologists focused on 'traditional' India for its major (West-contrasting) cultural principles and categories. Since Dumont has himself selected and critically evaluated a whole crop of such studies in his revised and complete version of *Homo Hierarchicus*, the reader is best referred to this book for his 'Preface to the Complete English Edition', 'Postface' and the corresponding citations in 'Notes'. Such Dumont-inspired contributions displaced earlier village and social change studies of the 1950s. The latter were found weak in 'theory'. The 'new' approach also rendered historically-situated India spurious because history simply stood outside the 'structural' ideology of the traditional Indian caste system. Correspondingly, the Dumontian fieldworker concerned himself with discovering hidden category oppositions and their significance within social conditions. Ironically, such a scholar, though studying India from within, remained preoccupied with verifying his structural theory, and again remained elusive and distant to the informant. He rendered India's villages sociologically secondary, and India's modernity ideologically spurious (see, for example, Srinivas 1976, for disputing Dumont's position on the Indian village, and Khare 1989, for a study of modern India's 'otherness' to the West).

Ethnosociology

This leads us to another major attempt to study India from within. It is McKim Marriott's 'ethnosociology' that grew out of another series of attempts, a counter-theory of sorts, spelled out over 30 years. With his early preference for 'interactional' over 'attributional' theories, Marriott (compare 1959 and 1989) claimed to provide an 'alternative' approach to study and understand India. Though this 'transactional' approach is worthy of a detailed comparative analysis (for its roots perhaps lie in an American sociology of formalism and pragmatism, recast as a 'Chicago anthropology' of India), we will confine ourselves to Marriott's general strategies for a study of India from within (and for a tacit commentary in this approach on India's otherness to the West).

Marriott's 'ethnosociological' approach incorporates some radical epistemological points of departure. After proposing an interactionist explanation of castes in India (see Marriott 1959), Marriott reveals, through a series of exercises (1968: 133–71; 1976b; 1987; 1989), his preference for, and a dependence on, certain formal 'sociological' tools, techniques, and three-dimensional representations of transactions. Essentially, his research proceeds in two phases. Up to 1968, as he scored the 'field-collected' caste ranking transactions on matrices, he illustrated his case-specific, logico-empirical analysis of village life (whether changing or non-changing) in north India. During this early phase, Marriott approached India, the non-Western other, for a 'scientific' (field and comparative) study. Despite his keen observations of the local scene, his overall approach emphasized certain etic distinctions (Marriott 1955). Though his field visits remained rare, Marriott proved himself to be a keen and sensitive fieldworker (Marriott 1966: 200–12). Reflecting cultural empathy and alienation, he keenly described the festival of Holi for its internal cultural content as well as its otherness. (Besides, to an Indian observer, in the same account the pragmatic sensibilities of a mid-western American coping with unfamiliar rituals of celebration also appear.)

Such an allusion to an 'early Marriott' of the 1950s and the 1960s is necessary to recognize the shifts he makes during the 1970s and the 1980s to construct an 'ethnosociology' of India. His review of *Homo Hierarchicus* (Marriott 1969) perhaps marked the transition, for within a few years he, with help from Inden, launched his 'monistic' approach to articulate 'flows' within the 'Hindu world' (and world-view) to reach 'analytical sociological models, comparable to the theoretical generalised social systems of Max Weber or Talcott Parsons...' (Marriott and Inden 1977: 229).

In Marriott's terms, such a departure argued that it 'would not be a bad objective for [Western social scientists] to make themselves—the knowers—somewhat like those South Asian objects that they would make known' (1976b: 195). His most recent statements (1989: 1–2) continue in the same direction: 'social science ideas ... can be developed from the realities known to Indian people.' Indian ethnosociology offers social scientists 'a second lens', 'a conscious alternative' to see through Western presuppositions and blind spots. Marriott and his close followers do so by pursuing their own distinct 'substance-flow' based view of the Hindu universe. This way they seem to be pursuing their own foibles—a formal, substantivist approach for rendering the Hindu's world concrete and systematic (and therefore 'real') in respectable Western scientific terms.[14]

Crucial to his 'construction' of ethnosociology, and directly relevant to our discussion of the cultural other, Marriott (1989: 1–6) provides us with some of his general assumptions and viewpoints:

(a) 'All social sciences develop from thought about what is known to particular cultures and are thus 'cultural' or 'ethno-' social sciences in their origins' (1989: 1).

(b) Western social science, though widely recognized, remains an example of 'ethnosocial sciences of only one limited ... type', and we need 'to expand the world repertory of social sciences' by 'working with a culturally related, but non-European people's thought about their own realities' (1989: 1).

(c) The social scientist should be fully aware about the implicit assumptions of 'the traditional categories of sociological questioning'. He should therefore not risk 'imposing an alien ontology and alien epistemology' on other people's thought and realities (1989: 2).

(d) The 'precipitates of Western social, intellectual, and particularly academic history' rarely fit 'Indian definitions of reality' (1989: 2).

(e) Yet Indian (or Hindu) notions and institutions are not 'impregnable' to Western-style analysis. 'Indian joinings' of what the West would dichotomize 'often point to *alternative*, especially transactional concepts of integrative value' (1989: 3, emphasis added).

(f) 'None yet appears to have attempted what is proposed here—following the Parsons and Shils method all the way to constructing an alternative general theoretical system for the social sciences of a non-Western civilisation, using that civilisation's own categories' (1989: 5).

(g) Such an attempt requires 'metaconceptual categories and descriptive terms' that 'remain congruent with the indigenously cognised features' on the one hand, and 'facilitate comparison' with Western social science, on the other. 'Some shifting of Indian meanings in a Western direction' is also undoubtedly involved but Marriott hopes such 'compromises' are 'equitable' (1989: 6).

(h) 'Together with the ethnosciences of other lands...', Marriott hopes, '[Indian ethnosocial sciences] may provide better bases for the future claim of an expanded, multicultural set of sciences to have that "*universal* significance and value", which Weber ... prematurely reserved for rational social thought in the West' (1989: 3).

(i) Thus, developed Indian ethnosocial sciences may, in his view, eventually 'take their place beside the Western ethnosocial sciences' (1989: 3).

Positioning himself distinctly apart from Dumont's firmly Europe-centered epistemology of the cultural other, Marriott views India's otherness in terms of Hindu culture's distinct principles and categories of transactions and the resulting knowledge of reality. Though India is more than the constructions of the Hindu world, we still need to know how (and how far) 'congruent' are his 'Indian ethnosocial sciences' to all that constitutes and moves the Hindu universe.[15] Is the Hindu universe limited only to transactions? The issue of congruency acquires added significance when his own analytic assumptions rest on Western science (i.e., his formal notions of consistency, simplicity and parsimony in 'transactions' and 'materiality'), while assuming compliance from Hindu conceptions of knowledge and reality. Does Marriott also, in the final analysis, work only with selected aspects of the Hindu universe? Does he also overlook the possibility that representational and interpretive devices of 'mathematical analogs' and 'three-dimensional graphing' could limit and distort Hindu conceptions (and expressions) of reality? As a test of Marriott's reading of the Hindu world, on the other hand, one might ask indigenous Hindu scholars (pundits and śāstris) to comment on Marriott's schemes. Some might find Marriott intriguing—even appealing, while others may dispute him.[16]

How do we make sense of some crucial achievements and failures of Marriott's ethnosociology? Among its achievements, particularly from the point of view of postcolonial social science in India, are (a) its bold and uniquely culture-sensitive approach to the cultural otherness of India, and (b) its readiness to make Indic epistemology a congruent and potentially 'equal' partner in reaching reliable and rigorous systems of knowledge. He is unsparing of 'the imperial style of Western ethnosocial science', and of a host of inapplicable Western concepts and distinctions. He finds 'processual relativism' of the Hindu ethnosocial sciences 'the most ecumenical of urges' (1989: 33). He also hints toward a universalistic social science that, as a climax of a 'multicultural' set of ethnosocial sciences, rises above the 'fears of parochialism and relativism'.

Marriott's ethnosociological approach encourages culturally 'accurate' ethnographies (see Marriott 1989, for his latest careful selection and interpretation of appropriate works).[17] Under Marriott's influence, if an ethnographer increasingly tends to become a textual and contextual exegete of aspects of learned Hindu thought, it is to discover flows (and 'fluidarity') of diverse substance-codes in diverse domains of transactions. So encumbered, a young ethnographer unfortunately might have far less time (or inclination) to learn from the field.[18]

Failures of ethnosociology, on the other hand, as already indicated, accumulate from one's predisposition toward one grand theory for explaining Hindu India or India as a whole (such inspiration usually originating in the West). Knowing India from up close makes such attempts increasingly less satisfactory. Ethnosociology is no exception in this regard. Though forging wide links, it still conveys to me that we can manage only aspects of the large picture. Confined to transactional domains, it lacks direct and sufficient capability to deal fully with the Hindu's sensual and suprasensual reality, especially when concerned with self, moral order, knowledge, experience, unconditional liberation, and the Absolute Reality (*jīvātaman*, dharma, *satjñāna, anubhava, mokṣa*, and the Brahman).[19] Such considerations fundamentally determine the Hindu's conception of being, karma, birth (*yoni*), and body (*deha*), and determine the admissibility of otherness, including of what Marriott is after—a verification of the transactional nature of the Hindu's 'seen' material and social world. As an approach, Marriott's ethnosociology has already attracted some comments and criticisms from philosophers (see, for example, several contributions in O'Flaherty 1980, especially by Potter and Larson) and anthropologists, some of whom find Marriott's approach as ultimately 'an anachronism' for Western social science (e.g., Daniel 1984: 54; see also Good 1982; Trautmann 1980).

For the Indian insider, ethnosociology remains silent on what Hindu culture and epistemology most vociferously assert—'The explanation of the seen is in the unseen' (see Satprakashananda 1965: 193, and his discussion of the place of 'suprasensual knowledge' within the Hindu notions of self, the worldly, and the otherworldly). As a philosopher has observed, Marriott continues to emphasize transactions over transcendence (or dharma over *mokṣa* or *pravritti* over *nivritti*; see Potter 1980), often producing the problem of indefensible distinctions and lopsided emphases in descriptions as well as in theoretical formulations.

Overall, ethnosociology represents one of the major Western approaches of the 20th century for understanding India (or analogously other such non-Western cultures) from within. It renders India's cultural otherness negotiable. Marriott's scheme is perhaps the first bold attempt to explore an alternative to an exclusively Europe-centered epistemology and world-view.[20]

For the 20th century, therefore, Dumont and Marriott, separately and together, conclude another chapter in the Western approach to India and its cultural distance. Though both claim theoretical differences between them (in terms of Western sociological assumptions), both study the cultural uniqueness of India (especially the Hindu culture and its world-view) from within. Both concern themselves with the learned and popular cultures of India, and both seek a single, internally consistent theoretical explanation of the diverse Indian social reality by applying the well-known 'scientific' criteria of simplicity, economy, and parsimony.

Although both scholars tried to view India beyond the colonizer's hegemonic 'other' (characterized by one-sided reportage on an epistemic domination of India), only Marriott could develop a much more rigorous and comprehensive conceptual apparatus to address some of India's distinct cultural insights. However, once we focus on India's ever-diversifying history, social situations and culture, Marriott's ethnosociological exercise tends to close in on itself by holding rigid views on 'substance', 'joinings', and 'fluidity'. Instead, to succeed, ethnosociology needs to invite openness, criticism and ingenuity (*patutā*) of a whole range of scholars, whether Indianists or not.

Critical Cultural Studies and Interpretations

Though Dumont and Marriott recognize the necessity of identifying Hindu India from within, both strangely shy away from the dominant Hindu way of dissolving the other—by the ideal of Universal Self (which dissolves all alterity; for the crucial Upanishadic conception of the Brahman, see Hume 1985: 32–52). We miss learning from them that Hindu India has its own way of dealing with sociocultural distance and alienation, and that its direct conception and expression are fundamental to Hindu India's predominant self-identity. Instead, Hindu India is *sociologized* by Dumont in terms of Durkheimian holism, and by Marriott (1989: 5) for constructing 'a general theoretical system' à la Parsons and Shils. Indian sociology gains most when it critically appraises both, and starts its own cultural critiques of ongoing researches.

Thus, in fact, it appears that the next phase is of careful cultural interpretation and criticism. It is increasingly characterized by (*a*) a general dispersal of the Dumont-style 'total' ideological contrast of India to the West; (*b*) a preference for alternative interpretive approaches to deal with India's regional and ethnic diversity; and (*c*) an effort to develop what may be called 'reciprocal sociology' between India and the West. This phase strengthens studies conducted from India of the West as much as those from the West. Similarly, instead of constructing a single grand theory (whether monistic or dualistic) to explain India or the West, now several investigators may prefer to conduct their analyses of substantive issues (e.g., foods, gifting, sacrifice, and principles of equilibrium and appropriateness) to develop a generally shared perspective on the larger picture. They may seldom feel the necessity to commit themselves for life to any single grand theoretical explanation.[21] Within such a picture, most Indian anthropologists and sociologists concern themselves with Indian cultural diversity and particularity.[22]

Though less frequently represented, the semantic or semiotic anthropology of the 1980s also focuses on meanings and interpretations of crucial textual knowledge and everyday practice. For example, one may consider 'the semiotics of Indian identity' with the help of Peircean semiotics because 'it provides an unexpected access to the inwardness of Indians and of Americans alike' (Singer 1984: 160). If the Indian other thus becomes less distant to a Western anthropologist, it allows a South Asian colleague to explicate the 'inside' and 'outside' of the Tamil's world by explicating the semiotics of 'substance', 'experience', and 'equilibrium' (Daniel 1984). Even more rarely, we encounter a 'semiological' study of India's view of the West, and of the West's internal otherness (Uberoi 1968, 1984). As Uberoi juggles the West's frames of familiarity and distance vis-à-vis those of India, he provides us with a valuable and scarce comparative commentary on the West's management of its own identity crisis. Some innovative efforts from India's political scientists are equally noteworthy, especially when they do not remain prisoners of the West's conflict theories and their production of otherness.[23]

Accordingly, the anthropologist's recent interpretive and critical approaches have increased reflexivity in their discourses, rendering the axis between self and the other as full of multiple 'voices', changing vantage points, and competing epistemologies—people's own vis-à-vis those of anthropologists (e.g., Babb 1987; Carrithers 1983; Madan 1987b). Similarly, as learned texts are interpreted as the locus of authoritative knowledge against people's social experience and its communication, they generate an anthropological critique of hermeneutics. Ideological texts sometimes become 'live' discourses, where words constitute a protest for challenging the entrenched equations of social and epistemic dominance (Veena Das 1982; 1986; Khare 1984).

Such an interpretive phase allows the anthropologist to address the contradictory, the chaotic, the emotional, and the mysterious within the informant's world. It is feasible because the investigator is not after the construction of a grand theory and is willing to test his own reasoning and conception against that of the people. He opens himself to the messages other people's epistemologies and ontologies provide (for a comparative discussion, see Ardener 1985: 47–70; Evens 1983; Overing 1985, especially the Introduction; Parkin 1982a: 1–51; Rorty 1980; Salmond 1985: 240–63). As a consequence of such initiatives a self-conscious investigator emerges, who watches the politics of epistemologies within his studies of other people's identity and otherness (Crapanzano 1980; Rabinow 1977). Ethnography becomes doubly reflexive. It concerns the anthropologist's intellectual world as much as it does the informant's, with a continuous construction of, and commentary on, the nature of the cultural other. A crisis of representation usually reflects a crisis in our assumptions about our own identity and difference (Fabian 1983; Whitten 1988).

Whether ethnosociological, symbolic or hermeneutical, an explanation of India's self-identity (and what it considers 'others') must ultimately reside in India's own cultural reasoning and historical experience. Equally important is the recognition of scholarship that proves that the two—classical Indian and Western—systems of logic and epistemology are in fact independently standing—and authentic—with comparable and congruent structures of significance (for a careful discussion of this issue, see Staal 1988: 1–56). As the Indian systems of logic and epistemology thus receive more attention by themselves (e.g., Matilal 1971; 1977; 1985) and in comparison to the European counterparts, we will not only have a genuine basis for congruency between the two systems, but we can also employ it toward the development of more rigorous universalistic formulations. At present, the otherness issues are usually defined, studied, and decided by certain basic distinctions produced by Western epistemologies alone (whether it is called power, class, ethnicity, alienation, or nation). Most often, therefore, we still know India primarily through a West-manufactured lens, or by our sporadic reactions to it. We require a systematic study of how India has, over the centuries, formulated its approaches to the other.[24]

Future Prospects

The preceding four approaches of Indian sociology, pursued since the 1950s, reflect a definite—but still limited—progress in dealing with the problem of the cultural other and otherness within India, and between India and the West. Though some attempts now show a greater sensitivity toward India as a center of reflexive cultural knowledge, the basic issue requiring our attention is a careful study of the West's (conscious and unconscious) alienation from, and processes of domination of, India (or other non-Western cultures). Indian sociology must examine the issue from *both* directions—to discover how contemporary India pursues its different values of otherness from within, and how it confronts as well as accepts Western modernity. A similar exercise is necessary when, within India, the Hindu world is compared with the non-Hindu other (Islamic, Buddhist, Jain, and Sikh). The other here refers to all those psychological, social, religious, historical, and philosophic differences which constantly mark the Indian's life. Indian sociology cannot afford to neglect such research.

Despite the sustained work toward its creation and rationale, a long-range survival of Indian sociology, especially as a prospering comparative discipline, depends on its research of the cultural other. Such a sociology has also to nurture deep intellectual roots and perspectives developed by Indian thinkers over time. As we have argued, at the heart of such a pursuit lies India's own dual cultural 'grammar' of otherness, one when it looks within, and the other when it faces the outside world, especially of the long-influencing West. India's recent social history provides us with ample clues about such a dual grammar of otherness. (For a historical analysis of some—internal and external—social forces in India, see Saberwal 1986.) However, this focus does not mean that Indian sociology can be self-absorbed or inward-looking. Instead, it must become 'reciprocal sociology', investigating Western ideas and explanations by non-Western (Indian and non-Indian) intellectual locations, commentaries and criticisms. Within India, issues of cultural unity *and* diversity must engage the same sociologist. He must attend to both as a part of the lived culture.

But in order to do this, Indian sociology requires a rigorous analysis of its own identity, including its otherness to India. We need a critical evaluation of the larger historical forces which produced such Western approaches to India as those of Dumont and Marriott, and of their generally limited receptivity within India. If Indian sociology itself has been a product of the post-War forces, it must be prepared to change with historical changes (including those now afoot in Europe and across East and West). Such a new Indian sociology may be increasingly independent to debate and evaluate various evolving positions of the West-based 'universal' (and thus also of the West's rationality and relativism; see Hollis and Lukes 1982). Recent appropriate exercises from India (Uberoi 1968; 1984) may have to be evaluated in terms of the hegemonistic nature of knowledge and representation on the one hand, and in relation to changing internal constraints on Western social science research, on the other.[25]

Internally, Indian sociology needs to enlarge its domain of interest and inquiry, bringing into focus long-existing springs of local and regional scholarship and knowledge. It requires that there be no unexamined dependence on (or automatic acceptance of) Western viewpoints. This would allow for a more open comparison and evaluation of those authentic studies that widely diverged in assumptions and outlook from those favored in the West.[26] To underscore the point of a larger intellectual landscape, I have purposely treated the works of Dumont and Marriott together, without dwelling on their West-located internal theoretical rivalry. We need to place Western works in the larger historical and intellectual picture of India. The general point for Indian sociologists is to translate also various forms of that otherness that Western and Indian scholars produce between them as they pursue their favorite intellectual predispositions.

Though started in the 1950s as a particular Western approach to view Hindu India and its cultural ideology, Indian sociology, as recorded in the pages of *Contributions* since 1967, has already been undergoing a slow but definite diversification (and even dispersal) in approach, content and perspective. It currently seems to entertain contributions exemplifying in some ways all the four approaches to the cultural other discussed in this chapter. Such a diversity is bound to increase with time, raising the necessity of fostering periodic critical reviews of major analytic approaches and their intellectual assumptions. The continuing role of the 'colonial mentality' is perhaps one such issue which Indian sociology can neither easily dismiss nor fully disown. The 'colonial mind' itself was perhaps neither all-knowing nor internally homogeneous. Nor was it equally successful all over India. If recent Indian scholarship wants to study the entire colonial encounter to control its cultural role in contemporary India, it has to make a long-term study of transforming faces of hegemonic knowledge. The exercises of Dumont and Marriott are instructive in this context—as well-researched explanations of India's identity and otherness. Though Marriott gets much nearer to India than Dumont, they still share more than they differ.[27]

For Indian sociology, there is still much cultural otherness from near and afar that remains to be translated and understood in Indian terms. Some of the enduring issues that so arise for Indian sociology to investigate are: India's own changing discourses on universalism and parochialism; implicit forms of cultural reasoning within such discourses; 'live' interrelationships between learned thought, regional variations, and local life-experiences; and multiple 'fundamental' grounds of truth validation and the consequent moral relativism. India-rooted Indian sociology, in such a complex endeavor, may have to undertake a more critical evaluation of its own sources of identity, both indigenous (*desī*) and foreign (*videśī*).

◄ NOTES

1. By 'Indian sociology' I refer mostly to distinct developments discussed in *Contributions*, the original and new series, since the mid-1950s. I prefer the term 'Indian sociology' over 'sociology of India' since it helps me underscore the original emphasis that Dumont and Pocock (1957; 1960) envisioned for their project. Historically, I distinguish between 'Indian sociology' that develops from within, reflecting the changing Indian intellectual temper, and that which reflects the colonial and/or Western value assumptions. Meenakshi Thapan's (1988) excellent paper was an encouragement to me in writing mine. She made my task easier by pointing out a central issue of Indian sociology: its limited ability, so far, to deal with the cultural other within India, and outside.

2. Widely different forces produce sociocultural otherness within a society and one could examine them from different theoretical positions. I confine myself (as do the scholars I review) to India's cultural discourses from within and their analyses. One could obviously take other positions to view India's internal strains.

3. The literature on the subject is vast and varied in Western philosophy, with some recent notable additions. For a wide-ranging and conventional discussion of the issue of 'other minds' in philosophy, especially for reflecting Wittgenstein's influence, see Wisdom (1956). For an anthropological analysis of the issue, see Fabian (1983); Marcus and Fischer (1986); Whitten (1988). For a critique of traditional Western positions on value, taste, judgment, and justi-

fication, see Barbara Smith (1988). She develops an 'alternative framework' by criticizing such recent thinkers as Derrida, Habermas, Northrop Frye, and Richard Rorty.

4. This has been so despite the best Western liberal tradition (and its intentions) that Louis Dumont and David Pocock may have represented. Recent studies alert us to the lingering colonial temper shaping the thinking of Indian and Western scholars of the period (see Nandy 1983).

5. My argument underscores the necessity of not reducing India's multiple cultural faces over time and region, for the sake of a simple theory or a 'system'. However, such attempts should also not overlook the internal devices of cultural unity.

My proposal emphasizes the role of indigenous forms of 'cultural reasoning and world-views', especially of the three long-standing major Indic traditions—Hindu, Buddhist, and Jain. These major players have long been involved in what Gilbert Ryle (1954: 1–14), in another context, called the 'litigation between [alternative] theories or bodies of ideas', shaping both the common sense and common knowledge of India—and the Indian.

6. However, toward the end of this century, the West's universalist position encounters difficulty when a protesting knowledge system (e.g., Islamic or Chinese) disputes the ultimate epistemic supremacy and authority of the West, and proclaims itself to be a separate anchor of ideological and cultural universalism.

7. In *Contributions*, during the 1970s and 1980s (as in other major journals), Marriott's ethnosociology could only receive insufficient intensive analysis and comparative evaluation (though it was frequently alluded to). This difference should be analyzed as an issue of disciplinary intellectual history, putting a requisite distance between the living personalities and our attitudes toward them. Looked at this way, ethnosociology has enjoyed only a limited general appeal and influence. *Contributions* also, accordingly, devoted its special issues first to evaluating Dumont's and Srinivas' work. Though undoubtedly Marriott's approach is far more refined, accurate, and rigorous in cultural terms than Dumont's, his style of presentation remains inaccessible. His 'Hindu science' and Western formal scientific method continue to be a misfit within ethnosociology.

Marriott's formalism (i.e., his transactional jargon, 'scientific' logic of parsimony, set theory, and multidimensional geometric representations) fetters him in approaching the multifarious (*vividha*) being and becoming of the Hindu world. The Hindu for him essentially becomes a transactional-porous-'body', with no room for a soul or a feeling self (or just a *jīvātaman*). The feeling-faith-guided-aesthetic-intuitive-experiential world of the Hindu can only be transactional (hence 'fluid') within such an ethnosociology.

8. Potter (1965: 241–67) presents what major Indic philosophies, in profile, have to say on such major issues as parts and the whole, causation, and the notions of 'freedom' or liberation. However, the anthropologist must suitably adapt such information for his use. Thus, for example, the otherness issue may relate to a host of classical conceptions of self, soul and universal soul, from the Upanishadic period; see Hume (1985: 23–32).

9. We should at this point consider how Indian sociology in the pages of *Contributions* has (consciously or unconsciously) employed different models and meanings of the West's other as its own. However, we presently lack a suitable background study. Meanwhile, as we have already remarked (see note 7), the Western other very often enters via sociology's formulations, even if the adopted view is emic. A.K. Saran (1963), for example, had very early remarked that Dumont's 'Indian sociology' remains alien to India (see Dumont 1966).

10. Whatever fleeting cognition of these is admitted, it is simply to yield to ever-dissolving momentary perceptions. In this context, the Buddhist philosophic 'deconstruction' of self or 'I-ness' (*anātmavāda*) is most radical. But even such a position cannot deny the everyday struggle with otherness (for the monastic lives of Buddhist monks, see Carrithers 1983).

11. Comparatively, some in Western philosophy have long debated the problem of knowing about the thoughts, feelings and dispositions of 'other minds'. For philosophers investigating other minds is not altogether the same as knowing about other knowledge by analogy, translation or other tropes (see Wisdom 1956).

12. For recent reviews, see Yogendra Singh (1983) and Srinivas and Panini (1973). However, Yogendra Singh's term 'Indian sociology' refers to all that has been studied sociologically in India in recent times from various theoretical positions.

13. Dumont's research program on India should be examined in terms of Dumont's reading of the modern ideologies of France, England and Germany. His view of India remains firmly grounded in the Cartesian 'ideology' of the modern West (with occasional critiques of its deformities during the world wars). In this way (while excluding the internal critiques and failures of post-war modern Western thought), he characterized India only as the West's perfect other—a society without the modern Western individual and a genuine politico-economic history. Ironically, however, this India (retrieved from a mixture of selective ethnography and Indological texts) appeared before the West only to reflect the West's own colonial archaism.

14. Physical bodies, material transfers, concrete spaces, food, blood, humors, alchemy, and mechanical 'flows' by heating and cooling (or other similar devices) constitute the main domains of analysis for Marriott's ethnosociology and its followers (e.g., Mines 1989; Moore 1989; Moreno and Marriott 1989).

    For some reviews of Marriott's work, see Good (1982: 36) and Daniel (1984: 53). One of the central disputes concerns equating the Western social scientist with his object of study, and dealing with the necessity of according India an independent—and equal—epistemic voice vis-à-vis the West. Proposing such an epistemic goal from the West remains exemplary. Indian sociology can only approve such an initiative, but only after examining some of its underlying ambiguities and assumptions. See note 7.

15. Marriott's general conception of the cultural other is difficult to decipher because of his silence on the subject. Though he carefully selects and employs other appropriate works—descriptive and theoretical—to produce his 'verifying evidence', such a procedure does not give us the required larger picture. We do not know how he approaches India's positions on knowledge vis-à-vis those that are Western. His view of 'science' also demands that we

know how he approaches debates between foundationalist and anti-foundationalist theories of knowledge within Western philosophies (e.g., Rorty 1989b; Taylor 1989).

16. I discussed in Lucknow in 1988, though unsystematically, some of Marriott's (1976a: 109–42) formulations with a few appropriate scholars of learned Hindu texts and daily practice (especially drawn from such fields as classical philosophy, Ayurveda and astrology). They discussed several contexts that interest Marriott. This way my informants tried to peek into a scholar's mind and his understanding of the Hindu world. One of my scholar-informants, in review, found Marriott's work to be similar to that of a university educated *śāstri*. However, when it came to reflecting the experience of the diverse Hindu universe and its *lived* sensibilities, several of my informants found Marriott remote (in Hindi, *vey basey kam par parhé adhika hain*).

17. Given a careful citation of the studies of students, colleagues and 'others', Marriott has developed a way of doing a sort of 'fieldwork' via other people's ethnographies. By representing and synthesizing these, he produces a kind of 'metaethnography' of his own to support his theoretical formulations.

18. This may be particularly true of young ethnographers from outside India coming to produce a study *of* or *on* India. Oriented to establishing or disputing a prevalent theoretical explanation, such scholars may rarely approach the field for unencumbered learning. While they theorize, local scholars often devote themselves to intricate details. Unfortunately, viewed over time, both tendencies, until coordinated, would yield unsatisfactory results for Indian sociology.

19. Marriott is however not silent on the liberation issue any longer. His Table 2 (1989: 14–15) summarizes the larger picture of a 'processual Hindu social science', and it includes reference to the Hindu's philosophic 'constants', where his transactional and mathematical analogs score 'empty set' and 'nonrelationality'. Are they conceived the same way by the ordinary and the learned (*jñāni*) Hindu? Though we lack appropriate ethnographies on dharma and *mokṣa*, such subjects as *jīva, ātman, parmātman, māyā, bhakti* and *sādhanā* directly constitute 'the realities known to Indian people'. These are *not* ethnographically empty; they only need to be studied as people account for them. They constitute the Hindu's active, indispensable voice.

20. By implication, the same approach must mean new challenges to better understand Hindu epistemology and how its reasoning patterns work within society. It also means a fuller explication of what 'an Indian way of thinking' is (see Ramanujan 1989).

21. For theme-based conceptual analyses, see Daniel 1984; Dirks 1987; Khare 1976; Madan 1987b; Parry 1985: 51–78; Raheja 1988; Zimmermann 1987. Though most of these generally uphold the goal of viewing India from within, they rarely investigate the Euro-centered epistemology of social sciences. Papers published in *Contributions* (new series) since 1967 generally support similar wide-ranging interpretive tendencies. It may be hard to find, for example, a staunch Dumontian among Indian sociologists and anthropologists working in India. If T.N. Madan has stayed closely with Dumont's work on India for over three decades, he studied, in my view, what Dumont had emphasized as well as ignored (e.g., 'non-renunciation'. See Madan 1987b). I

adopted a more critical (but constructive) stance toward both major—
Dumont's and Marriott's—approaches to comprehend India's learned and
popular cultures (e.g., for the Brahman's and the Untouchable's ideals and
practices on food, kinship, rituals, and alternative ideologies, see Khare 1976;
1983; 1984).

22. With independence, Indian social scientists increasingly study culturally and
historically particular faces of India. Even those aware of the India–West ideological divide often examine India for its ground-level regional, historical and
religious differences (Thapan 1988).

23. Rajni Kothari provides us with a valuable perspective on the cultural otherness that India and other non-Western countries face from the West. Kothari's
work depicts such otherness as crucial to evolving a non-Western 'alternative'
to modern political philosophy as well as practice. He raises the issue of
India's own version of modernity (see Khare 1988). He argues for a coherent
evolution of Indian political culture, especially in the wake of accelerated
social change and ethnic strife (Kothari 1970; 1976; 1986; for a review of
Kothari's work, see Pantham 1988: 229–46). Localized anthropological
accounts of dominant 'ideology' as a hegemonic discourse between the Hindus and 'antagonistic others' similarly need careful conceptual handling. Too
much emphasis on local conflicts tends to obscure the larger picture (e.g.,
Contusi 1989).

24. India, like the West, has produced, over time, several schemes to deal with
(a) the distinct other—the outsider and the stranger (yavana, dasyu, etc.),
(b) the similar other (Buddhists and Jains), and (c) the illusory other, a product of delusion and worldly attachment.

25. Simultaneously, the Western intellectual temper might also be changing toward a generally neoconservative, Euro-centered culture, accompanied by
declining investment in the so-called 'area studies'. Such a change has already
promoted the idea of doing 'anthropology at home'.

26. For example, we should juxtapose the studies of A.K. Saran (1963) and Marriott (1989) to examine their comparative assumptions about the Hindu's cognitive categories and cultural sensibilities (see also Madan 1987b: 161ff). In a
similar step, both these attempts could be studied against the appropriate insights and observations of A.K. Coomaraswamy on Indic civilization.

27. Apropos their claims of 'major' theoretical differences, Dumont and Marriott
stand most of all for understanding Indian society from 'within' (i.e., as formulated from their respective Western—French and American—locations).
Both evolve their distinct 'scientific' or 'formal' approaches to explain India
in sociological 'universals'. Yet Marriott (1989) reflects a better awareness of
the integral nature of the Hindu world.

2

Social Description and Social Change: From Function to Critical Cultural Significance*

I

This chapter argues for the need to re-examine the wider significance of the studies of social description and social change in India, the topics to which Professor M.N. Srinivas has made a series of pioneering contributions (e.g., Srinivas 1964; 1976).[1] Such a step is necessary because some recent influential analyses, especially those of Professors Louis Dumont and McKim Marriott,[2] point out new issues and problems which previous studies either overlooked or were unprepared to recognize. Meanwhile, we have questioned several sociological and anthropological assumptions about our method, descriptive representation and theorization, most notably scientific objectivity (see Agger 1991; Manganaro 1990b). In such a context of changing disciplinary assumptions, the works of M.N. Srinivas, which never clearly followed a predominant theoretical 'school', might be reviewed for their strengths and

* This chapter is a revised version of the article originally published in A.M. Shah, B.S. Baviskar and E.A. Ramaswamy (eds), 1996. *Theory and Method: An Evaluation of the Work of M.N. Srinivas, Social Structure and Change*, Vol. 1, pp. 55–78 (Sage Publications, New Delhi).

weaknesses. Though theoretically naive (hence unencumbered), these works still remain influential for describing the verities of Indian social life, often in striking styles of description, narration, and analysis.

An evaluation of Srinivas' work, in my view, automatically implicates the works of two other major contemporary scholars— Louis Dumont and McKim Marriott. A brief, stage-setting, comparative review is in order. For example, while Srinivas' view of Indian society rested on historical and cultural diversity, Dumont's 'Indian sociology', one of the most influential scholarly efforts after the second world war, chose to deal with Indian reality in 'ideological' terms, with the focus on the 'structural logic' of ritual status and power (Dumont 1980, also his other essential writings included therein).[3] Dumont thus proposed a new methodological point of departure: That Indian society must be studied 'from within', by its own cultural configuration of values, yielding what he called 'Indian sociology'. When juxtaposed to the wide ranging concerns of Srinivas' studies on India, Dumont's approach, in some important ways, remains incomplete, ironic, and paradoxical.

Incomplete because Dumont's accounts limit themselves to only traditional Hindu India. Ironic because Dumont's 'Indian sociology', while aiming to view India from 'within', actually establishes and highlights the primacy of modern Western thought for its logic of binary structures and 'total' oppositions. Dumont thus bypassed a rich and rigorous field of reasoning, relations, distinctions *and non-distinctions* which Indic (i.e., Hindu, Buddhist, and Jain) epistemologies had long developed and illustrated in their own societies. And paradoxical because Dumont firmly positions the West in the background as he describes India 'from within'. Actually, the result was to alienate India from its own conceptions of moral agent, political power, and cultural history.[4] From Srinivas' standpoint, to bring such a perspective to India is to see its culture only in certain favored aspects and essences. Little wonder therefore that Indian counter-examples, anomalies and exceptions should constantly dog Dumont's 'structural explanations'.

Similarly, despite Dumont's emphasis on studying a society in 'totality' (a lesson that Marcel Mauss, Dumont's teacher, underscored), his sociology continued to exclude (or only selectively include) the fundamental *essences* of Hindu India. Here, as elsewhere, the root problem in Dumont's work might be one of sometimes inappropriate and sometimes inadequate and misfitting selections, translations, and uses of 'central' Hindu principles and constructs. Rough analogies and the 'pure logic' of structural relations remained a poor, alien substitute for a closer inspection and translation of Hindu concepts and practices on their own. For example, Dumont's 'set theory of hierarchy' could hardly approach the rich fare which the classical Hindu models and popular uses had long developed on the crucial issue of 'identity and difference' or 'the one and the many' (Khare 1983). Nor does his notion of 'ritual power' adequately connect with the Hindu conceptions of *sakti*—temporal and spiritual. Similarly, Dumont's 'sociology of caste' starkly dismissed the Hindu panoply of formulations on the 'doer–experiencer' (*karta–bhokta*). To a critic, such examples convey that Dumont's ideas of the 'ahistorical', the 'social collective' and the 'holistic' (i.e., Dumont's encompassing and encompassed) unwittingly imposed on India some of the West's 19th century Orientalist formulations.

Further, Dumont, not unlike many other Indologists and anthropologists of his times, simply ignored the impositional role of Western knowledge, power, and discourse control while working on India. His 'scientific' scholarly approach, assumed the predominance of Western ideas, methods, and explanations even as he explicated India 'from within'. Locating himself squarely in the West, he found Indian reality historically remote, sociologically pre-individual, culturally pre-modern, and philosophically naive. Western sociology, in contrast, reflected for him a conscious control of its discourse by being external, exoteric, scientific, advanced, and universal.

However, a proper 'decoding' of sociological and Indological ideas requires multiple unpacking of subtexts from *both*—Indian and Western—directions. And yet, it is Dumont's pioneering works that lead us toward such an exercise. Placed within the larger sociological context, Dumont's work has been an influential 'alternative' to the conventional structural–functional descriptions and analyses. Whether it is India or Europe, Dumontian sociological program (see Dumont 1977; 1980), despite its flaws, shows us how one may compare dissimilar configurations of ideologies and values across complex cultures. Without such a comparison, we learn from Dumont, anthropology remains rootless and scotomatous.

In response to Dumont, on the other hand, Marriott's (1976a; 1989) 'ethnosociological' explanations take a different approach to study (but again largely Hindu) India.[5] Based on his recent essay, his theoretical inspiration comes from the Parsonian 'system of social action' and its pursuit of 'interactional' (relational) properties. Transposing certain classical Hindu formulations and ethnographic relations onto his three-dimensional 'cubic' representations, Marriott provides a sociological language to describe 'accurately' the essentially transactional 'Hindu world'. Doing so, he also claims to provide a paradigm for comparative regional ethnosociolog*ies* and a universal social science (see Chapter 1). Though his cultural reading and translation of Indian texts are rigorous and his explanations insightful, his 'sociological theory' imposes new and different burdens on the Hindu system. Committed to studying Hindu India by the 'realities known to its own people', he cannot let the thought arise why his 'sociological theory' would not be alien to 'the Hindu world'. Nor would he allow the question of Orientalist vestiges and representations even in his 'explanatory science'. Nevertheless, he needs to address them.

Such limitations notwithstanding, Marriott's 'reading' of Hindu culture, by itself, provides deeper and subtler formulations than does Dumont's. Marriott is best when he, with care, formulates and organizes the basic constituents and transactions of the Hindu world. His accomplishments, however, diminish or scatter when he tries to provide a sociological explanation which would *refute and replace* contributions of Dumont's dualistic sociology. Though Marriott's sociology may have different strengths, its weaknesses are similar to Dumont's. His abstract work (see MacIntyre 1981) also quickly attracts counter-examples, anomalies and criticisms for what it includes—and excludes—of the Hindu world. He reduces Hindu India and its lived complex reality to a few paradigmatic transactional strategies.

Though the latest round of discussions (Marriott 1989) explains more, ethnosociology must still adequately address (rather than dismiss or sideline) increasing empirical and conceptual criticisms (see McGilvary 1982, for some empirical questions, and the continuing discussions in the *Contributions*). A crucial question for our discussion is whether ethnosociology, as currently formulated, explains Hindu society more and better than Dumont's Indian sociology or Srinivas' social descriptions. After a point, unfortunately, not unlike Dumont's 'pure–impure', ethnosociology also settles on its own self-justifying (and self-limiting) navel—

the 'Hindu Physics' of 'substance'. An outsider may wonder if such a locus does not somehow take impetus from American pragmatism and its notions of a 'flowing' practical reality.

The preceding review of the two scholars' works mainly highlights the differences when juxtaposed to M.N. Srinivas' descriptions and analyses of Indian society. Contrary to Dumont's early protestations, Srinivas does *not* just 'describe' India. Actually, over time, Srinivas' sociological writings have stood the test of time rather well. He preferred to view India through its lived cultural diversity, with an open mind toward both endogenous and exogenous forces and processes of social change. To obtain a fuller (but neither an exhaustive nor total) picture, one must evaluate the West-based as well as India-centered social ideas and experiences, and their directions of social change. In such understanding and writing must also be found the seeds of a 'universal sociology', and a view of India which would be neither mysterious, unique, nor simply traditional.[6]

One of Srinivas' common concerns is to explain India by a range of (historically changing) ideas, representations, contexts, experiences, and actions. According to him, single, simple essentialist theories, however well crafted, do not adequately explain the lived, diverse and contentious India. (I found the same to be true in my studies of the Hindu traditional and modern spheres; see Khare 1983; 1985; see also note 11.) If Dumont and Marriott rest their schemes on India's selected age-old idealized essentialist principles, then Srinivas' descriptive sociology builds on the modern secular, the rational and the 'reasonable' (including its complicity with dominant Western academic ways). If most of Srinivas' work (like Dumont's) stands prior to recent critical debates on knowledge and power, his discussions of social change (e.g., Sanskritization and modernization) also rest on the inevitable and superior forces of Western knowledge and its authority.

So far, sociology and anthropology in India have largely steered clear of such critical issues, while recently historiography, under the focus of 'subaltern studies', has initiated its critical discussions (Guha 1989; for critical anthropological commentaries, see Manganaro 1990a; and Chapter 4 here). In comparison, Dumont's 'structural sociology' and Marriott's 'ethnosociology' debilitate themselves by being aloof, technical, ponderous, and self-important—all in the name of a theoretical explanation of India. Srinivas, on the other hand, shows that the sociologically complex and significant can be simply written and made sense of, without numerous alien methodological assumptions and a technical vocabulary.

Writing style and interpretation have been important to Srinivas over time, though one could not attribute to him any such critical literary aspiration as we have come to expect from, for instance, Clifford Geertz (1973; 1983). Similarly, meanings are crucial to Srinivas, though he could hardly be credited with utilizing Indian symbolic logic and hermeneutics. Most importantly, his sociological writings, not given to defend any particular theoretical position, remain open to cultural richness and subtlety. But, on the other hand, this also keeps his discussions unreconciled in some important ways. For example, we do not know if he ever tried to reconcile his subtle West-inspired humanism and equalitarianism to the robust and resilient caste-ordered customary India. For him, both are just there to take into account.

II

Let us now appraise Srinivas' selected works. Conventionally, we say that he 'used' the structure–function approach, directly or indirectly, in his ethnography, seeking meanings via functions, and providing a social commentary on the changing Indian society.[7]

Instead of reviewing all his writings, I will concern myself with only four writings (Srinivas 1952; 1964; 1975; 1976).[8] These writings, in my estimation, are largely concerned with empirical specifications, functional explanations and processual changes. Placed by some within Radcliffe–Brown's school of 'structure and function', Srinivas might be most evidently functionalist in his book on the Coorgs (Srinivas 1952; also 1964: Chapter 5). However, it is not the complete story for our purposes. Over time, he increasingly concerned himself with meanings. I find Srinivas' writings still significant because they variously weave subtexts and inform us (beyond rules and ideologies) about different locations, shades, and purposes of social meanings.

Most often, as the Coorgs study showed, Srinivas described those aspects of social and ritual practice that helped him explicate 'meaning' within and across contexts. Though textually it may be hard to link such a concern directly to Evans–Pritchard's shift from 'function to meaning' (e.g., see Pocock 1971; Dumont 1975: 333–34), it is not improbable. Srinivas often remarked on meanings as he identified and analyzed major social conditions and processes (e.g., vertical and horizontal solidarity; dominant caste; Sanskritization and Westernization). His work weaved, intuitively as far as we know, 'facts', 'meanings' and 'interpretations' together, but with what I would call balance and insight. It is these properties which open Srinivas' work to a discussion of the role of the writer, writing, narrative, and literary interpretation in 'critical anthropology' of the 1990s (see Manganaro 1990b). His distance from 'fashionable theories' served him rather well; it kept his 'descriptions' open to different readings.

Similarly, his methodological and analytic constraints remained unstated and implied. For example, while studying Indian social change, he (Srinivas 1964) seldom adequately described either the method underlying the selection of a major subject or of one example over others (see also Srinivas 1975). Yet his 1964 account of social coping mechanisms of diverse and contentious 'India' (especially after independence) allowed him to reach certain all-India sociological 'characterizations'. However, his conceptual assertions had a tentativeness, mostly because of his being an Indian social anthropologist or a sociologist, who had studied his own region and culture. He thus concerned himself with a 'double goal'—of modern scholarly objectivity and of that of a cultural insider. How? For example, 'we summon up all the willingness to think the thoughts and feel the feelings of the people whose life is involved in these facts' (Stark quoted in Srinivas 1964: 57).

Yet, if Srinivas at that time was for 'empirically rigorous testing' (see Srinivas 1964: 147–63), he seldom described in detail how such 'testing' was done. Though this 'mixed' methodological 'tool bag' conformed to the dominant India-study centers of Anglo-American anthropology (giving him required Western backing and authority in India), Srinivas was at his best when he grappled with social issues and changes intuitively. He employed his dual cultural (Indian and Western) sensibilities with success, including in *The Remembered Village* (1976).

In his 1964 volume also, I find him welding large chunks of empirical social data rather intuitively, essentially by extending an ethnographer's nose for contextual particulars toward India's diverse regional, macro-level social configurations. He (1964: 147–55) was made especially aware of this issue by his reviewers, and he responded by amplifying the advantages and disadvantages of his being a 'sociologist', who was also a Brahman from South India. He admitted the influence of such a factor on his work (1964: 152), and, according to the call of the times, discussed ways of 'reducing' such subjectivity for 'achieving greater objectivity' (1964: 154). There was, then, no need to question the goal of objectivity or of characterizing his reflections as a contribution toward 'reflexive anthropology'.

In contrast, a self-aware ethnographer's dilemmas now get wide attention. For an ethnographer must view the familiar from afar and the unfamiliar from up close (see Clifford 1981: 542; Geertz 1983; Manganaro 1990b). Similarly, an ethnographer must realize that a sociocultural condition involves a study of both rules as well as their modifications and transgressions. A social process yields conditional, incomplete, and open-ended results; it is neither about a simple notion of progress toward modernity, nor about a simple description of 'empirical facts' under West-inspired and West-looking 'scientific conclusions'. Srinivas, in comparison, generally viewed empirical data as yielding socially contingent (logically ambiguous) directions and culturally resilient changes. (Such a change may now be characterized as 'prestructural' by some scholars, and 'poststructural' by others.) He seldom talked of 'total structural oppositions and transformations'.

Thus, it follows that Srinivas' accounts (1952; 1964) remain strikingly open to conditional and qualified interpretations of Indian society. Such formulations, though cast in an empiricist's language, provide multifaceted clues which we now value under critical sociological approaches. Yet, Srinivas in this way synthesizes his all-India picture case by case and region by region, rather than favor a single 'mega-theory', straining to explain all of India by a single essence. (Compare Dumont and Marriott on this issue.) But to be conditional is neither to be muddled nor to exclude from one's study disorder and conflict in favor of order and structure. Thus, Srinivas' (1964: 160) remarks:

Conflict ought to be seen as inhering in social life everywhere. The institutional devices which every society has provided for the solution of conflict may work with greater or less efficiency, or the devices may work efficiently in some areas and not in others. There may be more conflict in some societies than in others, and in the same society there may be more conflict in some periods than in the others.... But conflict as such is an inescapable part of social existence, and should be of serious concern to the sociologist.

Srinivas (1964: 161) similarly argues for 'a positive attitude [especially of sociologists from developing countries] towards social change', while distinguishing between the apparent and real dimensions of change in a developing country. But the ability to make such distinctions sharpens when a scholar applies 'his mind steadfastly on the existential reality as contrasted with the book-view of society' (preferably by 'the study of a village or a small town'), when the unity as well as the diversity of India is 'borne in mind continuously', and when the intensive studies are 'supplemented' by a macro-study (1964: 158).

Srinivas' (1964: Chapters 2 and 4) discussion of Westernization and Sanskritization not only exemplifies the above intellectual location but it also concludes that the locational dilemmas are unavoidable for social scientists involved in a comparative cultural study. For example, Westernization, for Srinivas, is in various ways a complex, multi-layered, uneven, conditional, and competitive force of modern history, but he assumes ethical neutrality (e.g., see 1964: 48–56 on Westernization). Similarly, if it is polysemic (he uses the phrase 'living in a pluralist cultural universe'; see 1964: 75), it also has multiple results. As he remarked at one place, 'different aspects of Westernization sometimes combine to strengthen a particular process, sometimes work at cross-purposes, and are occasionally mutually discrete' (see 1964: 53–56, for illustrations).

A process of social change in India is invariably complex and he tends to consider it under specific social conditions, whether historical or contemporary (1964: 53). Questions of interpretation, implicit political attitudes, and reinterpretation only occasionally enter his discussion, especially when British and Indian cultural histories view the 'facts' differently. For example, consider his discussion of tolerance in Hinduism, and the remark, 'caste system made heresy-hunting unnecessary' (1964: 75–76). Indian thought, tradition, and popular history tend to overlap in such a subject as 'cultural tolerance', making him (as some scholars would say, from an upper-caste Hindu's standpoint) partial to internal devices of 'cultural adaptation' for social status quo.

For Srinivas, the conceptual significance of such cultural characteristics is relative, not ideological. Though he underscores the role and range of the cultural past and its resilience in India, he also remarks: 'The discovery of the past was not, however, without its pitfalls and dangers. It produced a certain amount of palaeocentrism in all educated Indians and, as is well known, a great past can be either an energizer or an opiate' (1964: 78–79). Srinivas must warn against 'xenophilia, palaeocentrism and communism, and the extreme idealization of Indian life and culture coupled with crude caricaturing of Western life and culture' (1964: 79–80). This 'balanced view' of Indian reality often attracts the educated Indian, 'the modern elite'. It, however, also fosters dilemmas of the 'logical middle', a condition Dumont's sociology must immediately dismiss for such a 'fundamental' opposition as the 'ahistorical' India versus the historical West.

In contrast, Srinivas finds contemporary India in the thick of historical conflicts. Yet his stance is conceptually cautious and 'politically neutral', reflecting the 'liberal' scholarly ethos of his times. If we juxtapose Srinivas' assumptions about Indian history to the concerns and criticisms now evident in, say, 'subaltern' historiography (Guha 1989),[9] we would get an idea of another recent 'shift' (apropos Dumont's and Marriott's) in scholarly concerns. But Srinivas favored his 'balanced view', defending contextually what would otherwise appear to be 'double think' (1964: 82):

> The very people who wanted radical changes in their society, and who were most articulate in denouncing its evils, spoke, when they were addressing the West, of the past glories of India, of the versatility and continuance of its civilization, of the many saints and thinkers India had produced through the ages, and the great and noble ideas they expressed. This was not 'double think', but only that different aspects of the same complex phenomenon were emphasized in different contexts to achieve certain definite ends.

Such a remark also shows how Srinivas would juxtapose and interrelate tradition and modernity to each other. For example, describing Indian society under change, he continues to rely on the bases of traditional authority and authenticity (even as they disperse under modern contexts). Thus he discusses, though briefly, the authority of the *Shastras* in castes and customs in comparative terms on the one hand, and of the application of reason to tradition in modern India, on the other (see 1964: 81–82). As a modernist, he notes how Westernization subsumes 'what may be broadly characterized as humanitarianism, by which is meant an active concern for the welfare of all human beings irrespective of caste, economic position, religion, age, and sex. Equalitarianism and secularization are both included in humanitarianism' (1964: 48). An important (and analytically revealing) qualifier, however, follows immediately in parentheses, recognizing the presence of an even wider notion of cosmic welfare in Indian thought.

In contrast to Dumont's India–West (traditional and modern) ideological opposition, Srinivas finds interstitial room for the goals of equalitarianism and humanitarianism within the complex Indian social hierarchy. In his zeal for achieving a clear and 'total' ideological contrast between hierarchical India and equalitarian West, Dumont simplifies and caricatures the thought and historical experience of an entire world civilization. On the other hand, Srinivas' allusion to the role of Western humanitarianism in modern India invites open inquiries (1964: 48–50). In particular, for example, we may compare the indigenous conception of social welfare to the Western one and examine the roles modernization, secularization, and Westernization can (or cannot) play in India under different cultural, historical, and sociological contexts (1964: 48–88; on Westernization, 118–46).

In Srinivas' view, however, a large part of institutionalized Indian reality is not only about inequality and hierarchy. It is much more, and paradoxical. Similarly, his discussion of secularism makes him see 'rationalism' in those traditional Hindu terms and concepts (including purity and pollution) which have 'a certain amount of semantic stretch', to allow them 'to move from one meaning to another as the context requires' (1964: 119–20). Secularization is found to be a 'mixed' development, where 'Hinduism has assumed a political form in the Rashtriya Swayamsevak Sangh (RSS) and the [then] Jan Sangh' (1964: 141, my interpolation). A secular government, thus, can also become 'an unwitting but powerful agent of Sanskritization' in India by prohibiting alcoholic drinks (1964: 142).[10]

III

The above characterization of Srinivas' work, while incomplete, draws our attention to an overriding point: the value of a careful context-guided description and analysis cannot be overestimated for understanding the diverse Indian social past and present. Whether one studies a caste, a village or a process of social change in urban India, this general commonsensical approach upholds. Yet Srinivas leads us to a tantalizing ambiguity as a text maker. As Srinivas' later book (1976) attests, even the memory of an early fieldwork experience could be a resourceful 'trigger' in such a pursuit. The ethnographer, with his 'inside' and 'outside' perspective, in such an exercise frames the account of field memories as (and for) field experiences. The author 'touches' and describes people through his memories, making a sociologist's scholarly objectivity largely a habit of the mind. But, on the other hand, his memories, however vivid, can seldom be empirically certain and complete, especially when decades old (see Srinivas 1976). Many details would have to be recovered/uncovered/invented for a literary-cum-'sociological' narrative. A fieldworker's memories of (and from) 'notebooks' cannot be a substitute for the actual ones. Srinivas leaves this ambiguous text before the reader.

His previous work, in places, I believe, also informed of a literary sensibility in sociological work (e.g., 1964: Chapter 5 for the roles of empathy, objectivity, micro- and macro-studies, and sociological analysis to uncover the social reality). A cultural empathy (an omnibus term) enabled the sociologist 'to understand what it is to be a member of the community that is being studied. In this respect, the sociologist is like a novelist who must of necessity get under the skin of different characters he is writing about' (1964: 156). This novelist-like role of the sociologist was mentioned again (1964: 157–58), but it had to await his burned notebooks and the writing of *The Remembered Village*. Yet the book could not be only a novel, for 'the sociologist is primarily interested ... [in] generalizations rather than the development of concrete particularizations' (1976: 158). By such a comment, if Srinivas stated his general preference, he also restricted the range of his narrative on Indian society. This would be especially true if his textual accounts were examined for how (well) they represented the cultural other within his *own* society (on anthropology as text, see Manganaro 1990b). However, empirical and interpretative tendencies clearly overlapped in the 1976 monograph on Rampura. Since Srinivas' memories and images of the village and its people 'reworked' what he calls 'social facts', his ethnography acquired a distinct tone and texture of narration. Thus, between the two books on the Coorgs and on Rampura, Srinivas' ethnography shifted from the scientific objective goal to humanistic concerns. But he hesitated to fully recognize and explore this shift. In both, instead, he wanted the 'empirical data' to be at the center of depicting and analyzing Indian society. On the other hand, though he only occasionally concerned himself with the content of what we now call popular culture, he always wrote on it elegantly and nontechnically. His earlier substantive concerns (e.g., village, caste organization, rituals, social dominance, and processes of social change) rested on a clear description of common culture on the one hand, and on a self-aware interpretation of value issues on the other. He approached his 'major concepts' the same way. For example, Srinivas (1976) found 'hierarchy' to be polysemous and interactional (mainly in terms of intercaste relations; see 1976: Chapter 6) under widely different contexts—land (Chapter 7), reciprocity (Chapter 9), and Muslims (Chapter 6). Adding a new direction in Indian ethnography, he discussed, though only briefly, 'face', 'friendship and enmity', 'gossip', 'envy', and 'sense of humour'. He termed these qualities of social relations (Chapter 9). Such topics helped reflect not only a sociologist's own aesthetic and social sensibilities, but they also identified his qualities as a narrator.

But those studied participated only indirectly in such a narrative, often with a face, but without a voice of their own.[11] We sometimes find Srinivas (1976) struggling to overthrow the prized scholarly distance (e.g., his depiction of departure from the field). On such occasions, I find him donning his old hat (empirical social science) as well as a new cap (a self-aware Indian aestheticism and its writing). Hence, where one influence ends and the other begins in such an ethnography is almost impossible to distinguish (and counterproductive), especially when the 1976 book is read as a narrative.

Overall, Srinivas (1952; 1964; 1976) uses ethnographic writing as a multipurpose template for reporting data, capturing Indian sociocultural conditions, and providing a sociological analysis. His analysis remained rooted more in 'empirical data' than on a critical evaluation of other scholars' ethnographies and theories. His writing, only rarely (see 1975), provided a sustained commentary or critique of another anthropologist's criticism. Only general (and mostly approving) comments are found on highly selected scholarly works of others. This style also agreed with occasionally providing disciplinary 'overviews' (see 1964: 155, for a remark on the internal struggle between sociology and social anthropology in India; also 158–63, for a general commentary on 'sociologists' in developing countries).

Put differently, Srinivas' attempts favored a certain 'reasonableness' in analyses and conclusions. But such reasonableness, in his words, should find support in the data put to

rigorous testing before they can become valid generalizations. The moral, then, is that an idea is not necessarily wrong because its originator occupies a particular position in the society. Its validity or invalidity has to be independently established. In the words of Bernard Shaw: 'The test of sanity is not the normality of method but the reasonableness of the discovery' (Srinivas 1964: 154).

Thus, resting on a morally relativized approach to society, he took a multifactorial view of social reality. The modern educated Indian, I should remark, would also often share such a 'reasonableness' in perspective. In contrast, Dumont's 'structural approach', based on fundamentally opposed cultural principles (e.g., hierarchy and equality, ritual purity, and impurity), would strike the same Indian as oversimplified, partial, and unjustifiably reductionist. If Dumont's approach to Indian society were akin to that of the lawmaker Manu, then to Srinivas 'Manu would be a bad guide for field workers; urban and uppercaste sociologists in India need to keep this constantly in mind' (1964: 152).

The Indian's 'reasonableness' actually points toward a larger Indian cultural and historical commentary on tolerance of diversity and inconsistency, especially after independence. For instance, his 'reasonableness' may not rest as clearly on what the West calls

'reason and rationality' as on what the educated Indian finds contextually 'appropriate', 'tolerable', and 'moderate' for an aspiring
democratic, secular, and modernizing India. Such a cultural ethos
of the modern, urban Indian renders the Indian cultural reality a
mixed bag—diverse and internally conflicted, but still neither unmanageable nor ultimately incommensurable compared to the
Indian's sense of 'reasonableness'. In my reading of Srinivas (e.g.,
1964; 1976), this general cultural sense repeatedly comes through.

IV

Finally, one could argue that in some of his social descriptions and
analyses, Srinivas anticipates certain aspects of the recent critical
discussions going on between ethnography and modernity (or its
pre-eminent social process—Westernization). I shall conclude the
essay with a comparative commentary on both, suggesting that
India needs a self-aware critical ethnography (which links with
but is not limited to Srinivas' initiatives) to address the increasingly
unmanageable subject of Indian cultural diversity. For example,
while discussing Westernization and secularization in modern
India, Srinivas (1964: 46–88, 118–46) offered a social commentary
on the dynamics of contemporary Indian history. Yet his concerns
remained very different from, for example, those of the recent
'subaltern' historiography on India (Guha 1989). He was essentially concerned with the social coping mechanisms of Indians as
they faced the rather inevitable and desirable Westernization
(1964: 50–56). As a concept, he found Westernization

> inclusive, complex, and many-layered. It covers a wide range—
> from Western technology at one end to the experimental
> method of modern science and modern historiography at the
> other. Its incredible complexity is seen in the fact that different
> aspects of Westernization sometimes combine to strengthen a
> particular process, sometimes work at cross-purposes, and are
> occasionally mutually discrete (1964: 53).

Clearly, Westernization for him was a social, but largely politically
neutral process. He assumed that, with scholarly distance as his
armor, the scholar could (and must) steer clear of all political

issues and power biases. However, recent critical debates in sociology would find such an assumption naive and untenable (see Agger 1991, for a wide-ranging sociological review). In a critical perspective, Westernization would highlight its strategies of power and control, along with a mentality which assumed the superiority of 'science and scientific objectivity' in human affairs. If it was never politically neutral, it also was *not all politics*.[12]

Today, it is a socio-political process which is neither monolithic nor conflict-free nor fail proof (e.g., Heilbroner 1974; MacIntyre 1981). I think Srinivas would also agree that if this process is desirable, complex, contingent and many-layered, it is also neither infallible nor 'gift-packed', nor a panacea. Sociologically, Westernization may first change the socially discrete and then the culturally fundamental. Either way, the process involves the introduction of alienation (and identity crises) in a host culture, by presenting 'better' (and 'correct') avenues of knowing, organizing, and interpreting social reality. But such 'new' ways, as Srinivas' discussions also indicated, breed wide-ranging conflicts in morality, consensual conduct, protest, justice, and fairness.

Unfortunately, India still lacks sustained critical debates on and evaluations of Westernization (and of Western critiques of modernity). Indian debates should include more participants and voices from all segments of society, rather than only modern educated Indians. This is crucial when India's alternative socio-political guide for modernization—the Soviet Union and its eastern bloc— has virtually dissolved itself. Meanwhile, if anthropology in independent India has offered theories of conflict, cooperation, resiliency, or compartmentalization to explain how traditional India adapts to the ever desirable modernity (e.g., Srinivas' studies; Singer 1972), its explanations still remain timid, and are often a prisoner of uncritical sociological assumptions. In such approaches, one usually values India for its passivity, docility and 'adaptability' for *accepting*, one way or another, the desirability of modern Western social assumptions and values. A critical, ground-level examination of that modernity which modern Indians profess and protect is virtually unheard. Many scholarly efforts may not consider the issue worthy of central concern (for a recent internal debate in the West, see Dumont 1977; Erickson 1974; Heilbroner 1974; Lears 1981; MacIntyre 1981). But they should.

Though Srinivas' work exhibits mild skepticism toward West-ernization and modernization in India, it is hardly sufficient for a critical debate. Engaged in establishing a major 'center of socio-logical studies' in Delhi, Srinivas, it seems, had shared all the controlling premises of Anglo-American social science and an-thropology. His sociology unfortunately seldom stopped to exam-ine either the Western critiques of Western modernity or the scant critical works of such pioneering (but so remote as to be almost mysterious) Indian sociologists as D.P. Mukerji (1958) and A.K. Saran (1963).[13]

To address the subject with substance, one must design such sociological and anthropological studies which put us in touch (and in dialogue) with clamoring Indian life and its intensifying conflicts and voices of protest. Our ad hoc, usually West-launched, and exclusive (and excluding) theories can wait, unless they help raise new and different questions. For social anthropol-ogy and Indian sociology, it means an increased role for *dialogi-cal* fieldwork and *reciprocal* ethnographic accounts (where one includes the specialist's and the informant's discussions of each other). Such accounts may help increase the investigator's aware-ness as much of himself and his 'science' as of the people he stud-ies. For him, ethnography would be at once a science, an art, and a 'reading' of diverse languages and intentions of his own and of those he studies.

Here, the ethnographer discusses the real, the metaphoric, the unequal, the unsaid, and even the surreal (see Clifford 1981: 539–64). He grapples with not only the structurally 'opposed' values in India, but also the culturally negotiable between the rational and the non-rational, the cooperating and the conflicting, and the 'seen' and the 'unseen'. The Indian ethnographer learns to make the familiar 'strange' so that he can systematize and ex-plain consciously what is explicit and orderly, and contingent and chaotic. Thus, as Clifford (1981: 548) had observed while summa-rizing Mauss' view, 'Ethnographic truth … was restlessly subver-sive of surface realities. Its principal task was to discover—in a famous phrase—the many "*lunes mortes*", pale moons in the "firmament of reason". The ethnographer concerns himself with "cultural impurities and disturbing syncretisms"' (Clifford 1981: 549–50). Quoting Marcel Griaule, as Clifford notes, 'Ethnography is suspicious, too, of itself…'.

Srinivas' *The Remembered Village* sometimes turns in the direction of the contingent, but it hesitates and returns to familiar ethnographic descriptions of everyday (and power neutral) 'reality' (see Clifford 1981: 553). Even such an ethnography, once in stride, is neither simply 'objective' nor 'subjective', but both in such a way that it enhances our ability to question the given and the dominant, and listen to the unrepresented and the remote. It amplifies the significance of what makes most cultural sense for society (see Agar 1982: 783). It also addresses the wider philosophical question: What is the nature and range of reality that ethnography should seek to study and communicate? One position is that 'the aims of ethnography in this regard are vague and the philosophical assumptions behind those aims poorly understood' (Jarvie 1967; 1983: 313). The other position argues that ethnography must become increasingly self-aware, socially responsible, and even-handed toward 'other peoples and cultures'.

Supported by recent developments in symbolic and interpretive anthropology, new ethnography questions the theoretically accepted and explores the socially neglected. *The Remembered Village* subtly moves in such a direction. It resonates with diverse cultural messages from a diverse, vibrant, and sensible rural India. However, if this India of the 1940s depicts controlled social conflicts and aversions, we now see how violent alterity, alienation, and antagonism increasingly churn the same culture, demanding a commensurate change in an ethnographer's assumptions, explorations, tools, and descriptions.

Marcus (1980: 508) rightly observes that the analytic significance of fieldwork and ethnography has greatly increased in anthropology in recent years, especially as symbology, phenomenology and hermeneutics have opened up new and different vantage points. In evidence is the rapidly expanding literature on the topic (see initial references in Agar 1982; Clifford 1981; Marcus 1980; Rabinow 1977; for a later summary, Manganaro 1990a). Such accounts examine their own discourse-forming and knowledge-controlling strategies, recognizing that no ethnographic representation can remain free of intentional biases and what is called the 'discourse politics'.

The issue matters whether one goes to study a distant people or one's own, or conducts government-sponsored nationally 'relevant research' (see Colson 1982: 253–62). Whether Western or non-Western, an ethnographer's cultural location (along with his personal biases) affects the conduct and profile of his study. Similarly, the ethnographer cannot overlook the issues of cultural distance, social differences, and power conflicts in favor of his structural theories of 'order' or 'system', particularly if the people point us the other way. If the ethnographer becomes professionally responsible for an adequate and appropriate comprehension, description, and analysis of such situations, then he must also introduce his self-critical cultural debates into anthropology's disciplinary history and practice (Asad 1975; 1982: 284–87).

A re-reading of Srinivas' work in the above context makes us aware of some major 'shifts' since the 1970s in anthropology and in Indian sociology. One now rarely devotes, for instance, a whole study to describe only a caste, a village, or an aspect of social change. But why not? The works of Dumont and Marriott partially answer such a question by their 'theoretical quests'. These may have altered the value and place of Indian 'social change' studies. We may also ask: What does the downgrading of social change studies mean for India, a developing country?[14]

The question makes us return to the changing conceptual role and criticism of modernity in the West. These concern anthropology as much as sociology. In many ways this changing debate *frames and informs* all that Srinivas, Dumont, and Marriott, separately and together, include or exclude as they sociologically describe and explain India. Located in a distinct frame of modernity, these three scholars bring to India their own preferred modern (read 'scientific') intellectual concerns, methods, and analytical perspectives. Though they studied India from 'within', only Srinivas, it seems, freely admitted those socially diverse contexts and values which mid-20th century India demanded. In comparison, Dumont preferred India to be simply ideologically opposed to modernity, while Marriott eschewed the tradition–modernity issue by focusing on India's 'paradigms' of selected classical transactional essences (or substances).

But to pursue a critical cultural perspective, among other things, one must now show how India, over the last two centuries, has developed its own distinct versions of cultural, political, and economic modernity, just as it has done by 'indigenizing' English, science and technology—the 'languages of progress' (e.g., on English language, colonialism and India, see Viswanathan 1989).

With English as a language of foreign domination, internal revolt, cultural and scientific regeneration, and political movements, India, I would argue, has had a direct handle on examining, rebutting, and transforming modernity—in all aspects, and with difficulty— for its own purposes. Our commentaries need to reveal both—the receiving and the responding—sides of such exchanges in India.

◀ NOTES

1. Written in the early 1980s for the Srinivas festschrift, this chapter now incorporates only a *limited* revision of the content and style, undertaken in the late summer of 1992.

    Those interested in following up the relevant recent literature on critical debates and anthropology are provided with references which include good bibliographies.

2. As I argue elsewhere (see Chapter 4), Dumont and Marriott extend each other's essentially emic studies of India. When viewed in the larger context of development of Indian sociology after the second world war, the picture remains incomplete until Professor Srinivas' work is simultaneously taken into account. Methodologically, Srinivas' studies complement—and criticize—the 'internal' view of India which Dumont and Marriott, two outsiders, separately and together, try to provide. When the three contributions are seen together, Dumont and Marriott must cluster together for relying heavily (and explicitly) on Indology and Western sociological theories, while Srinivas stands apart for his intuitive sociological formulations and homegrown cultural aesthetics and descriptive sensibilities.

3. Analytically, it may mean at times to distinguish between Dumont's own formulations on Indian sociology (see his writings and debates up to 1966 in the original numbers of *Contributions to Indian Sociology*, and up to 1980 in his revised and enlarged edition of *Homo Hierarchicus* and Dumont-inspired pursuit of Indian sociology by others. My concern is only with the former. I thus refer to only Dumont's use of the label 'Indian sociology'. Such distinctions are important to control the influx of other approaches and perspectives under the banner of 'Indian sociology'. A second round of critical evaluation of Dumont's Indian sociology may now be quite in order, provided we are prepared to make India *and* sociology its proper and primary subjects.

4. Other recent social scientists have rarely done much better. For example, Marriott's ethnosociological approach also tries to correct this inconsistency and explores Hindu classical formulations around only certain selected (academically popularized) forms of Hindu 'cultural logic'. However, he does not give any indication of a systematic comprehension of the subject from within. Nor does he explain the grounds for his selection of some forms of Hindu reasoning and the exclusion of others. And once he sociologically 'theorizes', the

sociological theory *naturally* assumes its superordinate epistemological position. He lapses here much like Dumont.

5. Such a claim should be carefully examined, especially when it methodologically shares Dumont's central premise to view Hindu India in terms of its own ideological (for Marriott, read 'cultural') formulations and concepts and their interrelationships. Not unlike Dumont, Marriott also reads selected Sanskritic philosophies and texts and selectively 'employs' their formulations to devise a distinct sociological language for seeking 'transactional' explanations (see Marriott 1976a; 1989; for the creation and extension of such a jargon around transactional—fluid and joining—strategies).

6. However, it is easy to retrogress also. For example, if the strategy is to return somehow to a pristine or an earlier sociological theory to disentangle oneself from the conceptual puzzle the recent efforts raise, the central problem will be sidestepped rather than resolved. The central issue is to open up the dominant sociological assumptions to alternative cultural translations and formulations, whether the exercise concerns Western or Indian social orders. Only such a procedure will help explore the case for a genuinely universalized sociological formulation. Meanwhile, issues of inter- or cross-cultural translation can neither be wished away nor rendered any less real.

7. Though obviously this is not all that his bibliography reflects, these are his sustained concerns directly useful to our exercise. The 1978 review symposium of the *Contributions* has greatly helped me in the selection and analysis of Srinivas' work. I draw particular attention to Madan's overview and Srinivas' 'Reply to Criticisms' (see Madan 1978).

8. These four studies represent a range of attempts to study Indian society. When an earlier work of Srinivas (1952) is compared with a later one (1964), a movement in focus, explanation, and perspective becomes clearly evident. Overall, the issues of empirical description and change receive constant attention. I shall argue that Srinivas' *Social Change in Modern India* (1964; lectures of 1964) is a sort of climax of logico-empirical and logico-meaningful inquiries in Indian social anthropology and sociology. It provided a larger historical, social, and cultural view of India, prior to *Homo Hierarchicus*. Most investigators were then tied up with their village, caste, and kinship descriptions, piecing together a regional picture. Dumont, however, had put forward his agenda for Indian sociology (and he had criticized Srinivas on his Coorg study). Similarly, Marriott's (1959) 'interactive' explanation of caste precedence and caste order had all the 'seeds' of his later 'interactional approach', though he, then, had focused on Dumont. Srinivas never directly evaluated any aspect of Dumont's work until the mid-1970s.

Srinivas' 1975 essay on the Indian village was significant in this context. It was written in response to Dumont's critique (for the discursive style, compare Srinivas 1964: Chapter 5). It offered a logico-empirical rebuttal, based on historical data, but it did not reach the standards of the 1964 book. It was as if his usual analytical acuity had eluded him in this essay.

Making an incident (i.e., the burning of his field notes in Palo Alto) his ally, he was engaged, it would seem, in a new genre of description. He evolved a social description based largely on his 'memory' of the fieldwork done long ago in a Mysore village. *The Remembered Village* (1976) represents more than an empirical description. It is a narrative in which an ethnographer discovers via memory a 'high art' to rediscover self and society. (For the place of memory in Evans–Pritchard's social anthropology, see Douglas 1980.)

9. This whole volume represents as well as culminates in several recent critical discussions on India's history, culture, and historiography. In particular, the reader may see papers by Gayatri Chakravorty Spivak, Ranajit Guha, and Veena Das.

10. Obviously, so much has happened in India since these lines were written. The Bharatiya Janata Party (the successor to Jan Sangh) 'swept' (especially northern) India during 1991. The so-called '3M'—Mandir–Masjid–Mandal—controversy continues to test the resilience of mixed Indian secularism and democracy. The 'Sikh problem' in Punjab tests the limits of both political and religious tolerance (and intolerance) within modern Indian culture. However, I have resisted to rewrite or expand the discussion here. See Chapters 7 and 8.

11. To my critical Untouchable informants, this would reflect the bias of an upper-caste Hindu scholar more than the fact of burned notes. If not voices, they would ask, 'Where are the remembered echoes, especially of those low castes who in the forties dared seldom speak, unless spoken to?'

12. Critical postmodern theories sometimes stress this point to the exclusion of other substantive issues of knowledge and inquiry. I do not. But nor do I dismiss the significance of witting or unwitting politics in human knowledge and its persuasive communication and acceptance (Chapter 4; see also note 11). In response to the critical non-Western reviews of their political strategies of dominating knowledge, the Western intellectuals now either vehemently protest the criticism or charge the critic with an untenable and harmful demand for 'political correctness', or dismiss the whole debate as a red herring. In America, there is already a battle cry to return to the Euro-centric knowledge 'core' and its conservative agenda.

    With his flair for 'only the substantive, reliable and authoritative knowledge', the Indian sociologist would easily tend to *dismiss* the whole critical debate as 'another passing fad' of the West. Without conducting its own independent exercise, such a sociology could readily accept the same conclusion that its uncritical Western counterpart has.

13. The purpose of such a critique obviously is *not* to confuse the politically 'right' and 'left' camps in Indian sociological studies. Rather it is to challenge the basic significance and productivity of such a simple ideological division under Indian sociocultural conditions. It is also to propose that now (at the end of the 20th century) we should juxtapose the works of Mukerji and Saran (in themselves wide apart) to those of Srinivas and Dumont to see how their sociological and philosophical assumptions on India and its tradition and modernity would enhance our understanding of the intellectual history of Indian sociology. We may note that Saran particularly tried to 'apply' early on India, selected strands of Western critical philosophy, with vague connections to nondualist Indian philosophy. But his mystifying brevity was his worst enemy.

    Throughout this chapter, I have also referred to shifts of perspective occurring in an investigator's career. I have shown how these shifts occurred in the cases of Srinivas, Dumont and Marriott. Though working with a smaller scholarly credit, I am also subject to such a shift. After describing, under 'scholarly distance', for decades north Indian Brahmans and Untouchables for their diverse structures of social actions and meanings, I am now increasingly inclined toward critical debates on contested ideals and representations in India (vis-à-vis the West). Perhaps it is as much a sign of my changing self-awareness as of social times and conditions in India.

14. Within anthropology and sociology, there has been a general decline in the intellectual value of social change studies. Several reasons may explain such a decline. For some scholars, the theoretical interest in the West has shifted from function and adaptation to structures and meanings. Others link this change to the postcolonial 'refocus' of the Western world and its intellectuals. To still others, structuralism helped establish *the* 'universal' supremacy of the rational order.

The attention thus shifted from the sociocultural 'development' of a society (a model on which Srinivas worked) to locating fundamental cultural constituents, categories, and meanings, irrespective of whether a society was 'developing' or 'developed'. As a logical consequence of the interest in abstract relational models, ideological principles were found to encapsulate the most, and the most crucial. To study social norms, therefore, meant to grapple with the 'core reality', while the content up for social change would, by implication, be superficial.

However, the paradox of this situation is especially evident to anthropologists and sociologists from developing countries. Everyday social experience and its conflicts rebel against abstract schemes and theories.

3

Dumontian Sociology and Since: Challenges Facing South Asian Anthropology*

I

As the world changes under contradictory forces of regional disputes and global markets, anthropology at the turn of the century faces change both from within and without.[1] One commentator recently labeled anthropology 'a much reduced science' (Scheper-Hughes 1995), and most sociocultural anthropologists (and only these concern me here) today grapple with a disciplinary crisis, especially when 'the towns and their populations, the countries in which they are situated, and the discipline of anthropology and the anthropologist himself have all changed radically' (Scheper-Hughes 1995: 22). Many find themselves examining not simply 'the data', but also how they study and write about questioning others.

If anthropologists study 'how natives think', then it is also about *how well* they comprehend, record and represent the 'natives' within a changing, contentious world. Thus, while some want to

* This chapter is a revised version of an article under publication in *Reviews in Anthropology* and is published here with the kind permission of Gordon and Breach Publications, Lausanne, Switzerland.

critically review the disciplinary 'canons' to address moral obligations across cultures, particularly the rights of the people studied,
others seek to reinstate the 'scientific' authority of the discipline.[2]
Wrestling with an assertive and vociferous world, many anthropologists find yesterday's 'normal facts', 'dominant orders', and
'standard explanations' controverted or insufficient. This is particularly true in a large, diverse, and internally conflicted society
like India, where the 'standard' modern sociological explanations
may sometimes either simplify or miss the changing social forces
and realities crucial to the people.

Anthropological writing, by definition, constructs itself on *dual
intellectual, moral and professional responsibility*: one directed
toward the people studied, and the other addressing one's peers
and readers. Irrespective of whether an anthropologist is Western,
non-Western or 'native',[3] all anthropological knowledge, however
presented, constitutes itself by explicating other people's knowledge, giving content and form to the discipline's notions of 'fact',
'reasoning', 'writing', 'authenticity', and 'accountability'. The structure of anthropological writing and analysis is, by definition, 'us'
versus 'not-us' centered, and comparative across cultures.

Such a disciplinary stance also recalls an issue that Louis Dumont (see Dumont 1966; 1980; Dumont and Pocock 1957), culmi-
nating his contributions to 'Indian sociology',[4] had raised while
discussing 'the anthropological community and ideology' (Dumont
1986a: 202–33). At its center are modern European ideological assumptions while writing about and analyzing the non-European,
non-modern cultures,[5] including the Indian.[6] Not only does this
discursive axis still largely continue to frame the anthropological
accounts 50 years after, it also sharply problematizes the unity
issue facing anthropology and anthropologists. And the same
issue becomes more complicated since anthropologists, for various reasons, tend to reflect in writing and analysis their own cultural, moral, ethnic, gender, and national locations (for diverse
attempts, see Burghart 1990: 260–78; Veena Das 1990a: 1–36;
1990b: 345–98; Tambiah 1986; Uberoi 1968).

The European and non-European ideological divide, framing
most anthropological discussions, is also found at the core of the
three recent major attempts at anthropological description and
analysis of India: Srinivas' 'field-view' of India versus Dumont's
structural and 'Brahmanical' (textual and contextual) analysis, versus Saran's foundational view of the Indian 'primordial tradition'

(e.g., Dumont 1980; Saran 1962; 1989; and Srinivas 1952; 1964).[7] The intervening decades, meanwhile, have seen several nuanced attempts at tackling the Western/non-Western (or the 'outsider'/ 'insider') divide in the anthropology of India, by both Western and Indian scholars. Let us recall here just two creative but different attempts: Marriott's (1989) comprehensive 'ethnosociological' approach,[8] and Veena Das' (1994: 133–44; 1995) recent interpretations of a series of critical Indian events, with distinct implications for a critical anthropological discourse.

Both attempts, though bold, struggle with the modern/non-modern axis of Indian culture and its contributions to the core of the disciplinary knowledge. Historically, the same axis has framed explanations of major events on the Indian subcontinent, especially as evident in the conflicting religious traditions, convoluted colonial and post-colonial pasts, gender discrimination, and deepening communal and caste violence on the one hand, and the emerging globalization of the Indian economy and popular culture, on the other (e.g., Ahmad 1972; Breckenridge and van der Veer 1993; Cohn 1987c: 422–62; Veena Das 1990a: 1–36; Engineer 1984; Guha and Spivak 1988; Raheja and Gold 1994; and for a general argument on moral obligations across the cultural and national boundaries, see Walzer 1994).

However, we also increasingly realize that the Dumontian ideological opposition between traditional India and the modern West yields diminishing returns for anthropology, unless it is fully opened up to diverse Indian ideas, experiences and crises, with a suitable reformulation of the major disciplinary assumptions and ethnographic practices. Only such a step can take us nearer to what an Indian reviewer recently wished—a genuinely 'cosmopolitan academic atmosphere' for scholarly exchange (Srivastava 1995: 312). This will be possible when neither the Indian nor the Western knowledge system is privileged for its own sake, when the Dumontian 'modern' neither excludes nor dismisses the South Asian debates with European modernity,[9] and when *both* Indian and Western scholars secure a 'level playing field'.

The preceding remarks help us situate better how the three books under review (*a*) account for 'indigenous' Indian conceptions and practices, ranging from the ancient to the recent; (*b*) seek an accessible yet culturally accurate and representative description and analysis of certain dominant religious institutions and practices; and (*c*) accommodate the recent historical and social changes in Indian and Nepalese societies on the one hand, and reflect on the changing disciplinary discourse, on the other.

II

Pursuing the subject of religion and society, the books under review diverge, and yet they significantly overlap in their goals, scope, evidence, argument, and analysis. All three make 'accessibility' a shared concern, while wrestling with enormous subcontinental cultural (textual, regional and local) diversity and complexity. Fuller calls his approach 'analytical', the one 'more prevalent in British social anthropology', (p. 8), while Gellner (pp. xvii–xviii), following the same approach, studies Newar Buddhism, both analytically (under Weberian inspiration) and 'on its own terms'. Heesterman, an anthropologically sensitive Indologist, depends almost totally on Vedic scriptural traditions to study sacrifices, rituals, and ritualists within the ancient Indian society, illustrating 'a paradigm of what Max Weber called "formal rationality"' (p. 4). Interested in civilizational comparisons, Heesterman repeatedly alludes to non-Indian traditions, from the ancient Iranian (Persian) to the Greek to the Judeo–Christian.

Heesterman's book is about understanding 'the origins and nature' of Vedic sacrifice by closely examining Sanskritic ritual texts (Brāhmaṇas) and manuals (śrautasutras). Whether among Vedic Indians or ancient Iranians and Greeks, Heesterman shows how sacrifice tries to tackle 'the riddle of life and death': It 'deals in the earnest way of play with the insoluble conundrum of life and death' (p. 27). Sacrifice is found to be a 'catastrophic center', 'a life-and-death contest', engaged in 'endless rounds of winning, losing, and revanche, the state of human affairs here and hereafter' (pp. 2, 3).

Four 'moments' (e.g., killing, destruction, feasting, and contest) structure the Vedic sacrifice, with successive ritual transformations of such moments until the individual sacrificer, by the relentless logic of ritual 'equivalences' (pp. 4, 80), renders sacrifice 'a transcendent realm of its own' (p. 5). Thus as a 'thoroughly reflected ritual', sacrifice shows how one's 'individual self', the ātman, interiorizes sacrificial fire, and how the self eventually encompasses and controls not only life and death, but also 'the seat of immortality … transcend[ing] both fire and community' (p. 215).

Detailed and erudite, Heesterman's account remains controlled, comparative and well-written. It is among the best the current Indological scholarship has to offer. It weaves a rich pattern as the concrete, the social, the ritual, and the speculative interrelate to tackle the successively abstract and the mysterious (e.g., from the sacrificial fire to the fire within, to the *ātman*). Hence his warning: 'the reader may well feel caught between detail and speculation' (p. ix). Simultaneously, Heesterman makes several anthropological observations and comments as he tells us how the Vedic notions and practices 'domesticated' sacrifice by successive ritualization, and how such steps compared with non-Indian textual traditions from Greece and Persia. We learn in detail how the Vedic conceptions, durations and mobility of fire (and water) developed, interrelated, and transformed the sacrificer (*hotṛ*), the priest, and 'the consecrated' (i.e., from *dīkṣita* to *uddīkṣita*).

These constituent transformations resulted in a sacrificial ritual still familiar to the Hindu (e.g., *agnihotra*, and its extension *prāṇāgnihotra*). These are marked by relations of contest and alliance, hospitality and gifting, and 'monistic ritualism' and the 'inalienable Self' or the *ātman* (Chapters 7 and 8). When juxtaposed to the Dumontian view of the moral individual, Heesterman explicates a chain of culturally crucial clues by which one understands 'self', 'Self', and the '*ātman* as the truth of the individual, the inalienable Self, and the seat of immortality' in India (pp. 216, 220). These forms and contents of the Indian 'individual' are civilizational in character and scope, and are ethnographically verifiable and sociologically significant. Dumontian sociology on India overlooked them to its disadvantage, relying only on the Western history of the modern individual.

Much that is anthropologically relevant—and ethnographically explicable—is thus presented in terms of the transforming self of the sacrificer, the place of 'mutual trust' (*śraddhā*) in gifting, and the differences between gifting and remuneration (*dāna* and *dakṣina*). Such a discussion has direct implications for the Brahman's status and its limitations (explicated via the logic of substitution; see p. 174ff; also 210–14; 220–22). Implications are also obvious for recent ethnographic accounts on Hindu 'gifting' and its comprehensive understanding (e.g., see Raheja 1988). Clearly central to sacrifice are the irreducible Hindu predicaments about life and death, and this-worldly versus the otherworldly priorities.

Heesterman pithily concludes by stating a paradox, 'The price of immortality is death' (p. 222).

Similarly, exploring the relationship between sacrifice and ritual, he remarks, 'Who says *sacrifice*, says *ritual*' (p. 45). But does ritual inevitably define sacrifice? Or, is sacrifice, in a 'developmental' sense, the precursor of ritual? Anthropologists favor the first formulation, while Heesterman here gets trapped between certain 'developmental historical' notions and a 'structural' explanation, fostering ambiguity in his argument.

Gellner's study is ethnographic and textual rather than text-based. Given to the everyday, lived cultural complexity of the Newar in Nepal, it carefully analyzes field data against the prevalent Buddhist and Hindu ideals, ideas and practices to decipher what the anthropologist thinks people do, and what the people think they do, in life. Tracing the content and affinities of Newar religion to Hinduism *and* to Theravada Buddhism (p. 2), Gellner's 'empirical' quest is 'to describe in detail how Newar Buddhism works' (p. 3). Thus his five chapters (6 to 10; pp. 162–306), about half of the book, explicate the 'Three [religious] Ways' of the monk, the householder, and the Tantric practitioner (for overview, pp. 3–4).

Attentive to the ideal–typical sociological (Weber-inspired) models, rules and 'instrumental contexts', Gellner's study revels in the contextual (i.e., the customary, the practical and the anomalous) Newar religious life. In his informant's words, 'There are religions enough for everyone to choose, just like vegetables in the morning bazaar' (p. 70). Gellner's rich ethnographic data present a well-nuanced socioreligious spectrum but, 'to theorize', he valiantly tries to distinguish, list, hierarchize, diagram, and translate and analyze a social fluidity, sometimes repeatedly on the same issue (e.g., see pp. 6, 137 and 337). He tries to capture the 'distinctness' of Newar Buddhism, from both the Theravada Buddhist and the Hindu standpoint, and searches for cultural 'constants' within swirling social complexity. On occasions, not unlike Heesterman's Vedic ritualists, who worked by establishing 'equivalences' between 'performing' and 'knowing', Newars also address this-worldly social and instrumental goals alongside those otherworldly (or 'obligatory', 'optional', and 'soteriological' goals in Gellner's terms, pp. 135–39). Thus, in general, the rituals, ritualists and even ordinary people on the subcontinent over the centuries seem to pursue a rather shared underlying cultural logic across a vast time and space.

But this book, despite its wealth of details and painstaking writing, wastes its analytical gains. Unlike Heesterman's, Gellner's conceptual goals suffer because he does too little too late toward the end of the book (see Chapter 12, p. 337ff). The major issues are repeatedly recalled by context (e.g., religious cosmologies, specialists, hierarchical relations, or instrumental versus soteriological goals), but, conceptually, little is done to them to yield a theoretical frame. His conclusions mostly reiterate the overriding role of situational contingencies in the Newar religious life. They establish a socioreligious flow of Newar life. It should have been a prized conclusion by itself for a study built with ethnographic 'capital'.

Fuller's book on popular Hinduism musters—and tries to claim—theoretically much more, and hence it deserves greater and closer attention. Synthesizing a range of recent anthropological studies and analysis, it effectively uses the same British 'sociological' approach that Gellner employs.[10] Focusing on the 'field-based' studies over those 'textual', his book, in certain ways, complements and qualifies Heesterman's account (e.g., see Fuller's Chapter 11, for his approach to the Hindu sacrifice–worship axis). Two main concerns shape the book, an overview of recent anthropological knowledge on Hindu religious and social practices, and an implicit 'sociological' interpretation and perspective on India highlighting certain anthropological descriptions and analyses of major Hindu institutions, popular practices, and social changes.

The Camphor Flame, a welcome attempt on a vast and complicated subject, admirably succeeds in its main objectives. It opens with a concise discussion of the subject's definition (e.g., of 'Hindu', 'Hinduism', 'popular Hinduism'), scope, selection of major topics and issues, and competing theoretical stances. By favoring 'synchronic, structural methods of analysis' over those of 'textual scholarship', cultural interpretation (particularly 'American ethnosociology'), and the 'critique of Orientalist discourse', Fuller makes his analytical preferences clear, while setting up a rather controlling interpretive frame.[11] The main goals of the volume are to present an 'up-to-date account of popular religion' (p. xi), with 'some implications for [social theory]' (p. 255); and to place specialist knowledge 'in a broader anthropological framework', making Hinduism and India 'intelligible to a wider readership' (pp. 3–12; xi).[12]

After recounting the status of the major subjects of anthropological inquiry in Chapter 1 (e.g., caste and varna hierarchies; Brahmans, renouncers, and kings;[13] women's status; great and little traditions; and indigenous categories and sociological representations), Fuller devotes his next two chapters to gods, goddesses and their worship. Here, as in other chapters, he tightly organizes the material around the institutional interrelationships the recent anthropological studies have reported on deities, holy persons, different caste groups, and ordinary people's practices. The summaries of selected 'ethnographic cases', usually drawn from at least two different regions of the country, help him illustrate different (rural and urban) varieties of 'popular' religions. A discussion of 'sacrifice' and 'kingship' occupies the next two chapters, followed by chapters on village rituals, and devotion and devotional movements, with particular attention to goddesses' and women's role in them. He rounds out his discussion with 'Pilgrimage' and 'Misfortune', presenting an account of Hindu ideas, actions and reasoning that stand behind the causation and consequences of good and bad happenings in life.[14]

Under the mid-century Dumontian sociological frame, Fuller chooses to stay mostly with the upper-caste 'dominant order'. There is, for example, no index entry on Untouchables, and the book does not accommodate their or other backward castes' resurgent cultural, religious and political movements, social conflicts, power struggles, and counter-ideologies. Other recent studies, as already noted, increasingly respond to such changing Indian social reality by addressing religious conflicts (ideological and popular), contested rites and divinities, communal strife, and 'subaltern' views (e.g., for critical remarks on anthropologist's predilection toward the 'order' over social conflict, contingency and 'protest', see Veena Das 1989: 310–24; for recent comprehensive arguments, see Veena Das 1995; Khare 1984, Chapter 2 of this book).

Similarly, his account of 'the fundamental relationship between the two interpenetrating fields of sacrificial and devotionalist religion' (pp. 253–54), the core of the book, could have reflected the Hindu social reality more accurately by including a few anomalies, ambiguities, creative alternatives, and protests (for some persuasive examples, see Zelliot and Berntsen 1988).[15] Thus when the book is viewed as a whole, its criteria of inclusion and exclusion of subjects and its implicit 'theorizing' make one wonder about a larger methodological question: Do 'modern sociological analyses' still somehow try to 'tidy up' other people's social reality to suit a favorite anthropological frame or analytic/interpretive stance?[16] Unfortunately, such a stance, however subtly introduced, and despite early disclaimers, must still be directly—and adequately—addressed. To some, discovering 'the dominant structure' or 'the order' in a society might be somehow synonymous with finding 'what really happens', and thus also with reestablishing the discipline's 'scientific' reliability and authority. Equally clearly, other anthropologists, however, may 'resent the role of [such] anthropology as a purveyor of dreams' (Veena Das 1994: 144; my interpolation).

Approaching Hindus as the cultural other, Fuller lands himself in a rather vexing issue by observing '...to try to construct a picture of popular Hinduism through indigenous categories alone would *not do justice to the Hindus' own capacity for self-reflection*' (p. 11; my italics). This hardly explained remark not only seems to misjudge the place and the role Hindu conceptions have within Hindu culture, but it also casts, even if unintentionally, a patronizing shadow on his contemporary Hindu friends and colleagues.[17] The issue appears in the larger context of the author's decision to emphasize the 'field-based' over 'the textual', instead of treating the two domains as largely interdependent and circulating bodies of knowledge. For Fuller (p. 6), while 'ethnography—not scripture—is both the major source of evidence and the touchstone of interpretation', he nevertheless is found recognizing what we all recognize: a 'marked improvement in scholarly cooperation between anthropologists and Indologists' (see p. ix; and the book actually depends on several major texts and textual scholars, including Biardeau 1981; Heesterman 1985).[18]

However, the central issue here is how far (and how well) a sociological/anthropological account explains the social reality that people face in life. The issue would be paramount when we find over 800 million ranked and fractious Hindus trying to relate to, and live with their 330 million (and now perhaps many more) equally ranked (and jealous) gods and goddesses. Add to the picture the increasingly violent Hindu, Sikh and Muslim religious confrontations in contemporary India, and we realize why 'popular' Hindu religion becomes an enormously complex, socially forceful but conflict-ridden subject, attracting many, but hardly any adequate, theories, interpretations, and commentaries. But only the concluding pages of the book allude to some of the major Hindu religious conflicts (pp. 256–61), leaving the reader with many unanswered questions.

Such contemporary conflicts acutely comment on what some now call 'runaway India', revealing also a 'runaway' side of the popular Hindu gods, goddesses, devotional rites, religious movements, and counter-movements. Perhaps the divinities, 'for their own unfathomable amusement' (to redeploy Fuller's phrase; see p. 253), today are far more excitable, cantankerous and contingent, just as their devotees and protesters are. Under such conditions, the sociological findings, however carefully controlled, concisely presented and argued, must also remain socially contested and sociologically contingent (see Veena Das 1995: 54).

III

Raising issues of wider anthropological concern, Heesterman, Gellner and Fuller attempt (by variously combining the textual information with field data) to make sense of the Indian subcontinent's *multiple* pasts and social realities in each other's terms. Heesterman and Fuller place the study of sacrifice at the center, showing how it transforms into 'ritualism', 'devotionalism' and even the current Hindu world-view (see Fuller pp. 254–55, and Heesterman 1985). And of the two, Fuller's study, given the diverse learned, vernacular and local writing on the living Hindu traditions, particularly faces a formidable task. Yet, when viewed as a whole and under its own terms of reference, it pulls together a cohesive, representative, and accessible account of the selected aspects of popular Hindu religion and society.

Simultaneously, the three studies under review also raise a cluster of interrelated larger analytic issues. These concern 'historical' versus 'mythical' reality, Western versus non-Western epistemologies, and the anthropologist's changing scholarly locations, interests and quandaries.

Fuller's 'field-view' of Hindu religion particularly sharpens the focus on the 'historical' (versus the 'mythical') in India. Though a long-standing civilizational puzzle and a scholarly conundrum, many modern scholars, including Heesterman, Gellner and Fuller, start by accepting the primacy of 'the historical'. But the Hindu's belief in the 'eternal' (e.g., the eternal or *sanātan* Vedas and the 'eternal moral order' or *sanātan dharma*) nevertheless remains a massive social fact, staring a modern scholar in the face. Some Indian scholars have called it the 'primordial tradition' (see Saran 1989). Since this 'ageless dharma' still guides the core Hindu ideologies, institutions, social attitudes, and world-view, and, since it also frames some of the most crucial conflicts (including the recent Ayodhya 'temple–mosque' dispute), the 'mythical' versus 'historical' debate may be actually far from resolved. Rather, the issue is becoming increasingly crucial, as the 1980s showed with the serialization of the *Ramayana* and the *Mahabharata* on television. Given the critical social role of the mass media and a major film industry, it requires continued careful observation, study and analysis of how myth and history come out of each other in India (e.g., see Cohn 1987c, for a pace-setting discussion of interrelationships between history and anthropology; and for a critique of 'the historical mode', see Nandy 1995b: 44–66).

The usual anthropological response, as Gellner and Fuller well exemplify, has been to let ethnography become more than 'microhistory', recording and explaining how the living religious beliefs, myths, and rituals play themselves out against changing historical conditions. But knowing how routinely and effortlessly myth and history in India interrelate meaningfully, ethnography cannot but evaluate both in each other's terms. If anything, such transformations have only multiplied, accelerated and magnified with the advent of the modern mass media.

Correspondingly, the issue has also been woven into the shifting interests of disciplinary focus in the last 50 years, though with increasing emphasis on the historical. For instance, if the mid-century 'village studies' were replaced by those explaining India by castes, caste ideologies and social hierarchy (à la Dumont and/or Marriott), the discipline now marginalizes these, including the quest for a single 'universal' underlying theory or explanation for India as a whole. Instead, one now examines Indian sociocultural life by issues, in all its lived complexity, including the social *anomie*, conflicts, contingencies, and resistance (for a range of reviews and remarks on such shifts in anthropological studies of India, see Veena Das 1994: 133–44; Fuller and Spencer 1990; Chapters 1 and 2 of this book; Madan 1966, 1994).

The same anthropological focus now extends to examining the role of the modern Indian state in inducing shifts in power relations and raising new cultural conflicts, social debates, alternative historical (subaltern, post-Orientalist) perspectives, new political claims to homelands, and rights with justice (e.g., on ethnic violence, secularism, colonial representations, popular religious communication, industrial disasters, and human rights, see Dirks 1992; Khare 1987a; 1990; Madan 1987a; Tambiah 1986; Zelliot and Berntsen 1988). The mythical and the historical, and the traditional and the modern are thus found to lock horns once again in India, but now not to illustrate the primacy of modern Western ideology, but rather those critical conditions and issues that directly involve ordinary Indian people and their vital practical interests.

Complementarily, from the other side, the anthropologist's own location and identity, however grudgingly admitted, frame his/her work, influencing the operating analytic assumptions, interests, writing, and perspectives.[19] At the end of the century (and the millennium), not only are the people themselves—the anthropological subject—restive and more self-aware, but anthropologists and their readers are also a far more varied, demanding and critical lot. Our 'disciplinary authority', a weak and nebulous one in any case (Geertz 1994), increasingly rests on having something to say that the people under study and interested readers would find perceptive, fair, and useful.

Well past any simple Indian/Western or traditional/modern dichotomy, most anthropologists working on South Asia today critically compare the 'Euro-American' conceptual and descriptive tools with their Indian counterparts. Similarly, Indian scholars closely examine both sides, where some retain a 'critical unease' toward not only certain Western hegemonic forces and knowledge structures, but also toward the state-initiated modern public culture (e.g., Nandy 1987; 1995a; see also Chapter 1 of this book).

But it seems the discipline still cannot fully get past what started with Dumont's mid-century locational debate on Western anthropology and anthropologists vis-à-vis non-Western India. It returns to us in different forms, and in different debates. Consider in such an intellectual and disciplinary context the recent exchange between a Sinhalese and an American anthropologist, Gananath Obeyesekere and Marshall Sahlins, on the Hawaiian views of Captain James Cook (the later Hawaiian's god Lono). Starting with distinct historical and cultural assumptions about the Hawaiians and the role of anthropological analysis, each scholar examines the same colonial encounter to reach clearly different interpretations about the Hawaiians—their memory, cultural representations, meaning-making devices, and 'rationality' (see Obeyesekere 1992; Sahlins 1995). Criticizing the other side, each, from his own intellectual location and social background, claims to represent the Hawaiians more 'accurately'. If Sahlins stands for not eliminating 'Hawaiians from their own history', Obeyesekere stresses Hawaiians' 'practical rationality', with European colonial games exposed by the mythologizing Captain Cook.[20]

The two anthropologists debate that persistent issue of 'accurately' representing the other, ostensibly under scholarly rigor, but not divorced from their different cultural backgrounds. Once again, however, the debate must end inconclusively. It is an issue that the 'anthropological community' must constantly try to reconcile but forever only incompletely, since its practitioners cannot but be a product of diverse human cultures. Dumont had made a similar observation some time ago (1986b: 233): 'If uniting through differences is at the same time the aim of anthropology and the characteristic of hierarchy, they are doomed to keep company'. But *how* does the discipline unite *in practice* while exploring and explicating people's cultural differences against the cultural backgrounds of ethnographers and anthropologists? Anthropologists might attempt to discover, under scholarly rigor, contextually shared (or issue-based) cultural grounds, communication structures and moral responsibilities, while recognizing and understanding (rather than denying) their own differences of age, gender, culture, race, and national location. It is a necessary complement to what anthropologists then do with—and for—those studied. Such an anthropology rests on an unwritten yet binding notion of interdependent and 'co-responsive' cultural communication as much among the anthropologists themselves as among the anthropologists and the peoples studied (see Chapter 4 of this book). The Western and non-Western discourse locations may thus learn by trial and error how to develop contextually interdependent anthropological inquiry, knowledge and significance for the next century.

Anthropology on the Indian subcontinent, by necessity, must now reflect a similar direction for dealing with increasingly divergent debates on complicated—and violent—historical and cultural changes at home. While the discipline can no longer outright 'apply' a theory conceived and formulated elsewhere, because its assumptions and implications would clash, it also cannot afford to isolate itself from global anthropology. It must enter into a fruitful wider intellectual dialogue, weaving relationships between the local, the national, the multi-centered, and the global (which is both European and non-European in scope and character). The Anglo-American disciplinary influences become a part of such disciplinary profile, influencing and getting influenced by a subject and issue under discussion. Nor, similarly, can the discipline perpetually paralyze itself in the debate where either Dumont's (1986a) ideology of modernity or Saran's (1962; 1989) self-privileging 'primordial tradition' left it decades ago.[21] Instead, one now critically debates major disciplinary assumptions and frames of analysis within the changing world of people's rights and the scholar's moral obligations.

Though several recent studies variously address this emerging cluster of disciplinary concerns (e.g., Geertz 1994; Nandy 1995a; Scheper–Hughes 1992; Chapter 4 of this book), Veena Das (1995) explores new and significant directions in a wide-ranging analysis. Consider, for instance, how in India the person, the agent, might be emerging as an experiencing, speaking, and rights-claiming locus ('the victim' in Das' material), and how such persons take on the forces that the Indian caste–class and the state release. To account for such situations, Das views the discipline as culturally more experiential, morally textured and historically responsible, while recognizing the loss of 'certainty' in knowledge, and that the social scientist's voice is only one within a 'plurality' of battling voices in today's world (Veena Das 1994: 143). However, she misreads or simplifies the strong and continuing grass-roots role of cultural traditions in today's India, along with their ingrained reasoning patterns, and the resulting Indian social 'resiliency' and 'practicality' (see Chapter 5). Throughout this century, major Indian traditions have increasingly battled among themselves and selectively against modernity and the modern state. Though neither side is above criticism or blameless, there is no end in sight to this tug-of-war. If anything, these struggles are increasingly serious, violent, and unpredictable, leaving the outcome uncertain where Indian modernity, secularism and the state are concerned (see Madan 1994: 51, for a summary of Srinivas' recent observations).

IV

Now, as anthropology on the Indian subcontinent increasingly turns to 'homegrown' issues—whether of competing moral orders, anger and love, domination, protest, violence, or injustice—the discipline is increasingly about cultural communication. Ethnographic writing, correspondingly, becomes narrational, polyvocal, reflexive, dialogical, and rights/justice-sensitive (e.g., Veena Das 1990b: 345–98; Khare 1984; 1990; Nita Kumar 1994; Narayan 1994; Raheja and Gold 1994; Trawick 1990). Slowly but surely thus moving toward a *post-Dumontian phase*,[22] anthropology now breaks down and renegotiates the Indian/European ideological divide on the basis of the prevailing issues and interests. A refocused rigor in scholarship and ethnographic accuracy also appears as a result, recognizing flaws in both *under* and *over*-interpretation (for excellent ethnographies, see Raheja and Gold 1994; Trawick 1990; for a recent philosophical and literary debate on the issue, see Eco et al. 1992).

Put another way (see Weiner 1995: 14–21), anthropology must stand up 'to and for that spirit of human uniqueness and resiliency', despite the deepening changes and challenges facing the discipline. On change, notes Geertz (1994: 131), 'It is not just ideas that are no longer what they were. The world isn't either'. Nor are the crowding challenges posed by the looming ghosts of Marx, Gramsci, Foucault, and even the non-European Said. The discipline today (not unlike philosophy, psychology, literature, and history in the recent past) invites either 'end of anthropology' pronouncements or a defensive 'recapturing anthropology' posture (Fox 1991; Scheper–Hughes 1995). Both ways, we know that it is a difficult 'rite of passage' for a discipline specializing in studying the cultural 'rites of passage' of the world.

Yet the several already cited recent works, with their new departures, hold promise (e.g., for 'an anthropology-with-one's-feet-on-the-ground', see Scheper–Hughes 1992; also pp. 4, 28). Today, when any depiction/representation can raise issues of cultural appropriation, manipulation and control over others (Geertz 1994: 130), and when anthropological '*mis*understanding' and 'not-understanding' of culture are the issues of discussion (Fabian 1995: 41–50), the discipline can hardly afford to continue the status quo.

Some discussions further consolidate the post-Dumontian disciplinary phase (consider together, for example, Veena Das 1995 and Scheper–Hughes 1992), particularly when anthropological reasoning, analysis and writing communicate and collaborate with the reasoning and perspectives (whether with or without writing) of those we study. In such a view, all 'sociological reasoning', however 'scientific' or 'modern', is, at some point, culturally and historically as situated as that of the people themselves (see Khare 1993c). Most crucially, the anthropologist's 'local counterparts' today expect (and sometimes even demand) *communication under parity*, not polarity, to share *their* cultural knowledge. Anthropologists, after all, work on other people's intellectual property to write, represent and understand it for the common good.

But such a formulation amounts to what Geertz (1994: 130) calls 'game change'. It also breaks the Dumontian ideological Western/ non-Western opposition in a thousand different ways, introducing new notions of knowledge production and ownership, and receiving divergent messages and commentaries from Indian traditions, regional histories, and the modern Indian state. Given the resulting chaotic public and intellectual culture, an analyst recently remarked on the Indian public culture's 'ability to confuse and exasperate', while proposing a 'plural' rather than the West-centered human future (see Nandy 1995a; 1995b). This stance looks 'for a language of social criticism that will not be entirely alien to a majority of Indians', and locates those 'cultural forms and languages of being and thinking that defy the logic and hegemony of the modern West' (Nandy 1995a: ix–x; dust jacket).

Michael Walzer (1994), a political philosopher, also raises a similar debate within the West, by focusing on the 'politics of difference', equality, and moral obligation, both locally (a 'thick' version) and globally (a 'thin' one). Nandy's 'plural human future' thus encounters Walzer's 'many-sided self', inviting anthropological sensibilities to flourish across the Western and non-Western divide. It also means undertaking an ethnography of both 'thick' and 'thin' cultural knowledge, but under conditions of parity and fairness for'all concerned. Let us hope that this post-Dumontian anthropological phase, thanks to Dumont's uncompromising logic of dichotomous ideological structures, will show how to communicate and negotiate anthropologically better *across* the dominant and 'other' centers and systems of knowledge, but only under conditions of parity and fairness.

◀ NOTES

1. This chapter, here slightly revised, is under publication in *Reviews in Anthropology* as a review article on three recent books: J.C. Heesterman, *The Broken World of Sacrifice: An Essay in Ancient Indian Ritual*, Chicago: University of Chicago Press, 1993; David N. Gellner, *Monk, Householder and Tantric Priest: Newar Buddhism and its Hierarchy of Ritual*, Cambridge: Cambridge University Press, 1992; and C.J. Fuller, *The Camphor Flame: Popular Hinduism and Society in India*, Princeton: Princeton University Press, 1992. Unless referring to another publication of these authors, I will give only page numbers of the books under review.
2. The 'scientific' in such contexts attracts several meanings, including an emphasis on, and analytic preference for describing 'the dominant order' for its 're-petitive' (and hence 'verified' and 'standard') social properties. See also note 8.
3. Anthropologists, even those 'native' (a term no longer an oxymoron; see Narayan 1993), routinely use the knowledge of the people under study (whether of one's own or of another culture) to compose their account. Increasingly, however, the discipline and its practitioners face questions about the discipline's unity and authority within a changing world (Dumont 1986b; Geertz 1994).
4. Here and in the title of the paper, 'Dumontian sociology' stands for the distinct systematic sociological formulation and discussion that Louis Dumont initiated. We could also call it a part of the much wider 'Dumontian sociology', a subject of continuing intellectual interest outside India (e.g., see Mark 1994).
   I am grateful to Dr Joel Robbins for bringing Mark's study to my attention.
5. Though 'oversimplified' in empirical and historical terms (see Halbfass 1988), this ideological opposition still guides the dialectic of anthropological discourse. Let us note, however, how firmly Dumont ties both anthropology and comparison to 19th century European modernity. Using 'European', 'Western' and 'modern' synonymously, he makes India of the past and the present merely 'traditional', a total logical opposite for Europe. In such a committed modernist view, all 'postmodern' criticisms, even those of mid-20th century Europe, must remain discounted, if not totally dismissed.
6. Unless specified otherwise, the term 'India' in the article refers to a shared cultural and civilizational region rather than to the Indian nation-state. Such a

stipulation is necessary to cover the ground Heesterman's (on ancient India), Gellner's (on the practised Buddhism and Hinduism among the Newar of Nepal) and Fuller's (on popular Hinduism in today's India) books demand.

7. See also Uberoi (1968) for an early attempt to consider 'science' in the context of the Indian state and 'self-rule' (*swaraj*).

8. Marriott's (see Marriott 1991: 295–308, for his critique of my views) ethnosociology ultimately falls short of resolving the Western/non-Western dichotomy in knowledge. Without going into details, a close reading of his latest response also shows a striking gap between his writing and its reading by his critics, particularly Indian reviewers (see Marriott 1991: 295, 299, 300, 303, 305, 306). Marriott's claims about an ethnosociological 'construction' of the Hindu world become not simply *more* 'comprehensive' and 'powerful', but also dramatically sweeping (Marriott 1991: 297, 305).

9. For a substantive account of contacts between Indian and European thinkers, some productive and others not, see Halbfass (1988).

10. By following a core of major Western sociological formulations (e.g., Durkheim and/or Weber), the practitioners of this approach, with minor differences, usually end up 'verifying' the structure and applicability of 'the standard' sociological principles and explanations across global societies and conditions. For a better recent attempt largely in the same vein, see Milner (1994).

11. Fuller leaves such an impression particularly since he makes many conceptual moves from the beginning to contribute to 'Indian social theory', but only through weak disclaimers or indirect hints (p. 255) rather than a systematic full discussion of his approach for the reader. The writing attempts a sort of 'stealth' theorization, a stance that puts readers, even specialists eager to learn from his structure of exposition, to a distinct disadvantage. For a similar but subtle framing in another discussion, see Fuller and Spencer (1990: 85–105).

12. By providing an appendix on the Hindu calendar, a good glossary, and a 'bibliographical guide', Fuller distinctly helps the reader. They make the book accessible. However, on the other hand, his efforts to edit and control the ethnographic details of illustrative cases become overly stifling, particularly for students, as some of mine (and others) have already remarked. But the issue is unavoidable for such a knowledge-synthesizing volume, and on most occasions I find Fuller editorially very judicious.

13. On the Brahman and the renouncer, see Heesterman, in the book under review (see p. 5, pp. 79–83, most of Chapter 5, and pp. 184, 187); and elsewhere (1985), for his insightful contributions on the subject.

14. Here we finally have a discussion of the three most crucial and interactive principles of learned and popular Hinduism—karma, dharma, and rebirth. It is belated and restricted at this point, though this is the religious language most known to and popular among Hindus.

15. Several selections in this book deepen, expand or diversify the picture of popular Hindu devotionalism (for a short but pithy descriptive relationship between the divine and the devotee, see Karve 1988: 3–6).

16. Related here is also the question of the lurking shadows of Orientalism in the modern analysis of popular Hinduism, an issue Fuller decides to dismiss

largely out of hand (p. 254; pp. 9–11). But the issue does not go away. (Compare Breckenridge and van der Veer 1993, for a wide-ranging discussion.)

17. Such a comment opens a Pandora's box. For instance, one may wonder exactly which Hindus the author is referring to—those educated and Westernized, traditional literati, experienced but illiterate city dwellers, or literate/illiterate villagers. If the reference is to all, it makes a very different anthropological point about how the 'natives' think (and how anthropologists think 'natives' think), than if it refers to only one specific subgroup. Either way, the remark confounds the issues of 'natives' and of the nature of anthropological knowledge. On the same point, compare the recent debate between Sahlins and Obeyesekere, discussed below, on the Hawaiians' role in representing their own cultural past.

18. During this century, the fractious Hindu society has not only further opened its sacred texts to a spate of writing and commentary, but also to radical political meanings and protests. For example, an activist untouchable organization, Ambedkar Mahasabha, recently launched fresh protests in political forums and newspapers against the *Laws of Manu*, equating 'Manuism' or *Manuwaad* with 'the hegemony of the upper castes' over the low castes and Untouchables (*The Pioneer*, 17 July 1995, p. 1).

19. Though their writing still only indirectly expresses such concerns, anthropologists, especially when facing divisive national, ethnic or social conflicts, may sometimes explicitly write for very human—even biographical—reasons. South Asian anthropologists have rather continuously recognized the role of such factors in anthropological writing. For example, see Veena Das (1995); Srinivas (1964); and Tambiah (1986). Besides, illustrating a similar approach in Latin America, see Scheper–Hughes (1992), who shows that good scholarship and a distinctly close and committed involvement with the people studied are not incompatible.

20. Even reviewers of such debates may openly favor one side over the other. See Fagan (1995). Writing virtually a paean to Sahlins' 'mesmerizing authority', Fagan charges Obeyesekere with uncritical assumptions, 'inventions', 'sloppy reasoning and analysis', and a 'fatally flawed' thesis about the Hawaiians, Europeans, and the Western culture. The same review, however, also recalls that Sahlins 'felt obliged to compose' his 318 pages in response because Obeyesekere's book had 'won awards and was praised for its penetrating originality'.

21. Given their ideological positions, Dumont and Saran must remain forever irreconcilable. If Dumont finds the history and development of human cultures (and hence of anthropology) forever dichotomous and modernity-bound, Saran renders the Indian tradition sui generis, complete, and presumably outside of or beyond history. For Dumont, similarly, all the classical or recent Indian critical scholarship on the modern West cannot be taken seriously. Europe is made above, impervious to or dismissive of non-European knowledge. For Saran, at the other end, the modern West, it seems, can never have the necessary conceptual basis (and tools) to understand India.

22. To some, including Fuller's book under review, the post-Dumontian phase may be conceptually unnecessary, even inadmissible. To others, particularly

Marriott (1989; 1991), ethnosociology may have already staked out such a watershed claim at least two decades ago. To still others, the interrelationships between the Hindu 'eternal', history, India, and anthropology must remain open to continuous inquiry (e.g., Cohn 1987a, 1987b: 18–49, 632–82; Guha and Spivak 1988; Khare 1993c; and Nandy 1995b).

4

The Other's Double—
The Anthropologist's Bracketed Self:
Notes on Cultural Representation
and Privileged Discourse*

I

The Other has been a subject of much discussion during the last decades. It is as if we have rediscovered it with renewed urgency as the Western liberalism of the 1960s and 1970s declined and the minorities and the postcolonial non-West demanded recognition of their *own* political presence. However, our subject, the Other, or 'not-us' seems to be as closely intertwined with our knowledge (cultural, historical, and political) of ourselves as of others living at other places and in other times.[1] During most of this century, a period in which we saw the rise of scientific temper and techno-logical solutions, we may ask whether we really understood the cultural Other (or its double—the self or ourselves) any better than we did in the past. Despite our recent plentiful critical literature

* This chapter is a modified version of the article originally published in *New Literary History: A Journal of Theory and Interpretation*, 1992, 23: 1–23 (University of Virginia, Charlottesville, USA).

on the Other, we might ask, are we any better in our comprehension and recognition of the historical and political placement of the Other as 'we' (whether situated within the West or the non-West) continue to secure an advantageous politics of privilege for 'ourselves'? If anthropology recognizes that the self is the Other's double, the anthropologist shows how, as he appropriates the Other to reconstitute his self, he learns to recognize an irreducible presence of the Other.[2]

My argument in this essay is that the self–Other dialectic is now historically so poised that to study the Other invariably means to grapple ever more with its cultural diversity, on the one hand, and with its comprehensive, intrinsic, and irreducible presence, on the other. The issue now is not simply to represent the Other but to *recognize* it anew, with its own powers of recognition, representation, and persuasion intact. However, to recognize the Other this way is also to examine the *unresolved* issues of one's own self-identity, especially as we privilege the self via different critical accounts (historical, cultural, and political). But such privileging processes have a cost: they increase ethnocentrism, alienate the Other, and produce 'a crisis of representation'. Suggestions vary on how to resolve such a crisis. Some suggest a more empathic, dialogical interpretation of the Other, some simply want to return to 'describing facts', while those more radical want anthropology to drop out from representing others.[3] I find the first position attractive but inadequate to resolve the crisis. The second and third positions are nonviable, though for different reasons. If the second is outdated, the third is impractical, given the dependence of human cognition, language, and society on representations of some kind or the other. One might legitimately ask, could 'genuinely reciprocal representations' be possible even within anthropology, a discipline devoted to studying cultural others? If we want to answer such a question in the affirmative, there is no alternative to confronting issues of one-sided knowledge control and discourse dominance. But before we take up this point, we should consider a few general properties of multidisciplinary (including anthropological) approaches to the cultural Other.

Our recent discussions (literary, cultural, and historical) of the Other generally involve two stages: first a critique of the cultural definition and historical placement of the 'self' (or 'us') vis-à-vis others, for its politics of privilege, and second, our dissatisfaction with (and an inadequacy of) such a (postmodernist?) critique itself. However, these multidisciplinary discussions are still so 'fluid' that we lack defining languages of criticism and clear, unambiguous directions and positions toward the Other. The situation is becoming so convoluted that we now perhaps require a new breed of academic sleuths given to tracking where (and how) the recent ambiguous critiques and metacritiques of the 'self' (vis-à-vis the Other) start and end. Simultaneously, everybody knows that the processes of privileging the dominant discourse continue (sometimes with increased vigor).

However, to produce some distance between oneself and such inclinations, to consider 'alternative' ways of dealing with the Other, one generally accepted anthropological rule of thumb is to 'immerse' oneself in describing and understanding other cultures. If we do so and allow other cultures to provide us with *their analysis* of the self and the Other, we may see the alternatives the non-Western others come up with. Some cultures may actually so formulate their ideal and philosophical positions on the self–Other axis that they are able to (consciously or unconsciously) 'decenter' (but neither neutralize nor remove) the politics of privilege. In such cases (for a discussion of India's case, see Section III), the self, us, not-us, and others may get defined by a given or a revealed order of moral values and precedence, with assurances of self-renewal and self-justification.[4] When facing the problematic Other, such societies may choose to 'underplay' the visible forces of historical, cultural, and political distinctions to forge that invisible Absolute that ultimately annihilates all traces of the self as well as the Other (without leaving any traces; the reference here is to India's nondualist—*advaita*—philosophy).

Still other cultures may choose to deny a continuing existence to the immediate self, and lose it into what we may call the momentary Other (as in the Buddhist perspective, for example), until we dissolve both the self and the Other (leading to the Buddhist notion of vacuity). However, if an anthropologist considers such 'alternative' strategies of conception and interpretation of the Other, he cannot afford to be oblivious to recent critical debates on the construction (and deconstruction) of the self and the Other within Western intellectual circles. We need open exchange from both—Western and non-Western—sides if we do not wish to lapse into another phase of isolation and a subtler form of ethnocentrism.

This point cannot be overemphasized.[5] Today, viewed from a Western standpoint, when we are confronted with the cultural and political assertion of 'others', our 'modern' treatment of the self and us, it seems, has lost its acuity. For example, the modern observer's mask of scientific objectivity has disintegrated; his mirror of moral neutrality has cracked. The politics of domination and control of the Other, when it really matters, however, continues to occupy center stage, allowing the cultural distance between 'us' and others to bristle with ever new cognitive and historical differences, communication gaps, and subtle (often private) ethnocentric intolerance. As we reflect on these problems, we wonder about their impact on the expanding (and for some, threatening) presence of the cultural Other.[6]

A critic of the postmodern debates may want to argue that our quandaries in understanding the Other seem to be increasing in the same proportion as 'our' self-doubt. For the West, in such a view, it means closing ranks against creeping uncertainty for its primary and privileged tool of study and analysis—the supremacy of 'the logical, rational, factual inquiry'. Any doubt in this citadel weakens the desire (sometimes conscious, often unconscious) to project a historical and cultural superiority of 'our' tools as we represent and 'explain' the Other. But, paradoxically, if a modern cultural essentialism (often best illustrated by the achievements of Western science and technology) justifies a strong rationalist–universalist posture, it also significantly reduces the 'moral space' for the Other to represent itself independent of Western universalism. It alienates the Other from a true ownership of its own history. If anything, Western modernity, by its own definition, may have rendered impossible any simple domination and control of the Other. For it is often modernity which encourages the Other to learn and employ the tools of 'independent voice' and 'self-representation' to gain a distinct political and historical existence. In such a circumstance the same Western scientific universalism cannot turn around and justify its perpetuation of a hegemonic (that is, Other-controlling yet self-privileging) discourse.[7]

Similarly, though we have accumulated diverse 'empirical' knowledge on other peoples, with increasing focus on minority groups and dependent cultures (that is, on women, children, refugees, ethnic groups, and the tortured), more knowledge does not automatically ensure (and produce) a better understanding of the

Other. The issue of when (and how) to mark, or not to mark, the self vis-à-vis the Other still eludes us. Though we conceptually realize that the Other, like the self, is an irreducible cognitive template of human culture, we still seem only to fumble both when real life situations (in different historical, cultural, and political contexts) are concerned. It is as if the modern cultural temper still does not know how to deal with crucial issues of alterity—'the other I' or the Other's 'I'.

Apropos of Lévi–Strauss' comments (see note 2), these recent discussions focus on dealing directly with the anthropologist's bracketed self. Not only should it be unpacked step by step; it also needs to be treated as the Other's double: whereas the anthropologist aspires to secure a special privilege to describe and discern the Other, the Other variously reconstitutes his self, slowly but unfailingly. The more the anthropologist tries to bracket his self out of his professional accounts, the more he may find it impregnated with the presence of the Other. All of this goes on as he participates in (as well as criticizes) the modern cultural temper of his own society (and the profession). Some 'activist' anthropologists go even further: They join the Other for 'improving' its survival and strengthening its political voice.

II

For anthropologists, the Other thus invariably translates into configurations of cultural similarities and differences, yielding that cultural distance—Clifford Geertz's 'not-us'—that has always been 'out there' in various degrees for anthropologists to record, interpret, and explain. If the anthropologist does not do so, the implicit argument is that others would not only remain 'unaccounted' but they also could not be 'counted' within the scientific (that is, also the dominant and privileged) discourse. At another level, they also could not truly become 'our' (the anthropologist's) double. And if the Other cannot inform and enlighten 'us' (the anthropologist and his audience) this way, one wonders whether others would solely be studied 'for their own sake'. Could it be possible at all, given the anthropologist's palpably dualistic (us/them) cultural framework?

On the other hand, a major consequence of the others' existence has been to let us become more self-reflexive and self-critical, allowing *our* expressions and explications of ourselves to pass through that refracting prism that the Other holds up. But one could argue that this is another anthropological way of 'appropriating' the cultural Other. Given the unavoidability of some form of cultural hegemony and power discourse when representing the Other, the practical question now is whether such a power and privilege can be consciously rendered genuinely *reciprocal* (and put to good use), rather than be totally eliminated.

Though anthropologists take differing positions on the question, I shall mainly concern myself with certain recent debates in cultural interpretation and criticism. Instead of 'describing' the life of other peoples as 'objective accounts' or as 'emblems of exoticism' of the premodern mentality, these postcolonial, postmodern anthropologists now examine how the modern West's notions of self and 'us' construct and implicate the Other, but mostly within a privileged discourse on human history and meaning.[8] These anthropologists often examine themselves and anthropology's colonial roots as they 'author' the Other once again within their authoritative criticism of past approaches. Some ask how ethnography could survive if it *stops* assuming, appropriating, and representing the Other, and lets the Other be itself.[9]

Actually, critical anthropology has increasingly privileged 'ethnographic writing', where how we 'write' (that is, whether we produce a 'thick' description with the help of Western literary tropes, historical parallels, and philosophical allusions) about the Other is more important than the Other in and by itself. And if the Other never stands by itself, it, again, can never fully represent (or write) itself.[10] Though anthropologists' literary and critical 'writing' has overtaken the mere (that is, intellectually downgraded) 'factual descriptions' of the Other, and the ethnographer as a writer–author invents or 'constructs' for his informant a dialogical presence, the Other's 'voice' still remains dependent and muffled. This voice is only that which makes 'sense' and becomes 'audible' to the writer–author anthropologist. This new ethnographer is no scribe, and no mere historiographer of the Other, who recounts.[11] Instead, he 'authors' the Other—in a new relationship of dependence. If he is a critical 'interpreter' of cultures, he artfully folds and selectively spotlights the Other within his cultural, literary, and historical 'text' on 'ourselves', with the goal of 'refiguration' of a 'fugitive truth':

To see ourselves as others see us can be eye-opening. To see others as sharing a nature with ourselves is the merest decency. But it is from the far more difficult achievement of seeing ourselves amongst others, as a local example of the forms human life has taken, a case among cases, a world among worlds, that the largeness of mind ... comes' (Geertz 1983: 16).

The question is not only how, but *what* we should read in such a summation of the goal of anthropological inquiry. At the turn of the century, which formulations of the Other best sum up the anthropological position—the Other that is a ground for verifying 'our' superior knowledge, the Other that is not inferior but just a different (and often dependent) double of the self, or the Other with an independent presence, which is much more than what the anthropologist's different devices of representation can capture?[12] At present, anthropologists tend to oscillate between these positions, depending on their personal cultural location, theoretical preference, and aimed professional identity.

This 'waddling' may indicate that anthropology, Europe's discourse-bearer on the non-European Other, is still trying to come to grips with an assertive presence of the Other (and its implications). If the critical literary–philosophical–historical authorship within anthropology increasingly exposes what it cannot authoritatively represent and privilege, then such a criticism also reveals gaps—a lack and a fading (or the subject's *aphanasis*, in Lacan's sense)—within the knower, the anthropologist. This in turn erodes the erstwhile certainty of knowledge within the life and practice of a discipline. A reaction of dismay and acerbic disapproval against such a critique is therefore equally predictable, with a tendency to close ranks and guard the territory–boundary markers of the discipline, in the name of a good theory and proven scholarship.[13] However, such counter-criticisms notwithstanding, identifying the presence and consequence of the ever-varying cultural Other remains the life source of contemporary anthropology and life blood of the anthropologist. Given this fact, the anthropologist cannot dismiss the central message of such critical postmodernist debates. He must either devise new ways to recognize squarely the independent presence of the Other or face a deepening disciplinary crisis of legitimate representation.

In such a condition, where anthropology sustains itself on deciphering the cultural Other, any device which claims the anthropologist's self-independence from the Other looks increasingly contrived, even false. An anthropologist's self cannot any longer bracket itself off from the Other's dialogue, because the anthropologist lives in the company of the Other for years, not only to explain or interpret it in the context of his professional life (the 'I' of published pages) but also to deal with it in his personal life. Increasingly, the anthropologist now opens (rather than masks or hides) himself more and more as the Other jars him loose from the usual and the expected. Sometimes such encounters yield new insights (for example, the police raid during a Balinese cockfight and Geertz's resulting 'deep play'). Now a few convincing and prized ethnographies tend to be those which record a journey of self-discovery with the help of the Other.[14]

However, such an anthropologist still remains a captive of a self-privileging personal-turned-professional discourse, where the Other appears as a docile echo chamber, only too eager and ready to provide catharsis to the anthropologist's puzzled self. All issues of discourse parity, reciprocal knowledge sharing, and interdependent authenticity still remain unattended. To attend to them, we need a constant cultural criticism and historical reappraisal of the anthropologist's 'I' (personal and professional) to redirect its one-sided self-privileging tendencies.[15]

The root of such self-privilege may rest within the anthropologist's axiom of appropriating the Other's knowledge and employing it mainly to better understand 'ourselves and our own culture'. Individual careers of anthropologists thus often start with studying an 'exotic' or a 'different' culture, but end with writings on their own. Such accounts often emphasize how the Other contrasts and complements what 'we' are (and are not), and stop there. But such a praxis not only depletes the Other, it also denies that the Other possesses independent, universalizing, authentic knowledge. Some recent India–West studies provide an instructive example, mainly for appropriating the Other.[16] We may better understand this imperial relationship if we visualize the reverse condition, where either the subordinate Other produced knowledge superior to our own, or where the Other's knowledge displaced ours. However, what we need is genuine reciprocity in sharing knowledge.[17]

III

Thus continues the anthropologist's self-entangling odyssey of comprehending the cultural Other. Though far from straight-forward, it provides us a glimpse of some anthropological strategies as much for taking the cultural Other into account as for letting the Other 'speak' for itself. However, since these strategies still remain 'intrusive' in conception, expression, and explanation, and are largely rooted in the Western tradition of securing and maintaining a privileged discourse, we may now examine the Other from within another major cultural tradition in order to see how it not only 'explains' the Other but also how it secures a privileged position for its own world and world-view.[18] I refer here to Hindu India's approach to the Other, since its major philosophical schools have long taken differing positions on the issue (from radical negation to conditional acceptance), and yet pursue it for divergent cultural, historical, and political purposes.[19] Though a subject worthy of independent inquiry, we will remark on some major Indian approaches to the cultural Other essentially in order to illustrate certain distinct philosophical conceptions and strategies.[20]

Three strategies may be particularly relevant to us: first is to deny any intrinsic reality to the Other and to 'dissolve' its apparent perceptions within a 'seamless' (nondualist) notion of the Cosmic Whole (called Ātman or Brahman, the ultimate Reality); second, award only a contingent value and (qualified nondualist) presence to the Other until the ultimate Reality is realized; or third, propose a necessary and purposeful dualist (and dialectical) relationship between the self and the Other by treating the latter as a genuine manifestation of the divine. The first (and dominant) philosophical approach demands that every individual being 'work through' veils of illusion and ignorance to realize that all forms of otherness are illusory. This universalist view asks: 'How other can the Other be?' given its illusory character. This viewpoint, strictly speaking, renders the Other a nonsubject or at best only a pseudosubject.[21]

However, such a philosophy does not render the anthropologist's quest any easier. Concerned not only with the ultimate ideal, it traces the experiences ordinary and learned Hindus undergo in pursuit of such an ideal (including failures). In so pursuing the subject, the anthropologist proceeds not unlike the Hindu's own major athletes of spirit (whether a mythological Nārada, a Vyāsa or a Śukadeva, or a historical Ramakrishna), who try and try again to realize the ideal (or more accurately, 'make the ideal descend') within everyday life. If the anthropologist's task is to deal with the Hindu struggling every day with varieties of otherness (within himself and in his surroundings), it is also to see how such experience is squared with the otherness-denying cultural philosophy. This 'internal contradiction' over time has been a creative platform for numerous 'reconciling' philosophical debates and practices.

What is the significance of such an example for our analysis of the Other? It is primarily methodological and perspectival, a point better appreciated if we formulate the import of the above Hindu thought in terms of four cognitive-cultural stages: contrast, hierarchy, occlusion–fading–erasure, and dissolution. Though the Hindu starts (like others) with an everyday cognitive contrast of the self versus the Other, he can seldom retain it lifelong without introducing cultural, social, political, and historical notions of separation, rank, and privilege. The basic nature of cognitive contrast between the self and the other (*aham* or *svayama* versus *anya* or *bhinna*) is initially homologous to what major Western psychologists and psychoanalysts (for example, Freud via Lacan) propose in the West as the formation of the self (or its 'I') in infancy:

> This jubilant assumption of his specular image by the child at the *infant* stage, still sunk in his motor incapacity and nursling dependence, would seem to exhibit in an exemplary situation the symbolic matrix in which *I* is precipitated in a primordial form, before it is objectified in the dialectic of identification with the other, and before language restores to it, in the universal, its function as subject (see Bowie 1979: 122; also Lacan 1977a: 2).

However, once the formation of the 'I' is complete, and the child is socially and morally aware of the distinction between self and the Other, the Hindu's conceptual trajectory becomes distinctly different from the West's.[22] The taming of the 'ego' starts by hierarchizing its various degrees of nearness to, and distance from, plural others, forming what the Indianist may say is his 'caste-bound ego'. This ego refines itself with what is called the 'second birth' (especially as represented by the ritual initiation among the upper—'twice born'—castes), where issues of moral responsibility and hierarchy elaborately identify every person. Such 'me' and 'mine' and 'thou' and 'thine' markers produce the Hindu 'worldly existence' (samsārika jīvana), establishing a basis for examining the issues of identity and difference (samāntā and asamāntā).

However, such a hierarchical ordering of the universe is only one way to deal with the self/Other issue. The other route is that of self-control (that is, by tapas and tyāga), where expressions of 'I', 'me', and 'mine' become signs of ignorance (ajñāna), the work of divine illusion (māyā). Instead of hierarchy, this path emphasizes occlusion, fading, and 'erasure' of the ego (ahama and its consequence, ahamkāra), often by conscious modification of one's modes of thinking and personal lifestyle. This radical Hindu step postulates 'world renunciation' (that is, a systematically detached attitude and behavior toward the concerns of everyday life) for an erasure of 'I-ness' and 'otherness' (or a neutralization of one by the other). With such training, one inevitably confronts the regional, sociocultural, and psychological otherness that the caste ethic inculcates. However, since this is a difficult feat (of self-training, usually called 'yoga' of one kind or another) the above process should continue, the Hindu argues, until there is the total erasure—dissolution—of 'I-ness' in one's speech, thought, and action (vacana, man aur karma). Only very rarely does one achieve in life such a 'liberating' consciousness, the Hindu thought emphasizes. Yet one in hundreds of millions does realize it, as if to verify what the path-breaking philosopher–teacher Samkarāchārya (of the 9th century) said in one of his verses: 'A liberated soul [jīvanmukta] is "forgetful" [vismṛtiprāpya] of a sense of "me" and "mine", even when carrying on in this world. He realizes oneness behind multiplicity, drowning the distinction between "I-ness" and "this-ness" [ahama and idama].'[23] With this consciousness, the Hindu world renders the distinction between self and others not only redundant but ideologically inadmissible.[24]

The classical Hindu approach this way proposes a distinct resolution of the self–Other issue: it proposes self-control and personal training until one 'forgets' one's sense of self-based possession and privilege. With individual rather than collective training, the Hindu wants to render the self–Other distinction intuitively false, even a nonissue. In contrast, the Western critical tradition deals with the issue at the collective—social, political, and textual—

level, seeking its 'resolution' with appropriate (and morally 'good') politics of identity, history, representation, and writing. Anthropology falls somewhere in between, since, on the one hand, it wants to resolve the otherness issue by forwarding an appropriate (liberal and pluralist) 'cultural perspective', but, on the other, it sees inevitable political crises (and burdens) in the cultural representation of the Other.[25]

As for the ordinary Hindu living his everyday life, the self–Other issues occupy him from all sides. He grapples with an unremitting presence of historical, social, religious, political, and economic others. Yet in his heart he equally ardently believes (more accurately, 'knows') that the Other is only an 'illusion', a symptom of his ignorance. If this ambiguity constrains him every day as he faces himself and those he calls his own (*apne*) vis-à-vis the others (*paraye*), he also lives in that (in his view) eternal, indisputable, and superior knowledge of the seamless Absolute which renders all forms of otherness ultimately illusory. This personal, inner template envelops and supersedes even today's reality struggling with ever-sharpening, conflict-ridden 'others'. Ironically, this continues even as today's India bursts with pervasive alienation, violent protests, communal riots, and fundamentalist and counter-fundamentalist brinkmanship.

The Hindu in this way provides a distinct—if raw and ambiguous—privileging commentary on the Other.[26] At a comparative level, however, when the long Indian cultural history and its major 'texts' are examined, India, not unlike the West, shows a preoccupation with (*a*) a distinct cultural and historical privileging of self (or 'us') vis-à-vis the Other (and all empirical others); (*b*) a representation and control of the other's political voice for its eventual appropriation and 'assimilation' within one's own dominant traditions; and (*c*) a production of privileging, authoritative 'texts', making others identify their alternatives (and positions) in terms of these texts.[27]

IV

Let us briefly consider the preceding three properties (and the associated issues) in a more general context to see how some recent critical debates might deal with them. Such a discussion will allow us to comment further on the observer's construction of a discursive 'text' on the Other. From the other side, we will also discuss how the Other challenges the a priori privilege of the observer's knowledge, language, self-location, and explanation, seeking avenues of 'redressal', particularly those which could be built on the possibility of 'reciprocal knowledge'. We will again keep the anthropologist's dilemmas at the center of our discussion.

Conscious of the limitations of their representation of the Other, and thus also of issues of privileging their own discourse, some anthropologists now raise a host of crucial questions: How (and how well) do the conventional anthropological texts deal with the Other? Are they more *about* the Other than of or for the other? What type of knowledge are such attempts capable of producing? Do such texts somehow, by definition, remain incapable of 'reaching' the Other on its own ground? Do the postmodernist perspectives, on the other hand, clarify or muddle up the existing anthropological text, especially by introducing a self-reflexivity that dwells more on 'ours' or 'us' than on a genuinely power-sharing discourse with the Other? What could be the overall impact of such a condition when we face a crisis in cultural representation, and even in its critiques?

If dealing with such queries one by one is beyond the scope of this chapter, let us consider them for their general import to our discussion. To start with, for instance, even if we mistrust the entire postmodernist debate on the re-examination of self vis-à-vis the Other, its impact may already be inescapable for conventional anthropology and anthropologists. Similarly, though postmodernist debates within anthropology have had a limited clientele (that is, mostly those with a literary background) and an uneven impact, their implication for anthropological description, narration, and explanation of other cultures, for example, could be unavoidable. Today's anthropologist will probably never enjoy the same 'certainties' that Frazer, Malinowski, or even Evans–Pritchard enjoyed while explaining the Other.[28] With more knowledge of the Other than ever before, our understanding has increasingly become more contingent. Similarly, with increasing awareness of how his discourse feeds on a privileged ground that wills power, the critical anthropologist increasingly re-examines his assumptions behind his fieldwork, ethnography, and the place of 'universal anthropology'.

On the other hand, however, one could argue that there must be limits to such a 'deconstruction' of anthropological inquiry. If neither facts nor their representation (or interpretation) are free of the politics and privilege of knowledge (in Foucault's sense), how can the anthropologist, as a human being, be expected to rise above them in his cultural studies? Representations are unavoidable. They stand prior to, and are at the heart of, all human communications, and if anthropologists do not represent the cultural Other, others will (often with less care and forethought). However, with the fall of the transcendental observer, the anthropologist now well knows his limitations, whether he is an empirical 'fact collector', an interpreter, or a stylistic writer. He can no longer claim superior knowledge of the Other because of his grand 'culture theory'; he can only hope to present better knowledge in comparison to what *he* (or his peers) knew before. Similarly, he cannot entertain epistemic arrogance by representing the Other better than the Other itself can. To get away from such grand illusions, some suggest replacing representation with 'evocation', essentially to deepen our comprehension and apperception of the Other, and to get away from the business of securing unequal discourse privilege.[29]

However, such a 'cure' is infeasible and impractical if everyday humans and their cultural activities are to remain the major content of anthropology. Instead, anthropologists should try to have an ongoing critical evaluation of their 'presentation', 're-presentation', and 'representations' (that is, political voices and protests), allowing a review of their assumptions and approaches toward the Other. One of its consequences will be to scrutinize as much the 'established' procedures of empirical inquiry as the cogitations of postmodern critiques, allowing us eventually to develop more sensitive devices of representation.[30] Meanwhile, if certain steps expose the new zones of self-oriented privilege and power within familiar anthropological expressions, dialogues, and discourses, we should criticize them.[31]

But such exercises are still rare. They are hard to conduct and harder to be objective about. For example, when a recent evaluation of the well-known work of Margaret Mead showed us how a woman anthropologist's privileged self-location, despite her disavowal, yielded a privileged cultural account, we realized also how an anthropological text over time acquires an authority and history of its own within a national (here American) anthropological tradition. Practically an icon of American anthropology, Margaret Mead, depicting the Samoans, was criticized for her 'Eurocentrism', especially the way 'the other was absorbed within the self, swallowed up by the demand for America's self scrutiny' (see Gordon 1990: 151). Put another way, the case illustrates how the Other's double—a conventional anthropologist's bracketed self—privileges itself, even unknowingly, at the expense of the Other's identity and world-view. Such accounts may unwittingly illustrate an inevitable appropriation and disassembling of the Other. It is as if the anthropologist's self requires the Other to 'sacrifice' itself, to let the anthropologist become a distinct 'text-maker'.

Today's modernist anthropologist, a careful text-maker, thus elaborately discusses how to 'read' and 'write' ethnographies, new and old (for example, compare Geertz's earlier ethnographies with Frazer's and Malinowski's), to construct his/her own distinct intellectual location. This new anthropologist wants to be a persuasive writer more than a grand-theory anthropologist. But the question still remains: Should his texts be read within the context of his own biography or are they independent of his 'personal self'—to be read 'out of context'? The answer varies, depending on who is asked. It seems that, for an empirical anthropologist, his professional 'self' now suffers from an unhealing wound—the one that reminds him of *his* limitations in 'the scientific pursuit of the other's truth'. Simultaneously, he wants his explanations (as a piece of text) to be persuasive (at least before his peers). He tries to develop a particular genre of narration of 'reality' that is both persuasive and effective to his readers. The empirical anthropologist, a distinct text-maker, thus also follows the goals of effective communication and persuasion.

Viewed in terms of disciplinary history, just when empirical anthropology was becoming confident of its 'fact-oriented' ethnographic narrative (via its magisterial 'ethnographic present'), the postmodernist critical temper upset the disciplinary cart, raising new crises in, and burdens of, representing the Other. To be effective, anthropology can no longer evade meeting the increasing internal and external criticisms its proper subject matter—the Other—raises.[32] Similarly, an effective anthropological text (not unlike the anthropologist's self) must now recognize and respond to the vociferous, critical (rather than passive) Other, and raise a suitable disciplinary debate. If the anthropologist wants the reader to accept his presentation of the Other as reliable, he has to convince his reader that his narrative neither shuts out nor freezes critical reflexive exercises between *self de/re/construction and the Other.* This is because the anthropological dialogue and discourse must change with the changing Other—and the changing self.[33]

This issue of the continuous construction of the anthropologist's self-location directly impinges on his approaches to (and the politics of) the representation of the cultural Other. However, limits should be recognized. First, self-reflexivity cannot be an end in itself for anthropology, since it can lead to self-privilege. Second, the languages of cultural representation need refinement built on genuine sharing and reciprocity with the Other, rather than their abandonment, as suggested by some. The anthropologist and the Other cannot give up this dialogical language of representation. This language is them—each alone and together.[34] As long as they share each other's presence, they engage in a form of open representation and share their languages of communication. Anthropologists are thus unavoidably condemned to present and represent whatever they record and conceive about—and with—the Other. However, they need consciously to control their inward-looking self-reflexivity, especially as it appropriates and 'eats into' the presence of the Other. As the postmodernist debate amply shows, since representation invariably raises issues of privilege and politics of self within a discourse or a text, a control of self-privileging reflexivity is doubly necessary for anthropology to move beyond its beleaguered colonial past, and to avoid chasing its own tail.

However, in a balanced perspective, we must still ask: What does such modernist critical review bring to anthropology? Does it lead us toward a distinctly new and different disciplinary praxis? Or, more modestly, does it help check one-sided, disproportionate emphasis on self-representation in the name of studying the Other? Minimally, does it increase earnestness in the self–Other anthropological encounter? If the postmodernist temper does not help us with such questions and raises only issues of power, domination, and control in different guises for the self via the Other, we should know the limitations of such an approach. Perhaps, then, we need an alternative direction.

Though a separate discussion is required to deal adequately with the allusion I am about to make, I note at this point what an anthropologist recently noted as an alternative way to approach the Other. It is to view the Other under 'love' rather than under a will to secure self-privilege and textual power. I refer to Margaret Trawick's outstanding ethnography on the expression and experience of love within a Tamil family in south India.[35] Her self-reflexive but controlled and honest account may point toward an alternative direction. It argues that 'love' (besides power politics) is also a pervasive and potent human sentiment (and force) variously expressed across the self/Other divide as an alternative (but equally pervasive and potent) human propensity.[36] Not only may 'love' as a producer of dialogue and discourses better address the anthropologist's deeper personal motivations in studying the Other, it may also encourage the anthropologist's self-privileging discourse to inspect itself from an angle other than that which reduces everything to issues of contested power and privilege. The general goal still remains: How does anthropology better recognize the Other, allowing it to exist *side by side*?[37]

But what could be the nature of such an alternative dialogue, based on love rather than unending contests between unequal power discourses? To proceed any further, we would have to investigate how, under persuasions of 'love', the privilege and priority of the observer construct *and* deconstruct themselves to grant unconditional and open recognition to the multifaceted Other. But such studies would demand of the anthropologist that, first, he does not privilege his own cultural (and historical) notions of 'love' at the expense of those of the multicentered, multipositioned Other, and, second, that he does explore whether love (not unlike the concepts of culture, power, and history) carries a *universal* human content and purpose. Under genuine dialogue, love may translate as an intrinsic ground for recognizing the *equipolar* and *independent* authenticity of the Other's knowledge and experience. An earnest dialogue not only recognizes the Other's voice; it also accords intrinsically equal authenticity to the Other's existence and epistemology.

A genuine dialogue consciously maintains a sense for *reciprocating advantage at all levels* of representation and communication (whether oral, descriptive, analytical, critical, or synthetic). A reciprocating 'text' cannot consciously retain hidden—protected, unexamined, and unapproachable—notions of exclusivity, advantage, immunity, and superior rights when engaged in dialogue with the Other.[38] The observer–analyst, whether an 'insider' or an 'outsider' to a culture, here *cannot* privilege his knowledge, theory, or explanation such that it becomes somehow exclusive to him (or his few peers, excluding those studied). Instead, for reciprocity, he presents his results and perspectives for extending, completing and sharing 'our' knowledge with that of the Other. Even if it means better translating 'our rules of logic' with 'theirs'.[39] However, such goals require cultivation of gradual efforts that try to strike *contextually* appropriate and adequate strategies with the Other for producing equipolar, reciprocal knowledge. It survives on open communication, periodic mutually critical reviews, and adequate revision of assumptions and perspectives.[40]

At present, we have a plethora of reciprocality designating terms and phrases but without genuine, equipolar reciprocality for sharing human knowledge and experience across the self/Other divide. Such increasingly used terms as *dialogue, discourse, intersubjectivity,* and *self-reflexivity* variously testify to an ambiguous condition. It is ambiguous because this new postmodernist temper can go either way—toward a genuine openness or its genuine distrust (and the resulting entrenchment of Eurocentrism under various pretexts). Under the first impetus, for anthropologists the world over, could there emerge a truly 'reciprocal anthropology'? The anthropologist's 'reciprocal knowledge' between the self (or us) and the Other (or them) does not have to achieve an absence of difference, but only its more complete, equipolar understanding and communication so as to avoid one-sided privileges, advantages, and immunities.

◄ NOTES

1. Throughout the chapter I capitalize 'the Other' to refer to a comprehensive conceptual construction of alterity, distinguishing it from the empirical 'other' or diverse 'others' encountered by anthropologists as they document and explain human cultural diversity. Since not only anthropology but many other cultural traditions may also recognize a similar distinction, I do *not* privilege the distinction by calling it 'analytical'.
2. Though the formulation that our self is the Other's double is not new (see Schrempp 1989: 10–43), our failure to come to terms fully with such a formu-

lation continues. For example, Lévi–Strauss (1976: 36) offered us a subtle formulation of relationship between the self and the other in anthropological
terms: 'In ethnographic experience the observer apprehends himself as his
own instrument of observation. Clearly, he must learn to know himself, to
obtain, from a *self* who reveals himself as *another* to the *I* who uses him, an
evaluation which will become an integral part of the observation of *other
selves.*' The last italics are mine. Though I use 'him' to designate all anthropologists, it is only for simplifying writing rather than to maintain a 'sexist'
practice. The gendered Other, however, is an appropriate subject for another
paper.

3. These positions are now increasingly discussed. On dialogical anthropology,
   see Maranhao (1990: 269–300). For a comparative evaluation of alternative
   anthropological positions, see also Maranhao's introduction (1990: 3–47).
4. Such a case would significantly differ from the West, which increasingly emphasizes the politicization of the self/Other issue for contesting privilege and
   control, and which knows to resolve it in only one way—with ever more
   politics among the contesting parties.
5. A continuous, open dialectic between the self and the Other is necessary for
   the continuous attrition of ethnocentrism. If studying the Other in its own
   terms can produce one form of ethnocentrism, West-centered studies (even
   of self-reflexivity) produce another. Both require periodic criticisms and
   corrections.
6. A number of recent publications take up the subject from different directions.
   For example, for a discussion of the Other between anthropology and literary
   theory for privileged 'text-making', see Manganaro (1990a). For an 'internal'
   anthropological criticism of how anthropologists account (or do not account)
   for the Other, see McGrane (1989).
7. For an anthropological discussion of the issue of Western rationality and
   'other minds', see Overing (1985); for a non-Western anthropologist's critique
   of Western science by locating a 'dissident' strain within it, see J.P.S. Uberoi
   (1984). For a background debate, see Hollis and Lukes (1982).
8. The 1980s saw a proliferation of such anthropological self-criticism, usually
   taking off from anthropology's Western colonial heritage and history. For
   example, from the early 1970s to the 1980s Fabian wrote about 'the project of
   dismantling anthropology's intellectual imperialism' by rendering ethnography an intersubjective communication that must proceed under a 'coeval-
   ness' shared between the ethnographer and the informant. Besides those
   already cited, see Fabian (1983).
9. On the act of anthropological representation, see Fabian (1990: 753–72). I
   agree with him that the Other is always much more than the ethnographer's
   representation. However, a minor but important difference in my formulation
   (vis-à-vis Fabian's) is that I would like the Other to have the privilege and
   choice to present *or absent* itself (as it sees fit) from the ethnographer's discourse, making him learn as much from its presence as from its absence.
10. Though a whole range of publications now deal with the initial phase of criti-
    cism, we still wonder whether this critical phase has awarded any freedom to
    the Other. Or has it simply produced another 'us-based', one-sided scheme

of representation? For the first critical wave, see Clifford (1988); Clifford and Marcus (1986); and Marcus and Fischer (1986).

11. For a useful discussion of 'recounting' often common to anthropology and history, see Megill (1989: 627–53).

12. See McGrane (1989: 263–67) for a review essay on the placement of the non-European Other within different stages (the Renaissance, the Enlightenment, and the 19th century) of the 'Eurocentric idea of the progress of knowledge' (1989: 129).

13. Such polemical responses are sometimes general and sometimes they reflect particular disciplinary conundrums, but they are, I think, always instructive as much for what they say on behalf of the territory–boundary issues of a discipline as for what they do to exorcize the personal ghosts of such critics. For example, see Beidelman (1989: 263–67); and Moffatt (1990: 257–66). Many others could be cited, but these two comments suffice for me since they concern cultural anthropology and South Asian studies (my long-standing academic concerns), and reflect how a commentator can sometimes blindly claim privileged knowledge of a discipline or an arrogance on behalf of other distant people and what they are after. The second citation (Moffatt's) could be particularly instructive, since it conjures up a vituperative commentary in the name of finding a 'good' culture theory on India. Usually, these also hide one's own ignorance and fear of the new and the different. Ironically, if such efforts seem to defend the Other in the name of a good, liberal foreign scholar, such comments continue to commit blatant Orientalist-style transgressions into the cultural worlds of the Other or the Other's other (India's Untouchables), based on a few months of fieldwork.

However, such examples of criticism in themselves would be of limited value to our general discussion, unless they also indicated a wider disciplinary restlessness, when our 'grip' over the main subject—a study of other cultures in other places and times—is brought into question by 'them'. This is so because now the multiple others (that is, near others, real others, other's other, dependent others, and so on) assert their postcolonial political identity and voice in terms (and expectations) different from those the anthropologist's liberal, tolerant, and 'do-good' stance can accommodate. Our usual empirical descriptions and 'culture theory' now increasingly fall short or flat. Usually, there are two different kinds of responses to the situation. One is to defend the status quo of the discipline by citing muddled thinking and inadequate scholarship of any one who tries to break the mold. The other response is to understand sincerely what the new ideas and changing behavior bring, especially when they directly come from the Other, with a message to modify the scholarly praxis.

For an idea of the launching of some basic arguments and debates on behalf of the non-Western Other, see Asad (1973) and Faheem (1982). For an 'accommodating' response from the West, see Clifford (1988).

14. Several good examples are now available. Some of the best ones show the anthropologist baring and shaping his/her self in the presence (or through the medium) of others. And doing so produces not only a fine-grained ethnography but a sensitive literary narrative and an unpretentious and defensible 'theoretical framework' (a prize the conventional anthropology seeks

most). On Asia, for example, see the book by Kondo (1990); and Trawick (1990). See also the oft-quoted studies by Crapanzano (1980); and Rabinow (1977).

15. The internal debate on this subject within anthropology takes several forms. For example, the 'empiricist' still wants to collect and count 'facts on the ground' *to explain the Other* even to the Other by a 'grand theory' (irrespective of the possibility that its explanations could be impositional and exploitative in character). The interpretive anthropologist, in comparison, remains open-ended. He not only 'writes' about the other but also constantly 'discovers' new relationships with the Other for consciously exploring the cultural and historical quandaries of his 'self', 'us', and 'ourselves'. To the first group, however, the second deals with interpretive and literary (even fictional) 'creations', constructed out of straw figures rather than field collected 'hard facts'. For such a review of the second position, see Leach (1989: 137–41). The second group, in turn, rebuts such a criticism by questioning the empiricist's collection of 'hard facts'. Are these facts not fabricated out of a self-privileging knowledge and history (including colonialism and its hegemonic strategies, where 'ours' dominates 'theirs')? See Cooper and Stoler (1989: 609–21).

16. Among recent anthropologists, Louis Dumont is perhaps most striking for studying the cultural ideologies under the us/them contrast. He examined the hierarchical and 'collective' ideology of India for highlighting the contrast and separation of the West's values of equality and individualism. See Dumont (1977; 1980; and 1986a).

17. While studies by Asad and others (see note 14) may illustrate attempts to establish a form of postcolonial anthropology of the non-West, examples of truly 'reciprocal anthropology' initiated from the non-West remain rare. For a comment on an 'alternative' Western intellectual tradition by a non-Western anthropologist, see Uberoi (1984).

18. In my view, therefore, not only does the Other always invite accounts by its very presence but privileged discourses are also integral to such efforts.

19. A note on terminology. I use here *India's* rather than *Indian* to distinguish my subject clearly from that of the 'Indian' (that is, American Indian) most familiar to American publications. Subsequently, I will employ *Indian* in this chapter to refer to the predominant Hindu cultural stance in India. My reference throughout is to that picture of the living Hindu which the learned and popular cultures, only together, compose. For such a Hindu ethos, culture, literature, and history must roll into one. As necessary, I will also use a few technical terms (mostly drawn from popular Hindi or Sanskritized Hindi) with adequate glosses. In addition to adding accuracy, these terms should help the reader get an idea of how a major non-Western tradition marks the issue of otherness.

20. Since Indian scholarly expositions are vast and philosophical positions internally diverse, such a caveat is unavoidable. My purpose is simply to allude to the fact that major non-Western cultural traditions have several established 'alternative' strategies to deal with the Other, sometimes running parallel to the anthropologist's relativist approach. However, I may mention an intriguing interpretation of the Other which McKim Marriott's 'ethnosociology' hopes to offer. Most recently, Marriott defined ethnosociology 'broadly as the

study of a society in terms of its own realities'. He also remarks that 'rather different "cultural others" ... are involved in this new work'. Chapter 1, along with this one, argues that India does not deal with the Other the same way as does ethnosociology. I find the latter framed and bracketed by Western categories of discourse—the 'context-free', the 'laboratory', and the 'analytical'. See Marriott (1991).

21. However, sociologically, the situation is *not* so simple. Actually, the Hindu constructs his everyday personal and social life around graded selves and graded others. The purpose of this 'worldly ocean' (*samsāra sāgara*) is to realize its illusory nature, on one's own, and separately for every being.

22. Though the difference is striking at the ideological level, one should not leave unexamined several analogical and homological similarities in Lacan's widely suggestive uses of hierarchy, lack, and fading in discussing 'the subject' and 'the unconscious'. For example, see Lacan (1977b).

23. The preceding characteristics allude to Samkaracharya's discussion of those 'liberated-in-life' (*jīvanmukta*). See his famous book of Sanskrit verses (Samkaracharya 1932).

24. For a recent discussion, see Mohanty (1989: 1–32). As a consequence, there is no idealized anthropological Other, but only illusory others and their projection of otherness.

25. Such a comparative sketch of the works of a discipline and of a 'culture from within' is useful to me for examining the usual dichotomy (and priority) posed between the outsider's and the insider's, the specialist's and the people's (or 'folk') knowledge. This allows us to open up the dichotomy that introduces and maintains a distinct privilege for the specialist's (and often the outsider's) knowledge, even if the 'indigenous thought' is equally rigorous and provides a genuine alternative.

26. Under a cultural interpretation, such ambiguity need not be just confusion but rather a profusion of meanings still being sorted out. For an exercise on reading Indian ambiguity, see Trawick (1990).

27. Thus it may also be remarked that India every day approaches the Other with the same rhetorical and political tools from which it, as a postcolonized other, now criticizes the West. But, then, India, not unlike many others, only plays out the logic the self–Other axis rests on.

28. As a related property, anthropology may not be able to 'resolve' the critical issues the Other raises the same way as some other disciplines (for example, philosophy, literary criticism, and even psychoanalysis) may. The Other the anthropologist faces is 'really out there' with its own polyvocal vitality and tradition. Such an Other can be neither totally subsumed nor dissolved, but only recognized for what it is by itself. Since such otherness continuously leaves ever new traces of difference for anthropology to deal with, the anthropologist can never be completely satisfied with his own quest for what a literary critic called 'a more insightful apperception of one's own backdrop'. Similarly, if a Richard Rorty-style rediscovery of 'philosophical Americanhood' can gain anthropologists' attention, it will be only to return to inquiring the Other more than before. See Loriggio (1990: 218–20).

29. My reason for proposing such a position is not that I do not see fully the ills in (and the power-neutral impossibility of) representation but rather it is our

(anthropologist's and common man's) psychological, linguistic, and social inability to stay away from representations. For proposing the evocative, see Tyler (1986). But such a position is found 'extreme' by those anthropologists given to empirical approaches. See O'Meara (1989: 354–69).

30. If the impact of postmodern debates on anthropology is not entirely clear to everybody, we need neither shun the critical debate itself nor hesitate in holding postmodern criticisms accountable to whatever they promise but do not (or cannot) deliver. Most postmodernist discussions have barely begun to address the issue: Does their criticism lead us to truly alternative modes of inquiry and perspective? Or does it simply leave us with a 'deep, unending skepticism' which goes nowhere?

31. Actually, the critical phase may have already helped open some texts, dialogues, and discourses to a gradual renegotiation with the Other and its irreducible presence. See Maranhao (1990: 4–5, 16–20, 345–50).

32. See Strathern (1990: 80–130). Whether such a split-self phase of anthropology would result in the dire consequences Jarvie posits remains to be seen: 'Are some anthropologists engaged in deconstructing their profession? Will they then ultimately jump into the dustbin of themselves?' (1990: 124). To my mind such a conclusion is alarmist. The critical phase for me reflects a necessary 'working out' of certain burdens and crises which anthropology gathered as it passed through the colonial and neocolonial periods. Appropriate critical—'deconstructing'—debates should actually be able to render the discipline more vigorous, provided the anthropologist does not create a self-reflecting hall of mirrors around himself, all in the name of either hard facts or stylistic texts, and get lost in it. As a discipline in constant dialogue with the Other, anthropology cannot afford to be without its critical perspectives, whether it is termed postmodernism now or something different in the future.

33. The usual way to express such an experiential 'fact' of the anthropologist's biography is to say that the anthropological fieldwork somehow touches and transforms the anthropologist irrevocably. He or she is never the same again, and his 'journey' of self-discovery starts rather than ends with fieldwork.

34. See also note 21 above. Apropos Tyler's (1986) proposal, I may also remark that as soon as an evocation is *expressed*, a 'text' is born, and along with it appear the privilege and control of the text and the text-producer. A dialogue, however equipolar or 'balanced', may also similarly remain tilted toward the one who begins it. Given such constraints, the anthropologist can only hope to approach better those *processes* of presentation and representation which he and the Other openly, evenly, and reciprocally engage in.

35. See Trawick (1990), especially Chapter 8, 'Final Thoughts'. However, the concept of 'love' is neither simple by itself nor free of the 'play' domination, power, and control have within it. Still, we start with a different overall frame, with significantly different implications for cultural representation and its communication.

36. Though we cannot develop this alternative here for the lack of space, it requires further systematic exploration, beginning with an examination of its connotative and communicative forces in human cultures and their urge to represent across the self/Other divide. In life, one does not simply stand demarcated and opposed to the Other in a game of power and privilege, but the

self and the Other constantly forge contextually appropriate reciprocal relations, emphasizing the roles of a dialectic and of a shared, conciliatory presence.

37. Though not informed by the 'love' alternative, for a general discussion of the anthropologist's privileged discourse, see Manganaro (1990a: 8–12). While examples of self-reflexive accounts, especially the postmodernist readings of earlier texts, are increasing (see Manganaro's bibliography), 'love' is still rarely seen as an alternative strategy. Among other reasons, one may say that 'love' in the West remains only an 'emotion' (in contrast to reason and rationality), and hence it is rarely seen as producing genuine history, culture, and politics.

38. A test of new openness in dialogue may be met when the anthropologist 'forgets' to privilege his 'theory' and 'analysis' over that of the Other's, and when both begin to work for completing rather than appropriating a perspective. It also means leaving behind the often implicit privileging adage: 'While informants describe and ethnographers "report", the theoretical anthropologist alone knows how to put "it" all together.'

39. Though the subject cannot be adequately addressed here for lack of space, the observer–analyst traditionally claims access to 'exclusive' knowledge and superior knowledge-building tools and epistemologies when studying the cultural Other. Reason, rationality, and the logic of contradiction, for example, guide the 'modern' analyst, establishing his superiority over those others less inclined to uphold these qualities within their discourses. However, anthropological studies now increasingly debate the issue by comparing the logician's logic with 'lived' logic, and argue for the crucial role of 'cultural logic' within human cultures. For an anthropologically sensitive discussion of logic and logical issues, see Schrempp (1989: 10–43).

40. Such a relationship involves reciprocal representation, persuasion, and evaluation, but it originates from *both* sides, without resulting in any built-in, long-term advantage or favor to either side.

Part II

Conflicted Self, Others, Violence, and Justice

5

The Body, Sensoria, and Self of the Powerless: Remembering/'Re-Membering' Indian Untouchable Women*

I 'Allow Us to Speak for Ourselves'

My anthropological encounters with urban Indian Untouchable women[1] during the 1980s were slow and difficult. I distinctly remember how during a discussion, an Untouchable woman's simple declarative sentence, the one which helps me start this essay, had prompted me to approach them for study in the summer of 1986. My memories and writing relate with and respond to *their* ways of remembering, forgiving, and forgetting within their world. We both are at the center of this essay, reflecting on each other and on our respective cultural locations and self-limitations. Our biases as well as empathies are a part of the same passage in which we learned to communicate better.

Extending my previous field experiences and studies of Untouchables (mostly men), I initially underestimated the social

* This chapter is a modified version of the article originally published in *New Literary History: A Journal of Theory and Interpretation*, 1995, 26 : 147–68 (University of Virginia, Charlottesville, USA).

complèxity of their concerns. They forced me to rethink our re-spective social locations. If they were considered socially 'the lowest' in India, then I was an Indian emigrant trying to capture their 'otherness' as well as their self-definition. Moreover, our distinct though overlapping interests guided us. These women wanted to improve their social lot to acquire a *positive* self-worth in changing India. They found in such an endeavor the goodwill and moral support of an educated Indian useful, at least locally. On the other hand, I sought to decipher and understand those who were culturally least known to me. To do so was also to learn about another crucial dimension of my Indian identity.

Despite the label of 'the lowest of the low', these women had a lot to say, I found, once directly approached and carefully listened to.[2] But initially my own subtle preconceptions (including per-haps my 'caste mind' and gender bias), I now think, also stood in my way. I recall how I had bypassed their 'everyday concerns' for such 'weighty matters' as reform ideology, caste conflicts, and political power struggles.

But, fortunately, I did not lose too much time. Once I was in their midst, their 'practical approach' to life was evident. If they con-veyed how (and how much) they still suffered, they also stressed their tenacious approach to life. Their powerlessness was thus paradoxical: it disabled as well as emboldened them. With a nega-tive social position, they felt free of the upper-caste[3] 'purdah mo-rality' and its constraints.[4] They effortlessly protested, mimicked, mocked, satirized, and challenged (when practicable) their sup-pressor and tormentor (*zalim*). Naturally, they wanted to make sure that I did not exploit them in any way. Nor did they want an 'educated babu' who would represent them 'for your reasons' (to quote their phrase). One local woman leader, I remember, had remarked, 'Try to understand our joy and suffering from where we are (*hamari khushi aur gam samjho vahan se jahan ham hain*)'.[5] Distrustful of political leaders and most modern educated Indians, who showed only 'hollow sympathies (*khokhli hamdardi*)', they were bitterly against such 'pseudo-protectors' of their rights and dignity. They sometimes found the educated Indian more igno-rant, condescending, confusing, and dangerous than an orthodox Hindu. To some radical reformers, the modern educated Indian was 'the new usurper and peddler of the sufferer's voice'.[6]

Before the fieldwork, these Untouchable women fit the frame of a faceless and mute 'subaltern', conforming generally to the Foucauldian account of a long-term, one-way exercise of social power, domination, and control. Long subjected to an unremitting technology of domination, they betrayed benumbed minds and 'docile bodies'. Foucault's forceful European historiography of different modes of objectification, especially in terms of the insane, the sick and the poor, resonated exceptionally well, I thought, with the Untouchables' current concerns.[7] Always subject to multiple 'confinements', social constraints, and 'moral policing', these women seemed a version of 'the poor' of 17th century Europe.

But such an interpretative 'fit', I soon realized, had to be subjected to a closer ethnographic examination. Even some of my Untouchable women informants once warned me not to drown their speech and experiences in those of others. 'Do not see us from behind a stack of your favorite books', was their admonition. They wanted me to 'hear' and 'see' them as they were before me. My response was, 'The account I write will have to be, recognizing the limitations, "ours"—yours and mine but open to mutual criticism.'[8] But once on this quest, I also realized that they, in turn, were pursuing their own personal and social interests, with distinct strategies for reidentifying themselves. In such a quest, they wanted 'to use' the academic writing for their goals. Also, they neither simply surrendered themselves to the dominant caste order nor sought a total separation from it. They used this social ambiguity to protest, maneuver, and negotiate; they placed themselves inside as well as outside the Hindu world.

Correspondingly, it was increasingly clear that I could not neatly 'fit' them in any single explanatory scheme, whether it was of the Hindu law-giver Manu or of such postmodern theorists of 'objectification' as Foucault, Bourdieu, and Derrida.[9] Also, I could not ethnographically treat their body, sensoria, memory, and speech as either historically nonexistent or culturally anomalous. Inviting reflexive sociology, their precarious social condition entertained wide-ranging self-questioning, turmoil, and resurgence rather than passivity and emptiness. Their powerlessness gave a distinct reality, justness, and urgency to their social experiences. And it often evoked, in turn, guilt in varying degrees among modern middle-class Indians, especially as they tried to hide their patronizing airs under a peculiarly postindependence brand of secular pretense.[10]

On the other hand, the Untouchables' powerlessness, especially as modified by reformers during this century, also helps them determine whether (or how much) to protest and reject different modes of prevalent (traditional or modern) complicity, appropriation, patronizing attitudes, and domination. However, such a strategy is not always easy, they concede. They fail and try again.

Such prevailing issues also affect an anthropologist's account, reflecting the social ambiguities, insecurities, and risks which people face in life. The ethnographer can do no less than try to describe and explicate, with appropriate attention to one's own subjective locations as well as 'scholastic fallacies', the Untouchable's prevailing attitude toward caste discrimination, on the one hand, and to exploring their social support, goodwill, and advocacy, on the other. An indigenous anthropologist faces special challenges in such a circumstance. His fieldwork and writing (and rewriting) must carefully try to negotiate a sort of 'minefield' set up before him by the subjective/objective, familiar/unfamiliar, superior/inferior, and insider/outsider markers. The issue is particularly difficult (and crucial) when the anthropologist and his informants decide to work together to 'write' what might be called 'co-responsive ethnography'.[11]

Mindful of the above constraints, I here write about how Untouchable women treat a series of crucial tensions surrounding their bodies, sensoria, symbolic gestures, and social memory. To redo these 'bases', for them, is to seek a distinctly different structural position—and a positive self-worth—for themselves. And to keep their ambiguous 'habitus' and its expressions and experiences in focus, an anthropologist must avoid committing what Bourdieu calls 'the short-circuit fallacy'.[12]

My writing, here and elsewhere,[13] concerns itself with three interdependent issues, one located inside the other: an ethnographer's exorcizing of his own ghosts of cultural and scholarly bias and self-doubt; an explication of the ongoing representations of the Untouchable's body, sensoria, self by selective use of remembering, forgiving, and forgetting for forging a positive self-worth; and an anthropological reading of the current use of politicized memories, social gestures, and private/public gaze for claiming a positive historical and economic location of their own in modern India.[14] If paradoxes, ironies, ambiguities, and parodies variously characterize such a quest, these significantly comment on how memory, politics, and powerlessness do (or do not) interrelate in India today.

For, as James Scott clearly shows, the weak rarely sit idle under domination.[15] They respond according to their own location, their estimation of crisis and injustice, and their sense of what is practical. They generate, as Scott says, diverse 'hidden transcripts' of differing effectiveness, whether a reformer's rhetoric, a body of vernacular literature or a serious political movement centered around distinct leaders and their anniversaries, named institutions, and memorials. Even if insufficient to reverse or overthrow the dominant's apparatus of power, such 'transcripts' may nevertheless pose increasingly serious political and social challenges, as the current events in India show.[16] However, the internal dynamics of Untouchable protest politics, where women still stay on the sidelines, is far from unified.

But some specific questions can now be clearly asked: How do Untouchables, men and women, *reconstitute* their own body and self in the face of unresolved fears, challenges, pain, and suffering within everyday life? How do they locate hope, tenacity, self-esteem, and respite within their daily struggles? How do they *re-position and use* their body, senses (particularly speech, hearing, and sight), and memory for forging appropriate social responses, including those of scorn, protest, and even bluff and bluster? To recoup and to survive, how do they sometimes employ forgiveness to forget and heal, and sometimes use memory (as a political strategy) to revive old conflicts in a new way?

But given my journey with them, and its role in seeking answers to such questions, I must first turn to my own experiences with them.

II 'Neither Your nor Mine but Our Words': Encounter and Writing

You write when we speak, but will you really write about what we say? Babus [educated persons] say one thing in front of us but do quite another when they turn their backs.

Words mean so much to us. Truthful, soothing words are so rare, while cruel words hurt us all the time. Our own words [have become] bitter, but our hearts are pure. Listen to us [carefully] and you will know yourself if it is true.

These quotations, coming from my field notes on opening conversations with older Untouchable women in 1979, set the stage
for my ethnography. Though we spoke the same language
(Avadhi Hindi), came from the same cultural region (Avadh), and
shared several major social and ceremonial events of the Hindu
calendar, the 'us'/'them' distance remained with us throughout
our journey. Over time, we learned to translate such distance into
'shared words and overlapping memories and experiences', but
we could not dissolve it.

Empirically, my journey with these women, though spread over
several years of periodic field contacts (and correspondence),
started in three Lucknow neighborhoods during the 1980s.[17] Starting with our life stories, we slowly worked toward the 'we' of
sorts, after several false starts. Given India's polarized and self-
inhibiting caste culture between a male caste Hindu and urban
Untouchable women, we struggled with several layers of social
biases and inhibitions, ranging from the purdah ethos, the urban
sahib culture, to that self-protective scholarly distance. Subtly but
surely, I sometimes also faced the lurking shadows of that Indian's
'caste of mind' which I thought I had largely erased long ago. My
encounter with these women led me to further self-questioning.[18]

During the mid- and late 1980s, they were often the initiators of
dialogue. Routinely sitting by the side of their husbands, brothers
or sons, they, after sufficient acquaintance with me, would
challenge me not to hide behind the upper-caste male norms. I
thought I was simply too shy and reserved toward them. Not
unlike many others, I also, then, justified those subtle masks and
biases by which the conventional 'scholarship' privileges itself
before its 'subjects of study'.

A few older women (including the midwife considered later on)
forced me, however, to change this attitude. They were persuasive because they, from the beginning, saw through me, an educated upper-caste Hindu, much better than I could ever analyze
their world. They were forthright about various issues—good,
bad, or indifferent—and about me. Unlike upper-caste women,
they did not hide behind social etiquette and politeness. Though
initially irritating, they made me open up and learn from them,
particularly about the distinct body 'languages' accompanying
their speech, anger, suffering, and social resolve. I also began to

decipher as their gestures and gaze began to acquire special meanings when normal speech failed or had to be curtailed.

However, their trust in me significantly increased only after two old women learned from my field assistant about my parent's family living in the same neighborhood of the city as these women's brothers. As expected, our families already knew each other and, fortunately, they had been on good terms. 'We can trust you now,' a prominent old woman had said, 'because you cannot run away from us any more. We know where your parents live.'

But with such trust also came definite social responsibilities for me. I now was a 'son', a 'brother' or an 'uncle' instead of an anonymous 'Babu ji'. I was expected to accept their hospitality and give them gifts on ceremonial occasions. Simultaneously, I noticed some veils had shortened, others disappeared and older women opened up about themselves and their family problems. Spontaneous conversations occurred about one's 'true feelings'. I now began to have glimpses of how (and why) these women made their bodies, memory, and speech the crucial battleground of self-identity. Though others considered it polluted, their body was the only thing that stayed with them lifelong. It was 'our only compass (*kutubnuma*) for charting our joys and sorrows'.

These women also saw their *multiple confinement* in terms of their body, and they tried to turn the confinement into their favor.[19] For instance, if their strong bodily pollution and karmic bondage brought about what Foucault (1984a: 124–40) might call their 'automatism of habit', their enduring confinement, then their own men, upper castes, and they themselves, together, devise perhaps a most self-confining 'prison' for themselves. But, paradoxically, the same confinement gives them the 'license' (or as upper castes quickly say, 'freedom') to rebel easily against rules and traditions, making memory, suffering, and speech their crucial allies against injustice. Such 'freedom' is a weapon of both offense and defense for them.

My crucial task in such a situation was to see these women with all their paradoxes and ambiguities in place. On the other hand, they wanted me to see them only in certain ways. For example, they did not want me to see in them the images of my upper-caste female relatives, much less those of such Hindu female ideals as Sita, Draupadi, or Savitri. Conversely, I must not see in them a stereotypical, wayward, disruptive, and uninhibited female. I must see them, I was given to understand, as 'those striving against heavy social odds'. To employ a Foucauldian frame, these women found themselves so deeply inscribed by the 'technico-political register' of Indian society that their path of emancipation had to be self-initiated, slow, and deliberate (Rabinow 1984: 130). Finally, I had to observe how they distrusted the empty gestures of modern Western liberalism, of feminism, and of the 'enlightened Indian secular viewpoints'. Especially when duped, they raged against apocryphal promises, half-truths, and false compassion.

Thus, though of course a part of the larger Indian society, these women clearly emphasized their distinct risks. But their memories, however fragmented, uniquely anchored their tenacious self-identity, with simulacra of hope, rebellion, and renewal. 'Our memories are often the ledgers of others' injustice (*dusron ke annyaya*) and our struggle', they would often say. Their songs, stories, and hand-drawn wall paintings, while depicting the traditional motifs, incorporated messages of their suffering, hope, humor, and rebellion. They wanted me to see them in three dimensions—the sufferer, the traditionally rebellious, and the newly emboldened.

Complementarily, I had to deal with my 'bifocal'—nonresident upper-caste Indian and academic—identity, by myself and in their company. I simply could not be an external investigator for them, nor could they accept me as one of them. Instead, we were to challenge each other as we worked together and as we converged on a collaborative account of both of us.[20]

III 'Our Body and Soul under Their Shadow'

When we see them, their defiling body comes to the fore. If we are honest, we know we still recall them most for their polluting qualities. As we pass each other in the same neighborhood, we gather our garments to avoid their physical contact. I know it should not be this way, especially in today's India, but it still often is.

This was the remark of an upper-caste woman who lived just across the street facing several Untouchable houses, indicating how one's personal and social responses are still inextricably linked to the habits and the habitus in which one is born and brought up. This ground-level ethos changes very slowly, she conceded. In contrast, Untouchable women's remembering and forgetting only magnifies the injustice of this situation thousand-fold. For them, their present condition—sullied bodies but rebellious selves—demands that we recognize their cry for justice, especially since controlling social forces still continue to truncate, distort, or fictionalize Untouchable women.

For upper-caste Hindu women, however, Untouchable women still represent 'the most distant and dangerously impure'. If upper-caste women generally considered themselves ritually impure but refined, diffident, self-disciplined, and customarily docile and tamed, then Untouchable women, by common knowledge, were found unrefined, loud, foul-mouthed, uninhibited, uncontrolled, and uncontrollable. Their food, clothing, speech, interpersonal behavior, and sexuality—all separated them from those higher. But not only is the Untouchable woman the ritually lowest and socially outermost, she is also considered morally puny, with a diminutive, opaque soul. Her past bad karmas are even found to distort her memory and drain her of personal resolve to better herself. She is seen remembering and forgetting wrong things, at wrong times, for wrong reasons.

She thus gets either mostly ignored or misrepresented or misjudged by the surrounding society, according to Untouchable (often male) reformers. Though they have long disputed and rejected each one of such negative characteristics, they are seldom found to write about their own women in substantive cultural and historical terms.[21] In a major leap, however, some young urban Untouchable women have now begun to speak in the language of 'rights', claiming social presence and political representation in modern terms. But for the male reformers, such claims will remain rootless until the traditional caste morality, which distorts the karmic principles in order to perpetuate social injustice, is totally rejected.[22] Since the caste rules of purity and impurity fundamentally debase the Untouchable's body and self, precluding the formation of a positive self-identity, the only solution for them, they agree with B.R. Ambedkar, lay in the 'annihilation of caste' (*jati uchhedan*).[23]

But everyday social life reflects a very different reality. Dominant upper castes still control and variously constrain Untouchables' life events. Their body, sensoria, and memory, while ostensibly reflecting their experiences, remain secondhand, confined, and dependent. This situation is intolerable to young reformers, because the upper castes in this way render them 'hollow (*khokhla*) from within', and deny them any genuinely independent psychological, social, and moral center.

Upper-caste women, to use a reformer's phrase, 'cast our women outside womankind (*stri jati*)'. Some reasons are culturally well-known. Untouchable women are found particularly dangerous for their threatening sexuality and dangerous magical powers. But the culture remains equivocal on the issue. If these women are known to carry curses, the evil eye, inauspiciousness, and black magical spells, then they are also known to cure, heal, and avert misfortune. Of all these, upper-caste women remain most anxious about the Untouchable woman's uncontrollable sexuality, to use their own phrase, 'for luring our men away'. The Untouchable woman, this way, renders her defiled *body* a powerful weapon; it is, in a local phrase, 'a forbidden fruit [for upper-caste men]'. Paradoxically, the powerless thus becomes powerful by threatening the dominant caste order. On the other hand, if this is social recognition, it is still, argue reformers, backhanded and *negative*.

Given such opinions and evaluations, one needs better critical studies of both traditional and modern forces on shaping the status of Untouchable women in Indian society. But, unfortunately, modern sociological accounts of the caste system are not very helpful in such a quest, because most still continue to explicate the caste order as the all-inclusive social given. We thus know far more about how (and why) the Untouchable woman's body has to be defiling, rather than about the Untouchable women's view of themselves and how they might strive to change social odds for a better life. As a young low-caste sociologist–reformer in Lucknow had once remarked to me, 'Upper-caste sociologists, favoring the socially dominant, render the caste order so real, powerful and pervasive that there is little room left for our alternative (*evazi*) viewpoint. Modern educated Indian reformers and politicians are even worse: they exploit both caste order and us for their own selfish interests.'

IV 'Rhythmic Social Memory and Self-worth': A Neighborhood Midwife

This brings us to consider the significance of the Untouchable woman's personal efforts in reconstituting her self-worth. The fact that the woman under discussion, a midwife, shaped herself *before* Indian independence is all the more significant. It connotes a distinct pragmatic habitus and an ethos of tenacious personal struggle for social improvement when the society was far more rigid and closed to Untouchables.

As a midwife's life history tells us, one strove, even in the early part of this century, to develop a practical skill or capability outside one's traditional occupation. More importantly, one could render one's memory 'rhythmic' (*talmel vali*), to suit life's changing challenges. The midwife had once said in 1980, before the assembled neighborhood women:

> Our body and soul are wounded. Even our own men and women do not spare us. We women, young and old, suffer [because] we are so dependent on them for our survival. I always say, change with demands of time. In despair, try to forgive and forget. In happiness, remember good times but do not forget that suffering lurks nearby.
>
> Establish your rhythm [*talmel*] with both. But to gain in life, do something on your own. Sell vegetables at the street corner or go find winnowing work at the neighborhood grain shop. My midwifery shielded me from begging as well as injustice. For healing this body and soul, we need peace inside ourselves and some skill [*hunar*] to earn money with respect.... And, yes, do send your children to school.

I met the 77-year-old midwife in the fall of 1979 in Lucknow, in a neighborhood (Modernganj) described elsewhere (Khare 1984). With sharp memory and clear speech, she first appeared before me as a children's storyteller, sitting outside her small unfinished brick house. In the summer of 1993, 14 years later, she sat with her favorite great-grandson (2 years old) in her lap, alongside that ever present *pāndān* (betel leaf box), continuing either an unfinished children's story or mediating a family or neighborhood quarrel. But in 1993, now 90 years old, her eyesight and hearing had significantly deteriorated. Her memory was not what it used to be. She now frequently needed her daughter's prompting while recalling a past event. One of her daughters (aged 59), a 'ward maid' in a local women's hospital, lived only three houses away from her, and she supervised her mother's 'practice'.

Still, however, the midwife had a sharp tongue. Her wrinkled arms and slim fingers wildly gestured in the air when she was emotionally agitated. These contrasted against the 'steady hands of a well-known midwife'. Her language (Hindustani, speckled with Avadhi and a few parrot-like English words) was always colorful, detailed, and critical. She called patients/clients 'cases', as does a modern doctor. She was the *devi dai* (goddess-like midwife) of the neighborhood.

Named 'Munna Dai' (after her dead husband's name), and a widow since 1957, she was proud that she took good care of her children and herself. She was thankful that her parents gave her a strong body. Though heavily stained with tobacco, her teeth were still intact and her digestion good. She walked slowly but steadily. She felt particularly proud when people said that she looked younger than her daughter. Her secret: she was 'pure at heart' (*dil ki saf*). In contrast, as she had once remarked, a Brahman may have a 'pure body' but often an 'impure heart'. Ultimately, she knew, the 'pure heart' wins. In everyday life if she was critical of others and was criticized in turn, she knew how to forget and forgive. In summer 1993, she had said:

I do have anger and grudges, but I do not keep them inside me. I say exactly as I feel, when I feel. I have seen this world and fear nobody. Earning my keep, I still depend on no one. I am easily offended but I also forgive easily. My midwifery makes me remember [good events] and forget [the bad]. I remember births of scores of children by particular events, or by births of other children born [approximately] the same time. I like talking about people's problems, thinking I might be helpful. I remember people and events. [For example] I distinctly recall the whole scene—with color, people, faces, noises, bands, and horses and elephants—of that English Raja's *durbar* in Kaiser Bagh Baradari, Lucknow [a reference to the Prince of Wales visit to the city in 1921].

The midwife had thus developed a sort of personal 'alchemy' for inner peace, social coping, and survival. She strategically placed forgiveness (*mafi* or *kṣamā*) between self-worth and anger, and forgave both those who would—and those who would not—forgive her. For her, positive memories, positive self-worth, and a sharp tongue went together. There was no paradox for her here, for the first two virtues canceled out the third.

Over time, she had become a local celebrity. Even the pre-independence British, upper-caste Hindu, and prominent Muslim families had known the ways of Munna Dai. She was the one 'whose cases never developed sepsis'. Long before the reformers came along, she was the one who did not give in to the caste-assigned view of 'the sullied (*maila*) body and immoral soul'. She tenaciously saw her body in a positive way, with room for self-worth.

These qualities, she said, she inherited from her grandmother (father's mother), who was also a rural midwife living 30 miles outside the perimeters of late 19th and early 20th century Lucknow. Though very poor and suffering the cruelty of a local landlord (zamindar), the grandmother, her guru, the midwife recalled, never lost her courage and hope under adversity. On body and midwifery, Munna Dai said,

A midwife always considers the human body sacred. She knows that all bodies—of a Brahman and of an Untouchable—are born the same way, covered by the same mucus, blood, and fluids. Our skill helps bring a new life to the world, whether it is of a king or a beggar. With the first cry of the just-born, I thank God and look at my soiled hands with pride. Each time it happens, I feel a joy.

My grandmother gifted me a pure heart and a knack for 'reading' a woman's belly with nimble fingers. She used to tell me how her fingers 'saw' within the womb. Though illiterate, she 'read', like an Ayurvedic doctor, the full story of the mother and of the fragile life inside her. At 10, I remember I accompanied her a few times to her 'cases', just to move my trembling fingers over a mother's swollen belly. I felt so proud. My grandmother later taught me to recognize different signs and messages a pregnant woman's walk, cravings, limb movements, pains, and bodily odors emitted. We know much more about the health of the unborn this way than by tying a woman to modern machines.... She told me how to read the pulse of healthy and sick mothers, and of those who miscarried or delivered prematurely. I also learned from her the need of frequently washing hands and of heating and cleaning—and keeping clean—the knife or blade used for separating the umbilical cord.

But my grandmother also recognized the limits of midwifery. It is a special skill [hunar] we patiently and carefully develop. But we are neither God nor can we replace doctors and hospitals. A midwife must clearly know her limits. She should say 'no' to a complicated case, but without misleading or abandoning the client. I tell the patient as I see it. But even then my clients know that I am always available to them for [often free] advice.

The preceding shows how not only self-worth and a positive body image contribute to cultivating a rewarding skill, but also how these become the ground for re-membering positive social memories of the self, the body, and the community. Pains and burdens of untouchability and femininity are in this way made more bearable.

Munna Dai's skill flourished as much on such a self-image as on the strategic use of remembering, forgiving, and forgetting in helping others with their problems. Her superior midwifery skills, and the attendant fame in the different parts of the city for several decades, once made her observe:

Whatever else, I am always a midwife. Whether one is a Brahman, Thakur, Bania, Muslim, Christian, or an Untouchable, everybody, foremost, wants to see a live and healthy birth at the end of nine months. The questions of a son or a daughter, or a Brahman or an Untouchable, appear only afterwards. But our society is strange. The faces which are full of anxiety and perspiration before child birth, change quickly afterward. Instead of a valuable midwife, I turn into an old Untouchable woman, living in a dirty neighborhood. But it does not matter, they cannot snatch my good karmas from me.

Her daughter once told me that for years, the midwife had refused to take a fee from both the very poor and the poor orthodox Hindus. She did so because she helped the first and shamed (or at least so she thought) the second into feeling about his or her 'false superiority'.

The midwife often mimicked (gathering her own sari) how the same upper-caste mothers, 'who lay soiled and helpless before me during the delivery, found me defiling a few days after'. In contrast, she found the (pre-independence) British and Anglo-Indian families more accommodating. 'They made me forget that I was an Untouchable. Even Muslim families were polite', she remarked.

She also recalled on the same occasion how, against her husband's liking, during the early 1940s, she had become a 'ward attendant' for a few months to a British lady doctor. She accompanied the doctor to a local hospital and its maternity ward, and observed the doctor deliver babies. The lady doctor (though younger) somehow reminded her of her grandmother. Both taught her to be extremely clean and hygienic during the delivery, she thought. Her infection-free deliveries had later made her famous even among several elite families of the city.

In the summer of 1993, she had remarked, 'All is past now'. The recurring theme of body, pain, memory, and healing was uppermost:

> Though I spent this life healing everybody, this society continues to inflict wounds. The wound is here [pointing toward her heart] and here [pointing toward her head]. It is long infected, with oozing pus and blood, but nobody has given me a medicine for it. [Pointing toward the ethnographer] Can you, Babu *bhaiya*, tell me if they now have a 'fever drug' [meaning penicillin] against this sore, this suffering? Even Gandhi bā-bā [Mahatma Gandhi] misled us.

Such a comment, I argue below, encapsulates a new powerful *social gaze and a gesture* of the Untouchable at the end of the century. In this gaze coalesce their anguish, anger, resurgence, and rebellion, with a new politics of memory for reclaiming self-worth.

V The Gaze, Sensoria, and Self: A Politics of Memory

When others write about us, they misrepresent us; otherwise, we are mostly ignored or overlooked. This body is our book of

life. It records [*darz karti hai*] those numerous—some visible
and many invisible—wounds and scars of neglect and injustice.
Each insult reopens our old wounds and stiffens our gaze. We
forgive and forget some things, but insult is like an open sore.
Still, life must go on.

Today our eyes and ears are open. Our eyes convey our suffering as well as resolve. Our tongue, people know, never holds
back. Our gestures [*hav-bhav*] betray what is inside us. We,
then, loudly quarrel even among ourselves. With selfish officers, exploiting politicians and increased violence surrounding
us, our gaze has to say what we cannot say with words. We
need our wits [*hosha*] as never before. We can survive today
only if we remember what goes on [i.e., keep score of what
others do to us].

Three different Untouchable leaders (the first one female and the
other two male) on three different occasions made similar comments to summarize how they struggle today to redo their old,
negative social identity. Although they face an enormous task,
they must try now more than ever, they feel, by congealing their
stray recollections into an 'authentic social history', which can directly challenge and confront the dominant's history. But to be
genuine, they must reclaim their glorious, pre-Aryan past, weed-
ing out the very principles which sowed the seeds of their social
degradation and misrepresentation (in Hindustani *galat bayānī*).[24]

'The misrepresentation will go on as long as others write about
us,' was the comment of a local woman leader. But to write effectively, one must have more than education. Writing requires some
form of moral authority and social recognition, whether positive
or negative. Until that happens, as a woman had remarked, 'People [will] see in us only what they want to see. [Recalling a saying]
as is the color of your glasses, so indeed does the world look.'

But independent India, with the efforts of democratic leaders,
high and low (for instance, Jawaharlal Nehru and B.R. Ambedkar), brought them a major historical break. It entitled them to
adult franchise, democratic political representation, and the resulting ballot box (and 'vote bank') politics. These developments
injected a political language of personal and social memory, and
an opportunity for self-redefinition. As the Untouchable's body

acquired a new political and legal basis, his bodily presence, actions, and gestures spoke in the language of political rights and contests. Their sensoria became strategic and their gaze public and political, conveying messages and meanings for disputation of traditional morality. Their body was now not only ritually ranked (and karmic) but it was, more importantly, the locus of new economic protection, political representation, and legal claims and rights. Such a reconfiguration now undeniably awards them a compensatory morality and memory, and an enfranchising social compact and a 'voice'.

But such gains, given India's social history, remain tentative. Many gains remain isolated, uneven, fragile, and local, inviting ever more resistance and opposition from the dominant. This makes Untouchables distrust even those on their side. While hoping for emancipation, they still face, they assert, 'social insult, cruelty, and dishonor. Such experiences rip throu;h our body and soul.' As the midwife had once remarked,

> Most people still see only our polluted bodies. Our touch, sight, and shadow defile them. [It is as if] we have nothing else inside us. Does God not reside within us? I am nothing by myself. Our eyes, ears, hands, heart, mind, and word—all count for so little. Even our earnest intentions [irādā or mansā] are distrusted and dismissed.
>
> If this is not injustice, what is? It eats us from within. When will this [suffering] go away?
>
> [Still, ironically] it is the upper-caste people who cannot do without us. They need us every day to keep them clean!

But such statements reflect only one of the several positions untouchable woman take today on their current social dilemmas.

In the words of a middle-aged (single parent) mother, 'Without the assurance of a crib (pālanā) at birth and funeral shroud (kafan) at death, we struggle every day during our lives. Nobody is our true friend; all sooner or later abandon us, even our own men.' She realized only too well that, unlike the midwife, she could not feed her children only by challenging and confronting the rich and the dominant. She alone must fend for herself and her children, both within and outside her community. Above all, therefore, she must have practical sense. She must negotiate between what reformers and politicians urge and what is practicable (and advantageous) under a given circumstance.[25] Under crisis, she knows that, unlike the upper-caste women, she has the moral and social leeway for becoming more self-assertive and strident. Here her selective personal and social memory are as crucial as her selective forgiving. If memories of insult and abuse steel her gaze (*taktakī*), her forgiving and forgetting provide her the needed social space to remain practical.

But younger educated Untouchable women (in some ways not unlike their upper-caste counterparts) feel greatly disappointed with this practical compromise. They find the older women too submissive for appeasing the dominant. As in the past, this will never work, they assert. Deriving strength from modern democratic protection, the younger group wants to intensify its frontal political rebellion, resistance, and protest against all those who oppress. Their memory claims genuine historicity, their gestures convey defiant self-assurance, and their gaze (*ghūrnā*), when hurt, is unforgiving.

'We are women but definitely not like those upper caste or other women of privilege. We do not want to be just like them.' This statement announces a new axis of social defiance. Emulating upper-caste traditional or modern ways finds little favor with them (though upper-class ways attract the most). 'It is a form of slavery,' said an educated radical, raging against the sociologically proposed 'Sanskritization'.[26]

Simultaneously, young Untouchable women also see some crucial differences between their positions and the rhetoric of rights of a feminist.[27] The main reason given was: Since modern feminists and women's rights advocates in India still almost always tend to be from the privileged upper-caste, educated middle class, they mostly reflect the interests and blind spots of their own social and historical location. 'Most modern sisters (*ādhunika bahenē*),' they said, 'remain ignorant, and are often habitually distant, dismissive and biased.' 'Their "eyes" (*nazar*) cannot change until a social revolution which directly [affects] their vital interests,' according to a female *bhaktin* (devotee). 'Nothing will happen until they see that our bodies are made of the same clay as theirs. We both are equally pure [or] equally impure.'

Exploited but vigorous and alienated but not passive, the Untouchable women today defy any simple categorization. To themselves 'three-dimensional', with 'triple habitus' or triple practical sense, they are at once confined yet persistent, deprived yet sensible and caring, and suppressed yet alert and practical.[28] Although a part of the Indian society, they find themselves like no other. Upper-caste or modern educated women are no consolation to them, because they are too blinkered. Untouchable women convey this 'unique helplessness' by their strident speech, sharp gestures, and a smoldering private and public gaze, especially when wronged, hurt, and suffering. 'We, then, distrust everybody, even our own shadow', was often the remark. Simultaneously, their body, sensoria, and memory are rearranging themselves in respect to one another to claim (or in their view 'reclaim') a positive self-worth. This stirring is now wrapped, however, in several paradoxical foils—from those of traditional powerlessness to those empowering under modern democratic forces. No wonder these women sense a change in the wind, making them socially bold yet cautious in everyday life. Their sense of challenging the old and the traditional is sharper today, even as they grapple with ambiguity and uncertainty within their own memories, motives, and meanings.

My journey with Untouchable women, though not without trials and difficulties, did permit sustained social contact and eventually a reading of nonverbal messages. We repeatedly went about examining and re-examining each other, alone and reciprocally, as I tried to decipher how to recollect and write 'with' them rather than only 'about' or 'for' them. While on such a quest, these women—and men—educated me, rather implicitly, about their rich body and sensorial languages necessary to their speech and social messages. They amply conveyed how, often unconsciously, their social struggle today rested on selective—practically sensible and politically informed—use of remembering, forgiving, and forgetting. As I began to recognize these strategic 'languages of expression', I also saw how they, with their men, struggled to render, first, their episodic recollections into a distinct personal and social memory, and, second, the latter into politicized, rights-claiming social and public memorials—parks, schools, universities, and government buildings—for concretizing their 'community history' (*sāmājika itihās*). However, since they still find their social past and present too repressive, tumultuous, and painful, the struggle, they know, is far from over. They oscillate between hope, halting progress, and despair, while using their recent democratic empowerment as an all-purpose 'tool' of social reform and progress. Untouchables thus neither simply rebel nor meekly conform today. They increasingly hum their own tunes of battle, anger, suffering, helplessness, practical strategy, rebellion, and recuperation. Their diverse memories, some personal and others social, some touching their soul and shaping self-worth and others combative, and some factual and others mythic, proclaim 'The Untouchables, women and men, now exist and they count (...astittva aur mahattva rakhte hain)'. These were the words of Chandrika Prasad Jigyasu, the local reformist, in the early 1970s.[29]

◄ NOTES

1. The term 'Indian Untouchable women' refers mostly to those long resident in Lucknow, a city of about one million and the capital of Uttar Pradesh. This city, a major historical, cultural, and political center of north India, also actively participated in regional and national politics of low castes and Untouchables.

   Another important caveat: Though I here concern myself with Untouchable women, I do not make the discussion gender exclusive. Not only I but my Untouchable women informants also found the gendered stance unsuitable.

2. The first-person accounts on and writings by Untouchable women remain very rare. For an attempt at presenting these women's stories with minimal commentary, see Bhave (1988).

   My writing variously tries to keep these women's words and experiences at the center of the text. Some long quotations are rendered here as recorded, even if at times incoherent. The reader may thus get a sense of the prevalent expressions. In the words of a local woman reformer, 'Our words, crude and few, say well what we are. We do not need to borrow words from the learned.'

3. Though the term 'upper caste' in this chapter is employed in a recognized sociological sense (opposing 'low castes' and Untouchables), it is not problem free. As India increasingly shows, Untouchables, still most often the powerless, face increasing resistance from many middle or low-ranked castes which are locally or regionally controlling. Some low castes (e.g., Yadavs in Uttar Pradesh) are already a political force but their alliance with Untouchables remains shaky at the best.

   Given this social reality, I will also employ the phrase 'dominant or controlling castes' in my discussion.

4. Purdah or 'the veiling of women' has already been the upper-caste marker of social etiquette, speech, and morality for several centuries in north India. Still,

most upper-caste women are so closely associated with the veiling custom that low and Untouchable women are distinguished either by its violation or its total absence.

In practice, low and Untouchable women may observe purdah in selected situations (especially when newly married). Otherwise, their economic and social necessities overtake such customs.

5. Over time, I found that this cautionary suggestion had much wider significance for current scholarly accounts of dispossessed groups. It meant challenging the scholars to get out of the frames of such a hegemonic discourse as 'you tell us and we will write to represent you'. Although such a challenge is now well recognized, it sets an impractical ideal. Instead, we propose a 'co-responsive' account, where both form the text together as a result of their self-questioning and a mutually responsible, voluntary dialogue. As this chapter makes an attempt in such a direction, Untouchable women and I need neither underplay nor hide our differences in location, perception, and gender. Neither side has to become silent. See also notes 8 and 11.

Untouchables, especially women, thus insist that they be recognized for their *distinct* perceptions of ideas, conditions, and personal experiences. If they are neither socially unique nor isolated, they are also not, as they insist, 'just like all other Indian women'. To overlook this property is to deny them a right to represent themselves.

6. A strong remark indeed, indicating the increasing distrust of the selfishness of the urban educated. But this also obviously complicates the task of any 'modern Indian scholar', however well intentioned. I had no option but to let them form their opinion about me over time. However, I decided early on to learn about *their* views on what was (or was not) 'patronizing' to them, superseding the 'scholarly' (and supposedly secular and objective) view of the matter. My own stance, for the record, therefore, ranged from distance, empathy to inter-subjectivity, to instances of advocacy on their behalf.

Patronizing attitude (*samrakṣaṇa*), in general, we must realize, is a complex and strategic political act and value for today's Untouchable. By context, it may mean domination, condescension, control, and usurpation. They may endure or condemn it for their own good reasons. But a scholar's 'secular equality' is most often superficial and empty for them.

Simultaneously, in my view, while dealing with Untouchables, an upper-caste and middle-class Indian scholar, whether an anthropologist, sociologist, historian, or political scientist, often suffers from his or her own unresolved social guilt, even if it is masked by Westernized objectivity and secular equality. We often hide behind it many crucial problems of those we study, and of our own.

7. See Foucault's three interrelated works on the history of what he called 'the dividing practices': (1965; 1973; and 1977). Foucault's historical study of the triadic—life, labor, and language—discourse in modernizing Europe, in some distinct ways relates to the Untouchables' recent quest to articulate their concerns around the criteria of personal and social experience, 'clean' work, and claim to rights and justice. As I argue in this chapter, Untouchables focus on body, sensoria, memory, and self-worth to reconstitute themselves from both

the inside and the outside. And, in Lalayi Singh's words, 'to do so is to uproot Hindu domination, though slowly but surely'.

8. This approach to study 'the cultural other' rests on what I later call 'co-responsive ethnography', emphasizing two-way voluntary communication, with inclusion of plural voices and observance of all appropriate responsibilities, from the beginning of the inquiry. By its construction, writing, use, and consequences, this ethnography recognizes and builds on 'similarities and differences' in the goals and locations of both the ethnographer and the people collaborating for study. Second, as it proceeds under prevailing anthropological sensibilities in today's world, it thrives on attempts at explicating any tendencies of subordination and control by either side. Third, it accordingly promises attempts at only the *working*—rather than either the 'totally scientific' or perfectly 'nonessentialist'—*reality* and its accounts.

   For earlier related discussions, see Khare, Chapters 1 and 4 in this volume.

9. This remark also draws attention to specific inadequacies of traditional, modern, and postmodern theories to explain crucial aspects of these people's intensely painful and prolonged social experience. But, then, from an ethnographic point of view, all theories are condemned, by their internal logic, to succeed only incompletely under changing social reality. Human conditions and expectations are too variable and complex to expect any other outcome. Untouchable thinkers also concur.

   Though it is an issue beyond the scope of this chapter, I must allude to a few comparative classical sources and modern studies for giving a sense of the problem. For example, for Manu, the classical Hindu lawgiver, 'the insider', see Doniger (1991). For Foucault's discussion of how humans are made 'subjects', see Dreyfus and Rabinow (1982: 208–26). Comparatively, while India still lacks a rigorous social (and sociological) history of the subject formation or of what Foucault called 'dividing practices', some Indian intellectuals, following the European exercise, now often engage in academic debates on identifying 'objectification', condescension, and so on.

   Correspondingly, for Bourdieu's remarks on, and a discussion of his sociological approach to 'objectivizing', marked by his theoretical apparatus of 'habitus', 'field', and 'praxeology', see Bourdieu and Wacquant (1992).

   On Jacques Derrida's related crucial work on voice, presence, and representation (or the problem of misrepresentation), see Derrida (1972), and on a hierarchy between speech and writing, an issue central to Untouchables, see Derrida (1977).

10. This reminds me of the remarks of some of my academic colleagues during a recent international conference in India. As a scholarly ethic, they confused anthropologist's empathy with patronization of Untouchables. This is entirely a misrepresentation, hence unacceptable. It was irrespective of how Untouchables themselves saw the issue.

   An ethnographer, in any case, cannot overlook the changing content and evaluation of what the people now think does (or does not) constitute 'superior attitudes'.

11. See also note 8. As a genre, 'co-responsive ethnography' should be distinguished from those where either the anthropologist, in a traditional way, controls the discourse, or where the people's rights or anthropologist's self-

reflexivity render the account one-sided. Co-responsive ethnography emphasizes an exchange of cultural messages—and the appropriate responsibility—from both sides, but without assuming 'correspondence' or absence of
differences. Even 'reciprocity' may not always be assured. Compare my remarks on 'reciprocal anthropology' in Chapter 4.

For an illustration of a case of the anthropologist's self-reflexivity, see Crapanzano (1980). For continuing exchanges, across diverse shores, on anthropology and its discourse, see two comments by Hirschkind (1994) and Crain
(1994).

However, a crucial point is that 'co-responsive ethnography' continuously
seeks dialogue and communication among people, and between people and
the ethnographer, while keeping a rigorous eye on (and the explication of)
self-privileging assumptions, narratives, and explanations *from both sides*.

12. See Bourdieu and Wacquant (1992: 68–70) on sociologistic reductionism, and
Bourdieu and Wacquant (1992: 172–73) on 'gendered habitus'. Both Bourdieu's notions relate to the positions Untouchable men/women today take
vis-à-vis the dominant system. Sociologists dismiss rather too quickly the crucially mediating 'pragmatic habitus' the Untouchable reformer promotes, and
continue to favor the power of the institutionalized caste. They tend to mis-
read the dynamics of the Untouchable's 'pragmatic habitus' and try to fit it
neatly into a standard caste rank, class, or gender rubric.

13. The related unpublished pieces on Untouchable women which have been
already presented in lectures, conferences, or seminars are Khare (1993a) and
(1993b).

14. After my field discussions with Untouchables, the notions of 'gestures' and
'gaze' gathered additional interpretive significance as I read the reflexive sociology of Pierre Bourdieu on the one hand, and modern fiction, particularly
Kundera (1992), on the other.

However, the approach to these important notions remains here rather preliminary. Untouchables, under certain conditions, have to depend on these
rather much more than other people, and they encode them with a widely
fluctuating range of meanings.

15. See Scott (1990) for a very perceptive and wide-ranging analysis of how the
dependent resist and cope with the strategies and interests the dominant set
up within widely different societies, including the Indian Untouchable.

16. Though such changes are still a part of ever-adjusting party politics, a conditional low caste and Untouchable alliance is now evident. For example,
Indian news magazines now widely present an account of these castes upset-
ting the upper-caste power calculations in the major state of Uttar Pradesh.

17. See Khare (1984), for a description of early fieldwork in the three neighborhoods.

As already indicated, my social distance and psychological limitations de-
creased, however, once I learned to see Untouchables—and myself—in
larger social contexts, heard them directly, and understood their well-
nuanced social expressions. Simultaneously, I found 'the invisible determina-
tions inherent in the intellectual posture itself, in the scholarly gaze that he or
she casts upon the social world' (Bourdieu and Wacquant 1992: 69). And I
was no exception.

18. Professor Nicholas Dirks' creative phrase, 'caste of mind', is perhaps put here to a different use. My usage refers to those psychosocial predilections which an Indian, by being raised within the Indian society, may consciously or unconsciously carry with him or her life long. Untouchables helped me discover how, even after decades of living abroad, such a 'caste of mind' could subtly color my thinking and behavior. They held up a mirror to me.

19. My usage here takes after Foucault's conception of 'confinement' developed in *Madness and Civilization*, and adapts it to the Indian context. The Untouchable has historically experienced a long and multiple confinement in terms of physical, material, and social location, moral bondage, and ritual boundaries and restricted speech and expression.

20. An informant had once remarked, 'The only difference will be that we will choose not to write about you, but you—or let us say, you with our active help—will write about both of us.'
    See Bhave (1988). Convergence appears at several points between this book and my account, including a strong self-image and a practical sense displayed by Untouchable women, whether they come from western or northern India.

21. Even careful local reformers/writers like Chandrika Prasad Jigyasu may not be free from such a lapse. For example, see Jigyasu (1969), giving a generalized account of Indian women rather than the one focused on Untouchable women. Still, however, such perceptive writers/reformers are seldom totally oblivious of the incoming change. See also note 29.

22. The 'vernacular' (mostly Hindi) literature by local reformers explicates this point in detail. Their argument is that it is the caste distortions, not the karmic doctrine itself, which need to be rejected. For example, see Pariyar Lalayi Singh (1983). On an approach to sacrifice, see Pariyar Lalayi Singh (1966).

23. The reference is here also to B.R. Ambedkar's influential book with the same title (see Ambedkar 1945). The book argued almost 50 years ago, raising enormous controversy and debate in India, that Untouchability and caste order have long been so closely interdependent that to root out the first one must 'annihilate' the caste order itself.

24. For details on such a cultural ideology of Untouchables, see Khare (1984). The underlying reasoning of the Untouchable reformer (including Ambedkar) is that the highly essentialist Hindu thinking can be defeated only by a morally more compelling nonessentialist argument. The recent political gains empower such a strategy, but the need for its pursuit is not diminished 'until total victory'.

25. Comparatively, such a location and practical sense appears strikingly analogous not only to Pierre Bourdieu's emphasis on pragmatism and practical sense in the notion of *habitus*, but it also relates to American pragmatism and its concept of 'habit'. See Bourdieu and Wacquant (1992: 120–21).

26. For the proponent's statements on this mid-century sociological approach to social change in India, see Srinivas (1964). Although 'Sanskritization' as a caste systemic process of social emulation has endured well, this inward-looking concept, not unlike many others of the standard sociological analysis, has totally missed—or dismissed—whatever low castes and Untouchables have been up to during the same period.

Such neglect has been unfortunate since, as we show, it puts sociological explanations far behind the changing social facts and conditions. Appropriate efforts are now critically needed in India. European critical thought, as shown by Foucault and Bourdieu (among others), also had to come to terms with similar changes there.

27. For a review discussion of 'a gender gaze' (vis-à-vis 'a gendered gaze') in recent anthropological accounts of women, their bodies, and 'bodies of knowledge' in non-Western cultures, see Dominguez (1994: 127–30).

28. For a parallel discussion of the notion of 'double habitus' and the role of agent in habitus and practice, see Bourdieu and Wacquant (1992: 120–21, 139–40).

29. Jigyasu, already cited above for his influential writings, uttered these words in an interview to me in March 1972, in Lucknow. He was sorely aware about the exclusion of Untouchables 'from the history that really matters'. Given his way of thinking about Untouchables in an all-inclusive sense, his specific reference to women was rather rare. But he 'sniffed', as he used to say, directions of change much before others.

I reread my notes of the 1972 interview and found how at the time he had begun giving more attention to Untouchable women's issues.

6

Elusive Social Justice, Distant Human Rights: Untouchable Women's Struggles and Dilemmas in Changing India*

Consider then the enslavement of [women] who have lost not just political freedom but whose body, soul, and spirit have been enchained. How can their hearts ever be joyful?

Uma Nehru, *Stree Darpan*, May 1918; quoted in Talwar (1989)

A woman's bondage is of her body and soul.... We women are birds in a cage. We live and suffer alone. We survive by sheer hardihood [*dhithai*] and endurance [*jivat*]. Facing more hardship than all other [Indian] women, we Untouchable women live with adversities. These have become our friends.... Yet we long to be free as humans.

Munna Dai Chamar, 91, Lucknow, 23 July 1993

I Situating Human Rights

Throughout this century Indian women, high and low, have struggled for the social justice denied them, but since both suffer under

* This chapter is an extended and revised version of the article originally published in Michael Anderson and Sumit Guha (eds). 1998. *Changing Concepts of Rights and Justice in India*, Oxford University Press, Delhi.

vastly different social conditions, they have their own distinct stories to tell. Urban lower-caste, especially Untouchable women,[1] do not want to append themselves blindly to the upper-caste women's world. Ideal Hindu women like Sita and Savitri depress particularly those young, educated, and socially radical. For these ideals forever stigmatize them and their female ancestors. Their suffering, self-struggle, and rebellion, they know, is a world apart from the upper-caste women's, though they share the same womanhood. A woman reformer had remarked, 'Upper caste, rich women cannot be our *true* sisters as long as they exclude and put us down.'[2] But such feelings are still seldom recorded for their direct social message. They are lost within politicized casteism and social violence, or are drowned by 'uninvolved' scholarly interpretations.

Though these women's social struggles are historically well-known to India, this century has added a distinct language of personal and social claims as the British colonial Raj and the national independence movement, separately and together, have played themselves out. India's predominant traditional notions of justice and injustice (*dharmādharma*) are increasingly contested today, yielding critical social commentaries directed both inward and outward. Engaged still in 'digesting' this new upheaval in its culture and history, India today, paradoxically, tends to run simultaneously inward to its own notions of the 'self-evident', eternal moral dharma, and outward to the acquired modern secular and democratic citizens' rights.[3]

Anthropology, especially ethnography of people's changing reasoning patterns and practical strategies, may be particularly suited to address such a complicated cultural and historical tendency. Ethnography helps us see within that 'black box' that people use every day to distinguish between justice, injustice, and all the 'grey areas' in between. By placing people squarely at the center of the inquiry, ethnography takes us to people's changing moral–juridical reasoning while dealing with situations in real life.

Such an anthropological approach should also be relevant to both national and international programs for human rights.[4] For, to be successful with ordinary people, they must relate to people's everyday life and its practical struggles. In India we should know, for instance, what the ordinary people's notions of justice and injustice are, how injustice is ultimately defeated, where people draw the line for their tolerance, and how these relate to their moral world-view and cosmology, and to life's practical struggles. In society, we need to learn when—and how—Indians *negotiate* their deeply entrenched traditional notions of right and wrong (e.g., karma–dharma[5] or *mazhab* and *shariyat*) for everyday survival, and when—and how far—they are prepared to seek the support and protection of the modern state to improve their customary system.

Unfortunately, the human rights debate in India is still far too remote (and culturally 'new') where Untouchable women are concerned. Most often still culturally misrepresented, socially faceless, historically nondescript, and politically mute, these women (and their experiences and opinions) are socially bypassed. To initiate change, they must be directly heard, and not only heard but listened to for their distinct social reasoning and messages. This means that we do not dismiss the often oblique and emotional cultural language in which they speak. Sometimes highly sensitive, rebellious, and articulate, and sometimes distraught, silent, and traumatized, these women weave a contextually acute and persistent language. Some are loud—but candid and sobering—critics of the surrounding society in vibrant, self-assured voices.[6] Some are silent and submissive, and some unsure. Over time, as they spoke, they influenced me, however, by making me 'reset' my own sensorial thresholds as an ethnographer and a 'social other' (Khare 1993b; Chapter 5 of this book).[7] They demanded that I include their direct messages and distinct meanings, with as little modifications as possible, since they saw themselves 'as those who are exploited even by those exploited [their community]'. One could justifiably call them, in the subaltern historian's lingo, 'the twice subaltern'.[8]

As for the recent studies of human rights, the anthropological effort is still sparse but, fortunately, now not without some synoptic overviews (e.g., Human Rights Internet 1987, cited in Messer 1993b; Messer 1993a; Wright 1988; and references in Messer 1993b). Generally, most anthropologists still distrust the West-launched uniform and unconditional code of 'universal' human rights. Some others advocate a quest for 'basic human rights' for safeguarding human life and ensuring cultural survival (see Messer 1993a, 1993b). Between 1945 and 1993, however, many have critically examined the role of Western political ideology on non-Western people's history and society, on the one hand, and on the subalterns' claims for survival with honor, justice, and environmental responsibility, on the other.

Most anthropologists still remain reticent about advocacy, while some subscribe to critical postmodern pluralism, including occasional direct humanist/populist advocacy.[9] Among anthropologists, critical Marxist or ecological-humanist advocacy for 'social responsibility' remains rare where India is concerned (but see Berreman 1973; 1980; Gough 1963). And we only rarely see a critical anthropological exercise on the classical jurisprudential and cultural historical issues for explicating the Indian notions of moral 'rights and justice', especially in a comparative 'self/other' and 'center/periphery' perspective (e.g., see Khare 1991; see also Chapter 4 of this book). Now with sharpening internal caste, religious, gender, and political–electoral conflicts, such issues are still far from any special anthropological attention.

Recent Western social scientific and humanistic studies of equality, compensatory social justice, and democratic rights are also in flux. Some political philosophers, jurists, and legal scholars start their quest by making the West-conceived human rights universal, indivisible, and inalienable under political globalization, while others criticize such assumptions in the face of multiplying ethnic, cultural, and national interests and differences (compare Nozick 1974 with Walzer 1984; and on India, see contributors in Baxi 1987; Baxi 1992; and Baxi 1994b, on human rights education; Galanter 1984; Krishna Iyer 1976). But, as Walzer says, 'The effort to produce a complete account of justice or a defence of equality by multiplying rights soon makes a farce of what it multiplies' (1984: xv).[10] Yet it is a major challenge for the human rights movement, which still faces concentrated and dramatic violations wherever social conflicts overrun state protections and result in ethnic cleansing, genocide, mass starvation, and environmental destruction.

Recent Indian scholarly and jurisprudential debates remain internally divided on equality, social justice, and civic and ecological rights. Conflicting debates and continuing historical ambiguities surround halting advocacy for social justice (e.g., see Baxi 1987; 1992; 1994a; Karlekar 1993; Kothari and Sethi 1989; and Mathew 1978). For instance, if the British colonial and administrative culture introduced a modern notion of 'equality before the law', it also sowed the hardy seeds of 'modern' casteism and communalism. While ostensibly 'civilizing' India by introducing the

English language and by 'documenting' in it numerous political, economic, and legal claims of castes, tribes, rajas, regions, and regiments, the colonial rule entrenched a politics of divide and rule that independent India also mostly followed rather than controlled, ostensibly for the purpose of modernization.[11]

In such a context, despite the recent focus on the progressive but largely male-run Dalit movement, we know next to nothing about the lot of ordinary Untouchable women. We do not know how they coped during this century, shaping their community and its leaders. Those I studied in Lucknow often spoke about their 'new helplessness in Gandhi Baba's India'. They found themselves newly exploited when, among others, their own men and community leaders took them and their labor for granted. This occurs, in one sociological view, because Indian 'civil culture' is still too weak (see Kothari and Sethi 1989: 1–17).[12] It fails to see the need to protect women, even when facing physically threatening conditions. But India, given its 'warring traditions', has no alternative. It must create a strong, people-rooted 'civil culture', without overlooking either the reality of intensifying religious and caste politics or the necessity of a committed struggle toward a women-inclusive, postcolonial, fair-minded public culture (see Breckenridge and van der Veer 1993; compare Walzer 1984). It is quite an assignment for ordinary Indians that 'public culture' advocates.

So far, only small, tentative steps are evident. Foremost, Indian women now increasingly write about themselves and their conditions, while, at least in the cities, demanding better social treatment. Though far from adequate (or internally united), the effort is to make such accounts increasingly inclusive (e.g., Holmstrom 1991; Karlekar 1993: 1–30; Nagar 1992; Sangari and Vaid 1989; Spivak 1988, particularly Part 3; 'Truth Tales').[13] But still, ironically, Untouchable women and children remain conspicuous by their absence, except when receiving a fleeting glance in most accounts (e.g., see Nita Kumar 1994; Raheja and Gold 1994; but for a rare and substantive exception, see Trawick 1988).

II Seeking the Right to Survive with Dignity

In everyday life, the main struggle for the vast majority of Untouchables still concerns *the right to survive*. In their own words, it simply means access to 'sufficient food, clothing, housing, education, and a secure life, but never at the expense of our personal and community honor'. My Untouchable informants, women and men, called these their 'basic right to live life' (*zindagi jeeney ke adhikar*). At the core of their 20th century protest and rebellion, therefore, stand the demands to have, with social dignity, a sufficient and fair share of food, work, and shelter (compare Messer 1993b, on 'basic rights'). To secure these is to have 'the right to be human' (redeploying a legal scholar's perceptive phrase; Baxi 1987).

From the untouchable women's standpoint, there are four interdependent concerns here: (*a*) whom to approach to complain about the social injustice, neglect, and exploitation they still suffer; (*b*) how to climb over the social barriers that still exclude or silence them when they seek or claim justice; (*c*) how to bring men, whether their own or others, to join their side; and (*d*) what can be done soon to improve their daily life struggles, translating empty talk into more wages and secure and better work. But these concerns still remain unaddressed because, foremost, their community lacks social unity. Their men enter political battles only when major male interests are at stake. Whether Muslim, Christian, Sikh, or Hindu, every community cooperated but only as long at its own interests converged.[14] Untouchable women stood entirely excluded from such male equations.

But when approached, once in confidence, these women expressed their own opinions, views, and priorities on the wider social and political matters. The younger ones were far from disinterested. Once their responses were pooled together for an overview, they produced a scale of their widely shared social concerns, along with the content for their folk jurisprudence. On the first score, they were most concerned about:

- facing personal insult (*tauhini* or *beizzati*), verbal abuse (*galigalauz*), and humiliation (*apmana*) of themselves and their parents;
- performing forced, unpaid (and indentured) labor and services (*begar*), including what they called slavery (*gulami*);
- enduring sexual harassment (*ched-chaada*), exploitation (*śoṣaṇ*) and desertion (*chora dena*);

- suffering physical violence (*marapiti*) and risk to personal safety, including threats to life.

Such persistent social fears and concerns repeatedly evoked statements from these women about getting social justice in life. They yearned for what they were most often denied. Their only recourse was to recall what they knew to be the given truths in life. For example, one must have full faith in unfailing divine justice. When humans oppress and become unjust, divine justice takes over. It always punishes the oppressor and rewards the sufferer. In daily life, while one's bad karma can delay or postpone such justice, it can never be withheld. For the cosmic moral order (dharma) is always just. Equally important, one should fight injustice in life by whatever means available. One must protest, strike, or revolt—whatever works in one's circumstances. Based on such beliefs, the women I interviewed subscribed to the following widely shared Indian notions about justice:

1. With God, there is delay but no anarchy or lawlessness (*bhagvan ke ghar der hai par andher nahin*).
2. It is better to get justice late, rather than not at all (*der aayad durust aayad*).
3. One definitely receives justice but only according to one's past karma (*jaisa karo taisa bharo*).
4. Salvage what you can of a bad situation (*bhagtey bhut ki langoti bhali*).
5. Even a garbage dump's fortune revives (*ghurey ke din bhi bahurte hain*; in English: 'every dog has his day').

Putting to practice what they believed, older Untouchable women loudly and distinctly protested whenever they faced upper caste or any other exploitation. Agitated and wildly gesturing while standing in their own street, they would hurl abuse, insult, and curses at the offender, whether heard by the party or not. Once the anger was vented, they despaired at their own lot, recalling similar past occasions, previous injustice, and continued social derision and neglect.

Often in despair, they rhetorically ask: 'Who listens to us (*hamari kaun sunta hai*)?' 'Where do we oppressed women go to seek justice (*ham din-dukhi aurten kahan nyaya mangen*)?'

'What can we do in this men's world (*is mardon ki duniya mein ham kya kar sakte hain*)?'[15] Unlike their men, rarely did they care to seek solace in leaders' and social reformers' words. Some, of course, knew about Baba Saheb Ambedkar and his effort to improve their lot, but little more. They knew that their struggle was still going to be very long and hard (for Ambedkar's similar remark, see Keer 1954). Yet the situation was slowly changing. They found themselves surrounded by increasingly violent responses, on the one hand, and more open and flexible city surroundings, on the other. They realize that they now cannot afford to retreat socially. They already have antagonized both upper and middle castes (and classes), and a return to old, customary upper-caste patronage is both hollow and dangerous. They find themselves where they 'can neither swallow nor spit out what these times have brought us'.

III Justice under Karma and Dharma

Popular culture finds the issues of justice and injustice deeply related to karma and dharma. Yet the relationship is far from simple or unconditional when examined against the people's everyday practical needs and quests. In the traditional Hindu ideology, karma and dharma form the undisputed and complete basis for all the justice or injustice encountered in life. Karma and dharma are thus considered to be the bedrock of justice. In life, however, a quest for justice, or at least an escape from intolerable injustice, takes a far more pressing and practical turn. Unless it is totally hopeless, people either revolt against or run away from the unbearable situation. They *do* something to remedy the situation. This they do as a part of their dharma, for to fight injustice is also a part of one's dharma. An injustice that causes torture and extreme hardship is not endlessly suffered simply as a fate, a fruit of one's (or a community's) past bad karmas. In such a practical view, justice (*nyaya*) becomes the core of dharma, modifying one's passive acceptance of the karma-assigned condition.

My upper-caste and Untouchable informants readily converged on the issue. Dharma represented justice for both. By definition, injustice could never triumph over dharma, because dharma was self-evident justice, and it was the very source of all creation and the cosmos. But it was so not without a major caveat. Dharma decidedly triumphed over injustice 'only when injustice overflowed' (*jab atyachar ki hadd ho jati hai*). In such a system, as Untouchable reformers complain, injustice is tolerated until it accumulates enough to trigger the balance of dharma to set itself right. Such dharma is, however, considered today a necessary but insufficient compass of social justice for the oppressed, until it also becomes sensitive to people's lived pain and suffering, here and now.

In response, Untouchable reformers, especially the Buddhist, make Untouchables a part of humankind (*insaniyat, manavta, admiyat*) 'to escape the shackles of narrow Hindu dharma'. But as they do so, they realize that in life issues of justice (*nyaya*), equality (*samata*), and 'rights' (*adhikara*) still most often rest on the bedrock of rank and dharma. Castes continue to matter, from birth to death, even to those who have become Buddhists. The firm grip of caste and dharma continues. And those realistic also realize that they can only slowly reform or selectively subvert, but not uproot, this 'dharma' any time soon.

Older uneducated Untouchables, men and women, particularly continue to think about the moral duties and debts prescribed by the powerful karma and dharma principles.[16] Here also emerges the crucial role of the divine (*bhagvan* for the ordinary people), who retains the supreme power of intervention in the calculus of the universal principles of karma and dharma, but 'the will of the divine' is always mysterious and unknown to mortals. A devotee therefore sees all justice ultimately resting with the divine, and since divine justice, not unlike that of karma and dharma, can be only delayed but never denied, the weak usually take only a long-term view of justice and fairness. They seldom expect prompt justice, but their consolation is that the divine can never be ultimately unjust. All human, historical, and even cosmic injustices are, under such a faith, set right, but only under the divine will, and at the divine pace. One said, 'Whatever the divine wills, occurs' (*bhagvan ki kari sab hoy*).

Though exasperating to a modern social reformer and a human rights advocate, this deeply-ingrained cultural lexicon of karma–dharma and divine justice complex is shared widely by ordinary Hindus, Buddhists, Jains, and Sikhs in India. It *is* the people's jurisprudence, shaping the prevalent notions of social fairness and justice. It goes through periodic cycles of rigidity, reform, flexibility, as various saints, reformers, and leaders try to explicate it from time to time. It encounters petitions, protests, and upheavals, as well as a rising devotional faith 'in the intervening power of the divine will' (Khare 1991; 1993c). Many less radical but more devout low-caste and Untouchable reformers found the 'divine will' much more open to a genuine devotee's petitions (*sacce bhakta ki arzi*) than was the karma-ordained fate.

The subject was extensively discussed in the field among Untouchable men and women (old and young, middle class and poor, educated and uneducated) to get a sense of their *shared* reasoning and concerns about social justice:

1. Moral right and wrong and justice and injustice are a part of one's worldly existence and of one's karmic balance sheet.
2. Karma and dharma are those inexorable causative forces that explain all life events, including those of justice and injustice and reward and punishment. Together, these principles weave the most comprehensive explanation of and moral reasoning for personal and social duties.
3. But historically, the rules, uses, and meanings of karma and dharma are found to change, with changes in people's 'judgmental reasoning' (*dharmādharma*; see Khare 1993c). Rigidity in caste order has generally promoted exclusion, while flexibility encouraged social inclusion. Today, as the caste order and democracy confront each other, karma–dharma rules again attract new indigenous interpretations and emphases from social reformers, Indian popular culture, and politicians.
4. For instance, though marginal to caste sociology, the reformist (including the renascent postcolonial) Hindu impulse increasingly resurrects one's 'common dharma' (*sadharana dharma*) over the 'specialized dharma' (*viśeṣa dharma*) of caste rules, rituals, and duties.[17] The first dharma, based on the spiritual sameness of all creatures, promotes a shared sense of mutual care, avoidance of violence and injury, and a pursuit of fairness. It undertakes activities for everybody's welfare and attracts progressive reformers. Human rights advocates might locate here a convergent indigenous Indian impulse, worthy of reinforcement (e.g., see Basham 1964;

Baxi 1987; Chousalkar 1986). The common dharma ethic also attracts the less radical Untouchable social reformers.

5. Social reformers essentially fall into four categories. While those orthodox reconcile the situational with eternal dharma (for example, see Bhishma on dharma in Shantiparva of the *Mahabharata*, although the issue was seldom fully and convincingly decided), modern reformers selectively try to open the 'eternal' (*sanatan*) karma–dharma and customary caste rules to democratic social and political values and their development (e.g., consider Vivekananda, Mahatma Gandhi, and Vinoba Bhave's selective and limited approaches to reforming caste inequality). But radical reformers, old and new, either totally refute 'caste-accommodating' rules and ranks (e.g., Kabir), or pursue an anti-caste *alternative* moral order (e.g., as B.R. Ambedkar adapted Buddhism for Untouchables). Lastly, but very rarely, there might appear an ultra-radical thinker/reformer who rejects the entire Indic civilization to favor a truly external alternative (e.g., M.N. Roy's uncompromising communism).

6. Most contemporary Indian reformers belong to the second and third types, variously discovering 'bridges' between the common—*sadharana*—dharma and caste-structured inequality to reach working compromises between tradition and democracy. Though far from successful, such efforts during this century have repeatedly promoted the idea of 'common dharma' by calling it either 'human morality' (*manav dharma*) or simply 'public service' (*janatājanārdan ki seva*). Mahatma Gandhi distinctly built on the latter as an instrument for strengthening the 'common dharma'; though ultimately unsuccessful, his efforts led to a first ever 'public' challenge to untouchability.

7. Traditionally, as shown in Bhishma's expositions in the *Mahabharata*, the 'caste-by-personal-action' argument has seldom succeeded in India. Though he tried to reconcile 'caste-by-birth' with 'caste-status-by-personal-merit', the exercise was far from convincing or complete. Simultaneously, however, caste members were asked to voluntarily pursue the lofty values of common dharma: truthfulness, compassion, abstention from injury, recognition of other's rights,

self-contentedness, and freedom from malice (see Chousalkar 1986; Rege 1985).

8. Despite its rather anemic social history, 'common dharma' still provides the strongest 'internal' argument for becoming fair and just to all those marginal, weak, exploited, and protesting. To overlook these means to indulge in *adharma* and earn bad karmas for one's future. Major early and medieval reformers (from Buddha to Kabir and Raidas), with such reasoning, made common dharma their moral terra firma for attacking the birth-based *jati* or caste system and its inequities, while modern reformers like Ambedkar and Gandhi, in their separate ways, tried to resurrect a common dharma for the people about to set up a modern democratic India's tolerant civic and public culture. But subsequent events have repeatedly dashed such hopes, sidelining both Gandhi's reform of Untouchability and Ambedkar's reformed Buddhism.[18] (For Untouchable leaders'/reformers' approach to Buddhism, see Jigyasu 1984; Khare 1984; Pariyar Lalayi Singh 1966.)

Though most Untouchable women rarely raise the points or the issues which the above formulations of the learned convey, their eyes remain on general karma–dharma considerations all their lives, reserving occasions to criticize and protest against those unjust, according to the situation, 'to score against Brahmanism' (*Brāhmaṇvāda* or colloquially *bambhanautapana*). Such social criticism is frequent, heartfelt, and spontaneous. So, they also pour scorn on modern liberal reformers, including feminists and any hidden human rights advocates. Suffering from intensifying daily social conflicts, these women distrust 'the upper-caste sisters, who try to reform us only from a distance, only by lip service'. Often facing the wrath of their oppressors alone, these women now protest, bluff, rebel, cajole, or compromise to get a helpful social result. It is they, after all, who challenge and extract more concessions from the caste Hindu, and with much greater ease, than their own men. At home, they also sing devotional songs in the praise of the divine Rama and Krishna, and yet vigorously 'protest upper-caste injustice and exploitative Brahman priests' (compare Kothari and Sethi 1989).

IV Strategies of Seeking Justice

These women's quest for social justice today is far more stressful, but focused. They suffer more, yet dare more. This is possible because they, more than most other Indian women, traditionally enjoy *more* social options against men's control. They customarily can (and do) 'run away', divorce, and remarry. They enjoy far more behavioral freedom in practice than upper-caste women. Viewed sociologically, such 'options' might also be at the core of their traditionally rebellious, hard-edged and sharp-tongued self-identity. In the Untouchable women's view, however, upper-caste women lack such 'freedom' because they lack personal tenacity and social courage.

By being the lowest, socially most silenced and excluded, Untouchable women feel strangely emboldened. It is they who turn their abject powerlessness into a sort of subversive social power.[19] For whenever crucial for survival, they are found to challenge and flout both traditional religious authorities and local community leaders. Even if it sometimes means severe social sanctions.

From the other side, the orthodox Hindu world still continues to treat them as representatives of *innately polluting, negative womanhood.* Behind such inequality is also hidden the view that dismisses these women's own ability to remember, identify, and educate themselves. Their words, senses, and sensibilities are doubted, discounted, and dismissed. Their thinking is rendered 'empty' and unreliable. Put in a socially radical language, these women exist, as an educated Untouchable woman once remarked in rage, 'only to verify the age-old Manu-imposed subhuman status on us'.

But in everyday life, Untouchable women have that paradoxical docile-yet-rebellious social face. They suffer, rebel, and devise rational strategies to secure a more favorable (and just) social outcome for themselves and their families. Their struggle for justice, and their whole social world, revolves around their households (i.e., their children and the aged, with or without their husbands). They endure stress, physical beating, and domestic abuse 'only for our family's sake and its welfare'. Ironically, however, the most frequent and major episodes of unanswered (and unreported) violence and injustice against these women also occur within or around their households.

Thus while women live for their families, their males group them with 'children' (hence in Hindi a man calls his family *bal-bacche*). As an Untouchable man put it, 'Women are like children, who need succor, protection and safety in return for obedience. Whenever disobedient or out of bounds, they require—and justify—some thrashing, discipline, and control.' Repeatedly, when angry and quarreling, husbands 'punished' (i.e., physically beat and confined) their women, and justified themselves by saying that they did so 'as much to save these women from themselves as to protect our own honor and family's welfare (*unke bachav aur apne aur ghar ki raji-khushi ke liye)*'.

Wife-beating, often justified by older women, was considered routine, while educated men in their 30s (or below) found the practice 'less justified, but still sometimes unavoidable'. They explained, 'Children need more control and punishment than women, but some women invite men's blows by their own actions and hard-headedness. Normally, mothers, when necessary, punish girls while fathers thrash their sons until they mature (*jab-tak pakke nahin hote*). But we also know of women going astray. Then, what can one do (*tab koi kya kar sakta hai*), except beating them until they fall in line?'

Young married women, in contrast, complained that men were seldom able to see things women's way. They remained too self-centered, and placed their personal comfort, name, and social honor uppermost. As mothers-in-law, older women encouraged and abetted their husbands' (and sons') physical violence and domestic abuse, they thought, 'to keep their own control over the family'. But the same young women, as daughters, supported their mothers and grandmothers for 'controlling our brothers' brides'. Younger women thus had a contradictory feeling toward older women: As mothers-in-law they were detested, but as mothers and grandmothers they became a moral guide for one's own social behavior.

Unless highly educated and economically independent, younger women still accept gender discrimination as a social given. It rarely counted as a problem of outright injustice. Older people particularly found the educated youth 'wrongheaded' in this regard. They countered, 'How can one be unjust to one's own children—to one's own blood—while disciplining them, teaching

them the ways of this world? It is all crooked and misguided thinking that today's schools impart.'

Within such a social milieu, the content and definition of what
is partiality, bias, unfairness, or 'injustice' depend significantly on
one's age, education, and social circumstance. If city schools and
colleges now expose Untouchable youth to some of the modern
Western notions of equality and individualism, including a vague
sense for claiming social rights, then their families and neighborhoods still strongly assert customary social conformity and famil-
ial obedience. But enough is slowly changing to let 'the youth of
new light' (nai roshni ki javan pirhi) at least verbally question traditional injustices. Grown sons now rebel when their fathers beat
their mothers, and even some daughters spurn their mother's 'unjust control over us'. Yet local reformers find the pace of Untouchable social reform too slow and feel increasingly disillusioned and
impatient.[20]

In everyday life, Untouchable men and women seldom find the
issues of justice/injustice in clear opposition. Instead, governed
by the general cultural notions already discussed (see Section II),
they see in life a whole range of gradations between justice and
injustice. Some of these are routine, others tolerable and negotiable, and still others intolerable and unacceptable. Here, for example, is one such popular scale:

– 'delayed justice' (e.g., late rewards, restitutions, and late male
  progeny);
– 'customary justice' (e.g., socially expected 'mildly' inequita-
  ble and biased justice with ranked rewards, deserts, and pay-
  ments);
– 'tolerable injustice' (e.g., customary but *unfair* moral, social
  and economic transactions, reflecting [even mocking] people's low rank, ritual impurity, and lack of social honor); and
– 'intolerable injustice' (e.g., arson, rape, and murder for personal, caste, or political revenge or retribution).

But underpinning it all still remains that already-discussed multivocal but ambiguous 'divine justice' (daivik nyaya or bhagvan ka
insaaf). Whenever human devices for securing justice and fairness fail, this cosmic divine justice is always there. Its unfailing
'balance of justice' (insaaf ka tarazu) rights all wrongs.

Untouchable women firmly subscribe to this 'self-evident' divine justice, but without giving up practical ways of getting justice, even if it takes offending an employer or accepting help from a local politician. The politicians these days also encourage these women to vociferously protest and collectively petition 'higher authorities' if it brings some positive publicity. In a Lucknow neighborhood (called Modernganj and described elsewhere; see Khare 1984), some women collectively protested several times during 1993 to seek 'fair compensation' (*thika/ucita muavaza*) after (*a*) a woman had severely injured her hand at a sawmill, (*b*) a neighborhood girl was beaten, (*c*) a 10-year-old boy was left paralyzed in a hit-and-run road accident, and (*d*) an upper-caste family withheld payment from a domestic maid servant for several months. In each case, these women, with their men's help, demanded (and received some) compensation after carefully deliberating on their plan of action.

They saw themselves sometimes in the old ways of their mothers and grandmothers, and sometimes as urban, politicized women, led by a local woman leader. They decided their response case by case, balancing risks against possible gains. But most realized that they could not remain passive or mute any longer. Nobody stood up for them. The mother of the paralyzed boy, for instance, had observed, 'Facing the loss of limb and livelihood, we could not have remained silent. Unlike upper-caste women, we often have no secure shelter or support. We have no corner in which to hide and cry. Even our tears move nobody until we shout and demand justice in the streets.'

But a local low-caste woman leader, running a local dalit women's reform group in Lucknow in 1996, felt that their struggle had not become any easier. In her words, 'to get a picture published in a major daily newspaper that we know a minister or the Chief Minister reads is one thing, but to get a sum of money or employment from them for a starving mother and her children is quite another. Much more difficult is to get a politician to pass a law favoring us Untouchable mothers.' She found unsympathetic men, of high and low castes, still tightly controlling political power and purse strings. However, they were always eager to preside over an occasional politically beneficial public ceremony for giving token awards to widows and destitute children. Those suffering felt angry and frustrated. In a primary schoolteacher's words:

After suffering for hundreds of years, we well know what is injustice. It surrounds us; it has wounded us to the core. But if our grandmothers and mothers, for generations, courageously endured innumerable atrocities, often silently, we cannot take them anymore. We must fight for a better life for our children. Blatant injustice [*khullamkhulla beinsaafi*] makes our blood boil.... When helpless, we quarrel, and often take out our frustration on our little children. But what can we do? We stand alone. Tell me, how would upper-caste women know what we really go through?

But such radical women's voices are still rare. Most, even when educated, still seldom write about themselves. Though this situation may change with the upcoming more educated younger generation, most male Untouchable reformers/writers (including sympathizers like Jigyasu; see Jigyasu 1984) still monopolize the community voice. They continue to appropriate or assume their womenfolk as they write 'for' their women.

V Today's Content and Measure of Injustice

Untouchable women are thus sometimes clearly self-assertive and sometimes fearful, passive, and receding while seeking to get fair treatment from society. When assertive, again in the primary school teacher's words, 'We may be the lowest [*atishudra*] for others, but we are neither without pride nor a glorious ancestry. Our religion is not Hindu, Buddhist, Muslim, Sikh, or Christian. We belong only to *manav dharma*—the religion of humanity. Nobody is above it, and nobody can take this away from us.' (For similar statements years ago for Untouchables as a community, see Jigyasu 1984; Pariyar Lalayi Singh 1966.) But her aunt, visiting from a neighboring village, and in the company of younger women, was cautious: 'I fear your such bold talk. You are young and your blood is hot but do not forget the brutal upper-caste wrath, especially in villages these days. We have to be careful. In our village, Thakurs beat our community members and sometimes burned our houses whenever we raised our head.'

A young girl, a high school student in Lucknow, and her friends, however, joined the primary school teacher in criticizing the timidity of the old woman. Younger people, she said, now engaged upper-caste youth in debates, criticizing many upper-caste customs and values. But her mother, a middle-aged maidservant, was not that confident even in Lucknow. She complained about the continuing injustices in an untouchable woman's life:

Parents confine us as a young girl, while as a wife we have to face lifelong cruelty of a drunk or lazy husband and his relatives. As a mother, we have to endure our own disobedient sons. Outside the house, arrogant and mean people—men and women—still insult us whenever they can. But there is one change: Now at least [here in Lucknow], we speak up, shout back, and sometimes even make the offender pay.

At this point in the discussion the schoolteacher had interjected once again, observing:

Whenever I can make the offender pay, I feel vindicated, like a human being. It is not only tit for tat. It returns to me what is rightfully mine—my self-respect. It is only fair. It returns to us something so unique which only we, a people facing injustice for so long, can feel.

Expressing the same social boldness, a few young university educated women wanted to 'desanskritize their community's ways—downgrading or discarding upper-caste rites and customs'. Yet the same group was practical enough to readily cooperate with upper-caste Hindus in offices, schools, and factories.[21] To survive today, they said they knew what was practical and what was practically contestable, avoiding major unnecessary social confrontations.

Put another way, it means that the society still cannot secure uniform *positive social rights* for Untouchables. One has to struggle for them piecemeal and according to one's circumstance, though, in law, the Indian Constitution had awarded these rights to them soon after independence in 1947. Similarly, inalienable moral and juridical desserts, based on civil rights or an intrinsic new moral self-worth, are still not possible (for some comparative notions of desserts in Western jurisprudence, see Galston 1980; see also the next section).

Here the ordinary Indian's lack of cultural expectation for 'prompt justice' also plays a definite role. Daily customary domination is no injustice until it crosses into some form of violence, and such transgressions are a cause of concern only when repetitive. Only *unbearable* injustice (*asahya annyaya*) evokes divine justice. In life it means that one demands justice, particularly compensation, only after significant suffering or crippling bodily harm or loss of life. Comparatively, Untouchable women are increasingly more vigilant. They raise a social alarm when facing partiality, neglect, and discrimination, and doggedly seek a solution when injustice directly and severely affects such crucial concerns as:

- their or their husbands' livelihood;
- the feeding and daily care of children, the old and the sick in the family;
- personal danger faced by domestic violence;
- rights to (and at) work, again with attention to personal honor and physical safety; and
- threat to marriage and community honor.

The real struggle of a young Untouchable bride frequently starts, first, with a careless, lazy, irresponsible, and drunk husband. In the families studied in Modernganj (as already indicated, a 'progressive' neighborhood in Lucknow), six out of 10 households had to face more than one alcoholic man, at some time or another in their family lives. Brides knew well how drunkenness, unemployment, poverty, and unprovoked physical violence surrounded them like a 'tightening noose around our necks' (*galaghontnevali phansi*). Social and sexual indiscretion occurred, insisted older Untouchable women, only when some young women broke down under this unbearable suffocation and agony (*asahya ghutan aur tarapan*).

Second, irrespective of their husbands' dispositions and habits, these women, as already noted, must single-handedly care for their children and family. It is their primary duty (*khas farz*)—'and a birthright' (*janma ka adhikara*). Without 'the special social care and protection available to upper-caste women', they must earn money *and* bear children and raise them as their own (but ultimately for their husband's families and relatives). They thus cannot afford to be as docile, confined, and totally male-dependent, they argue, as upper-caste women. If it makes them look rough and quarrelsome, they do not make any apologies.

Third, within their families, Untouchable women often fend for themselves alone, while suffering physical abuse and domestic violence. Their husbands were often the culprits rather than protectors. In the words of one woman, 'They themselves often abuse and assault us (i.e., engage in *galigalauz aur maarpeet*).... Sometimes they do so by habit, sometimes for our faults, and sometimes out of sheer frustration.' Equally often, these women resist (including, when unavoidable, physical battle). A mother of four, raising her children alone, remarked:

We have to control and contain these unjust men. They fear our harsh words [*karve bol*] and our loud shrieking and shouting [within the locality]. Though I do not know how educated women revolt today [against their men] in your [i.e., the ethnographer's] society, nor do I care, but we Untouchable women cannot take violence and injustice silently beyond a limit [*ek hadd ke bahar*].

But their 'harsh words' alone are seldom sufficient to get them justice from the larger society. Here they must have their men's support. But men support them most when either their own women (i.e., mother, sister, or daughter) do not oppose, or when their own interests and social honor are at stake. With such social pressures, no wonder women do not readily talk about their husbands' violence. Yet, once in confidence, some women related to me cases of sexual abuse and physical assault, including broken bones, bleeding (*khoon bahana*), forced confinement, and starvation. Still, few men knowingly wanted to inflict an injury that would involve hospitals, police, courts, and politicians.

Fourth, Untouchable women struggle often with their employers, especially those in their locality. This is where they live and seek work for livelihood, and this is where their children must learn to survive. With traditional *jajmani* relationships and the colonial 'sahib-servant' dependence largely defunct in a city like Lucknow, these women find upper-caste households and other city employers highly capricious, dismissive, and exploitative. The employers, in turn, see low-caste and Untouchable workers as 'uncontrollable' (*bekabu*). In the words of a neighborhood merchant (December 1993), 'they extract ever greater concessions from the government, and from all of us. Untouchable women wait for an opportunity to cry foul. We are weary of them. They shout slogans at the slightest pretext and condemn us irrespective of whatever we do [to help them]. Now even the [U.P.] government has ordered us not to require sweepers' services before 8 a.m. See! now the sweepers' families come before ours!'[22]

Untouchable women responded by calling such merchants 'cruel slave-drivers'. Forced to work nonstop for 10 to 12 hours a day for a pittance, women returned home to cook for the family 'with swollen hands and tired, aching bones'. Once conditions became unbearable, loud quarrels, petitions, and even sudden strikes ensued. But their quest for job security and personal safety at the work place still remained precarious. This was because once the public or political pressure eased, the employers quickly reversed themselves, keeping these women at the receiving end.

Fifth, an Untouchable woman's social standing within her own family and community crucially rests on her physical health and a wage-earning employment. Once unemployed, the same women who earlier received social attention within their families became mute and helpless again. Their men's attitude became more repressive and confining (for a parallel cultural logic of 'confinement' that dependence created for the European masses, see Foucault 1984a: 124–40). Husbands fought and bickered less, these women remarked, as long as they brought home wages and took care of the family. One woman, recently laid off from the local women's hospital, complained,

> Once without earning, we hear taunts and sarcasm within our families. I know. This is why I tell my daughters to go to school to acquire some skill [*hunar*]. They will have something to depend [later on].… What if my girls end up having both—an oppressive husband and [an exploiting] employer [*atyachari mard aur malik*]?

Such thinking, let us note, is largely born out of their hard life experiences rather than because of any direct government education or welfare programs. A feeling of being 'the utterly other' or 'the other's other' repeatedly occupies these women under such conditions.

VI · For Securing 'Essential Rights'

In summary, though socially still faceless and historically unrepresented, Untouchable women, once ethnographically recorded, show how they relate their experiences and expressions to domination, exploitation, and injustice, on the one hand, and to their traditionally robust (and recently politically emboldened) *individual* search for social justice, on the other. Sociologically, these suppressed (but hardy) women show how they try to create a distinct social–juridical space for themselves by their persistent loud social protests and demands until their oppressor is put on the defensive.[23] They fight their battle themselves, they insist, 'because nobody stands by us in adversity' (*kyonki hamara garhey ka sathi koi bhi nahin*). Such a personal self-assertion contrasts with the usual sociological view that all Indian women are passive, silent, and unwilling and unable to resist any domination by caste and men. Such a social profile should particularly interest those who want to promote human rights education at a grassroots level.[24]

But this view of Untouchable women emerged from 'co-responsive' ethnographic and historiographic strategies that directly involved these women in conveying their life experiences, opinions, and cultural sensibilities (on co-responsive field strategy, see Chapters 4 and 5). To uncover such narratives and personal accounts is also to take the first wave of 'subaltern studies' to its next logical step, where the oppressed directly compose not only their own self-portraits, but also show how, in significant ways, to challenge the dominant everyday, and thus assert their right to survive with human dignity. Here 'expert expressions', however empathetic and subtle, and however politically correct, postcolonial, and intellectually persuasive, remain only poor and temporary substitutes (for helpful opening subaltern debates and advocacy, see Guha and Spivak 1988; see also Baxi 1992: 14; on postcolonial issues, see Breckenridge and van der Veer 1993).

Sociologically, some activist Untouchable women challenge the dominant and the powerful not to remain only as silent victims.

194 ◁ Cultural Diversity and Social Discontent

They claim to rewrite cultural and legal histories of the 'victim' and 'victimage'. Most others are, however, as our second epigraph suggests, a distinct mixture of despair and hope, and new self-doubts as well as willed hardihood and endurance. They persevere despite the knowledge that their own community and the larger Indian society—their jury, witness, and judge—are still largely dismissive toward them. Given such a condition, they are very often severe critics of unjust Indian (and not only Hindu) social traditions, faltering modernity, rising violent conflicts, and distant and hollow slogans of women's reform.

Thus, while for the expert, 'structural injustice' may continue while the interlocking caste, religious, political, and economic forces do not radically change, these women cannot afford to just wait until all this happens. Instead, they discover hope as they extract small social victories in everyday life.[25] In pursuit, they now bend, when necessary, the traditional karma–dharma ethics to serve their concrete, practical needs to succeed or to receive more support from the Indian state (for the related Lucknow Untouchable women's efforts, stories and images, see Khare 1993b and Chapter 5), without waiting either for a radical political or religious reform movement.[26] Many recent reform groups and reformers in India already manipulate both Hindu traditions and modern democratic rights to further their practical and political interests.[27] They search for new practical ways to demand social justice in concrete life situations (compare Walzer 1984 on minority politics in search of social justice). But still socially the lowest and most exploited, Untouchable women do not expect the dominant to alter their 'unjust ways themselves' (for Ambedkar's relevant speeches on the point, see Bhagwan Das 1963; also Baxi 1992: 30).

So, where do these women, and Untouchables more generally, stand today in their quest for social justice? Overall, they are in a better social and psychological position to demand improvement, but are still far away from forging a new positive moral and social basis to claim *dessert* (i.e., 'the possession of some quality that places an individual in a preferred position relative to some good'; see Galston 1980: 5). Notions of caste pollution and discrimination still drag them down. On the other hand, they share the customary upper-caste morality, commonly enunciated in India in terms of one's moral duties and a resulting sense of reciprocated justice: 'Doing justice consists in rendering to someone what is due him and doing injustice consists in withholding from others what is due to them from oneself' (Rege 1985: 8).[28]

Though aggrieved, the Untouchable women I studied in Lucknow, however, did not become vindictive or unfair toward their oppressors. Instead, their strength lay in viewing themselves as socially bold and in challenging and subverting the dominant until they yielded at least some positive results. Culturally, their search for social justice in today's India enjoys greater attention in paradoxically both traditional (particularly reformist) and modern secular terms. The orthodox traditional center is on the defensive, while the modern state half-heartedly struggles to deliver on its promises. Yet, neither a Brahman (or a Thakur) nor a state official can now hope to get away for long with mistreatment. Both realize (with or without protests) what is now morally (i.e., under expansive dharma and liberal democratic expectations) 'right' to do.

Thus to seek social justice (*nyaya* or *insaf*) these days is 'normal'. It is a part of the new India. In urban culture, the public consensus also readily shifts toward the aggrieved, giving him/her the benefit of the doubt. Sometimes voluntary initiatives emerge in the cities to help those willfully wronged or neglected, relaxing, if temporarily, the existing institutional caste restrictions.[29] All such actions, though disconnected, embolden Untouchables and their women to challenge the existing social barriers. In some ways, therefore, Untouchable women provide a uniquely sensitive cultural barometer not only of what has been socially achieved but also of what is hoped next in their quest for social justice.

At the other end, the entire human rights movement in India faces its own struggles and dilemmas. As Baxi says, its politics is harder than that of domination, and its relationship to the modern state is full of ambivalence. A state may hide its inactivity behind its 'open' support for human rights, while specific political interests may stifle its activism.[30] Sociologically, this movement in India today remains cozily confined to those already a part of the state power structure or its legal institutions. Those pushing it for 'public good' as intellectuals and reformers often stand on the sidelines.

No wonder, talking about these to Untouchables might as well be talking about either a 'mythic garden of justice' (*insaaf ka sabzabagh*) or a totally unfamiliar, practically impossible hope. It is unlikely to change soon unless human rights advocates translate their concerns into popular terms and for lived social conditions, and unless they are ready to first educate themselves about the people's relevant experiences, expressions, and expectations. An earnest and unpretentious grass-roots approach is sorely needed, eschewing empty political promises where every desire of the oppressed seems to turn into a right, but only in words (for a similar remark by the Czech writer Milan Kundera, see Kundera 1992: 136). At the core, human rights for Untouchables, as for any human group, revolve around a demand for physically safe, secure, and sufficient work and wages, with assured fairness and social honor.

Despite all their courage, social persistence and small social gains, the Untouchable women's search for social justice is just starting. All the tough struggles are still ahead. They realize this much, and also the fact that their social past is a 'cage' still in search of its birds. And, paradoxically, they also sometimes look for their cage. Old Munna Dai's words (see epigraph) thus cannot but remind me of Franz Kafka's line—as well as its converse: 'A cage went in search of a bird.'

◄ NOTES

1. Though identified and internally ranked in specific *jatis*, 'Untouchables' for our purposes are all those who, as my Untouchable informants said, 'pollute others by touch, particularly all caste Hindus (*savarna*), and are excluded from sharing water, smoke, food, and marriage'. Though the term 'dalit' is now increasingly in use, I find this self-definition eminently suitable for my present purposes, especially since this account concerns older urban but largely illiterate women.

   The words, phrases, or sentences within quotation marks, unless otherwise specified, come directly from either my or my assistant's field notes, or from the transcripts of taped conversations and discussions with my informants and/or discussion partners.

2. The quip parallels a remark made recently by a woman scholar writing on feminist discourses and scholarship: 'Sisterhood cannot be assumed on the basis of gender; it must be forged in concrete, historical and political practice and analysis' (Chandra Talpade Mohanty 1984: 339).

3. The phrase 'secular and democratic' refers to modern legal–juridical domains of human rights, though secularism has historically diverse meanings, uses, and limitations in modern India. While Westernized Indians want to promote a 'secular civic culture for the Indian public', most ordinary Indians intuitively

favor practical sharing for an overall pan-Indian coexistence and survival. Yet all the problems are far from resolved. See Nandy 1990: 69–93.

4. In the international context, the late 20th century story of the human rights movement remains incomplete until globalization, a process reflecting multinational corporations and their search for cheaper labor and new markets, is also considered. But the two, the human rights movement and globalization, produce uneasy company for each other, especially when the first seeks to secure rights for the weak and the oppressed, and the second wants to do so only insofar as these rights serve to open up cheaper labor pools and new markets. See Baxi (1996). On some interpretive muddles that globalization produces for sociological theories, see Robertson (1992).

   Though outside the scope of my present concerns, as cheap labor, Lucknow Untouchables may not be that far off from the slowly creeping effects of globalization via India's open economy.

5. Here as elsewhere (Khare 1984), I treat karma as a comprehensive active/reactive principle of 'action'. But karma neither means a simple, passive 'rationalization of the status quo' nor does it only rationalize defeat. In life, it variously spurs people, including Untouchables, to willed and purposive action and practical strategies. To equate karma with merely blind fate or destiny is not just to oversimplify the reality but also to sustain a defunct Orientalist frame.

6. I have written elsewhere about my 'difficult journey' in the field with Untouchable women (see Chapter 5). Over time, they taught me as much about myself, as an ethnographer and as an upper-caste non-resident Indian male, as about themselves.

7. My studies of these women are based on intensive ethnographic field studies. The fieldwork was conducted in Lucknow, the capital of Uttar Pradesh, during 1979–80, and with related interviews during the summers of 1984, 1986, and 1988, and with a revisit in 1993.

8. The phrase draws attention to the Untouchable women's unique position in Indian culture and history. Their moral 'disabilities' intimately concern their intense lifelong impurity of the body and an opaque self and soul, as perhaps of no other on the subcontinent. Their almost total absence from the 'official', 'authentic' or even the recent bulk of 'subaltern' history is truly remarkable (though for a general plea for making the postcolonial subaltern historiography truly inclusive, see Guha and Spivak 1988).

9. The American Anthropological Association, for example, selected 'human rights' as the central theme for its 1994 national meetings in Atlanta, Georgia.

10. Compare Milan Kundera's (1992) observations about the same consequence seen when thinking of human rights issues for Eastern Europe.

11. Although often bypassed as remote and peripheral vernacular writings, numerous local (and some extremely perceptive) accounts today exist on 'atrocities against Untouchables'. More recently, news reports, occasional judicial inquiries, and regional reformist and political 'histories' also amplify the record. For example, see Kodian 1978; Shyam Sunder 1987; and the Justice Bhave Report 1974.

12. India's 'public or civil culture' is still largely rootless. It rarely involves the ordinary Indian. Instead, it is rather a world of that thin layer of predominantly

Westernized Indians that runs the government, national political arena, academia, and mass media. Politicians, academics, and newspapers address this largely select hall of mirrored public culture, conjuring up magnifying images for equating it with the whole of India.

13. Such literature is now fast multiplying in India (and *on* India coming from abroad), reflecting wide-ranging inspiration, including from feminists and human rights advocates. Unfortunately, the ordinary Indians and their indigenous cultural sensibilities and conflict resolution strategies still receive scant attention, though it is these which must directly suffer the consequences of social unrest and violence.

14. Though the Lucknow Untouchables I studied approached non-Hindu communities mostly for political coalitions or alliance, their overall attitude toward them remained rather skeptical. If they sometimes found Muslims, Sikhs, and Christians 'behaving better than caste Hindus', it all changed once their political interests diverged.

    The new Dalit politics, claiming to speak for 'all the exploited', is still a pipe dream for these older uneducated women, while those younger differ.

15. Though familiar Hindi expressions, they powerfully flag emotional strain, helplessness, and the surrounding social apathy, especially when used by Untouchable women within their specific life conditions. Often, such expressions led one to relate painful stories of personal suffering and survival.

16. But it is now a karma–dharma that openly rebels while following certain caste Hindu rules and social expectations.

17. For a related notion, see Saptarshi (1988: 251–63), especially Zelliot's and Berntsen's editorial note, where they refer to the concept of *manuski* to refer to 'the idea that each person is entitled to be treated as a full human being'. One wonders if *sadharana dharma* might not have inspired and informed *manuski* or other such regional reform formulations.

18. Ordinary Untouchables heavily depend every day on such a dharma–karma reasoning in which the difference between Hindu and Buddhist becomes rather academic. Islam and Christianity matter to far fewer, while some Christian organizations are rebuked for publishing 'Dalit theology' essentially to proselytize unsuspecting Untouchables (e.g., see ISPCK 1989).

19. Under extremity, the powerless tend to behave like their opposite—the powerful. In desperation, they dare challenge the oppressive authority with distinct courage and persistence, and pay the price. The orthodox upper castes, however, characterize this courage as either 'foolhardiness' or 'social arrogance'.

20. Untouchables in this century have experienced double disappointment, since not only did the Gandhian reform of the Hindu caste order fail, but the Ambedkar-led Buddhist alternative also petered out. A reformist Untouchable Buddhist today therefore directly links up with his community's electoral clout. Regional leaders like Kanshi Ram, Mayawati, and Mulayam Singh Yadav (the last two being the erstwhile Chief Ministers of Uttar Pradesh) today engage more in effective power-brokering among their followers and with those who can keep them in power (including their political opponents like the Bharatiya Janata Party), than in evolving a genuine Buddhist critique of the Hindu caste order.

21. Though a detailed comment is beyond the scope of this chapter, a radical Untouchable sociologist considered 'Sanskritization as a pure and simple

device for maintaining and justifying upper caste domination and control'. A young low-caste sociologist in Lucknow had remarked in 1993: 'What is Sanskritization if it is not a message of superiority from those who always want us to imitate them while they look down on us.'

22. The merchant was referring to a much-publicized order in December 1993, by Mulayam Singh Yadav, then Chief Minister of U.P., which allowed the sweepers morning time to attend to their own families before they started their public sanitary duties. In traditional upper-caste terms, however, a local merchant had labeled the order simply an election gimmick.

23. But there are limits to their success, especially when their oppressor resorts to physical and/or sexual violence.

24. Particularly relevant, for example, might be Professor Upendra Baxi's (1994b) initiative on Human Rights Education, whose manifesto specifically includes the following: 'Human Rights Education recognizes that patriarchy, fomenting myriad forms [of] subordination, repression, and humiliation of women, is the site and school for the worst violation of human rights.' And the following: 'It must imagine pedagogies which will convert the motto "Women's Rights are Human Rights" into maxims of action at the local, national, regional and global levels.'

25. The question of small-scale versus 'cosmological' changes appears here for Untouchables. Most 'small but concrete gains' still dwarf beside the traditionally entrenched ways of domination and injustice. Yet most Untouchables today see a unique opportunity, even a historic opening, brought about by none other than their own anti-Manu Babasaheb Ambedkar. As an anonymous reader of this essay had remarked, if such efforts expand to practical strategies, and if this looks like writing 'another *Critique of Practical Reason*', so be it. For indeed it is a momentous development for Untouchables and their women. Most of all, they are fighting it themselves.

26. Recently, however, a few younger Untouchable women, spurred on by the Dalit political movement, have joined protest marches in Lucknow and have even sent 'representatives' to other regional meetings to seek 'Dalit women's human rights'. Yet the majority still distrusts and doubts the concrete gains such sporadic gestures can achieve.

27. For a local event of uncompromising confrontation between Hindu caste order and Human Rights, see Saptarshi 1988: 251–63. And for a *bhajan* on securing rights for the low and the poor by a local saint, see Dandekar 1988: 223–50.

28. In modern philosophy as well, the protection of rights depends on not only distinguishing 'right' from 'wrong', but also on not doing to others what one does not want done to oneself (e.g., compare Galston 1980: 127).

29. The limits of such 'breakthroughs' must be equally obvious to the reader. They remain socially uneven, often more in the cities than in villages, and their social results accumulate very slowly.

30. Baxi (1996) repeatedly discusses such mutually constraining forces of the modern state. If one arm promotes human rights, the other works at cross purposes. In India the situation has been all too evident in recent times, and Baxi (n.d.) reviews it in yet another unpublished piece called 'State and Human Rights Movements in India'.

7

The Cultural Politics of Violence and Human Rights: Contending Indian Traditions, Narratives, and the State

I Violence, Victims' Narratives, and Human Rights

Violence today shows contradictory faces, roles, and meanings, some ideologically assumed, many politically contested, and others customarily followed. Human cultures give widely different meanings to violence, and even consider it necessary to creation and life. Still, after a certain limit, violence in practice is repugnant to all humans. When extreme, it produces anxiety, suffering, trauma, and terror among those directly affected. Its neurobiological effects are deep, and are both physically seen and hidden (Krystal 1969). Similarly, violence produces 'body memory' with lifelong effects, making survivors respond differently to physical stimuli, on the one hand, and live their entire lives remembering, mourning, and representing traumatizing experiences, on the other (Herman 1992). Those recovering feel a need to tell, retell, and mourn. While telling, survivors seek support and validation from the surrounding world as they relate 'what really happened', 'what was experienced', and 'what must be told to others' (Lifton 1967). Language and culture stretch to their limits as victims struggle to tell their stories to the incredulous world outside (Scarry 1985).

Today's electronic information-driven society seldom makes the required moral space and psychological and political attention available to victims and their narratives. Instead, experts usually claim center stage, including mass media commentators who construct for the public 'the real story of the how-why-and-wherefore'. While showing victims on the television screen, they tend to push them further into the background, since the main point of the story often is a surrounding political and/or economic controversy among major national and international forces for issues of dominance and resistance.

This century has repeatedly replayed such cultural politics of violence (e.g., as in the Holocaust, Hiroshima, and the Indian partition), spanning the local and the global, and, as this chapter argues, often directly limiting, distorting, or enhancing what gets socially recalled, remembered, and represented, including the formation of victims' narratives and of accounts of political blame and social guilt (Langer 1996: 47–65). The same politics often keeps ordinary victims from entering into normal social and psychological processes of mourning and recovery with the help of surviving relatives and friends. Usually, the perpetrators and spectators of violence get more attention and voice than victims themselves, though it is obviously the latter who hold most crucial clues about 'what really happened to victims'. Such a neglect and distorted focus may be regarded as one of the distinctive characteristics of modern violence (Kleinman and Kleinman 1996: 1–24).

The following discussion on India argues that victims' narratives are not only a much needed cultural corrective to accounts of contemporary violence, but also crucial for issues of social justice and any grass-roots acceptance of the human rights movement. Victims' 'violence narratives' provide us with that unique core of human experience of pain and suffering that is at once universal in some respects and local in others. We here uncover a whole range of contextual cultural expressions, verbal and non-verbal, that range across the bodily, the sensorial, the instinctive, and the deeply emotive and intuitive. We rediscover the value of 'normal' human life. Victims' narratives are a domain of simultaneous expressions of remembering, forgetting, mourning, and coping. As we locate violence this way within the inner and outer surroundings of the victim, we also trace how a violated, fractured self very slowly and cautiously tries to reconstruct itself once again within a highly fragile and uncertain world of hope, and possibly social justice (for some recent accounts and observations on India, see Veena Das 1990b: 369–91; 1996; Gopal 1991; Nandy 1995a).

The Indian human rights movement, when seen only as a legal or political statement or as a civic watch-dog commission, is very likely to miss this victim-based ground reality and its educational force. Though all such matters tend to turn into a complaint, an action file, a case report, or even worse: a statistic, there is much of direct learning and consequence in a victim's narrative for the movement. Since the victim's world is about learning to live with loss, trauma, and suffering, it is a life of many unspoken and un-explained (and inexplicable) stories. Questions of 'why', 'how', 'injustice', and 'why me/us' echo day and night. Even the normal world is so far off from them that it looks strange, inhospitable, and even cruel to them. For a victim, in anthropological terms, the outside world stands split apart, usually along the 'before' and 'after' division of self vis-à-vis the violent event. To try to reconcile them is 'like trying to join a snapped thread without a knot' (a Hindi saying). To include (and learn from) such perceptions is to bring the human rights movement to its most crucial human center.

Within such a commentary also figures the general issue of how anthropology approaches and understands violence. More than stating a culturally relativized view, we require disciplinary self-criticism for sometimes either assuming or ignoring too much (see Girard 1972; 1978; 1982; and for a critical review of Girard's work, see Kearney 1995: 1–14). If violence is seen as a sociocultural (cosmological, originary, and institutional) given for the human world, the question of limits, controls, and prevention appears equally quickly (on ancient Indian notions, see Heesterman 1993). If people render cosmological, mythical, and 'structural' violence as purposive, conditional, and even restorative to life, social violence is seldom considered 'purely' mythical, ahistorical, power-neutral, or mentalistic. The mythic sooner or later begins to reflect the historical, as Girard says, especially when 'the immo-lation of the "other" [occurs] on the altar of the "same"' (quoted in Kearney 1995: 1). Interwoven in daily lives and with people's cul-tural and 'multiaxial structural' past, violence and suffering pro-foundly affects the late 20th century human. It demands narration of experiences and making sense of suffering (Farmer 1996: 261–83).

The modern social temper also struggles to account for violence. If it is found unavoidable under some conditions (e.g., for 'the maintenance of peace' and 'law and order'), its prevention and control for public welfare are paramount in others. As a result, modern societies must carefully distinguish between (and manage, mainly with public-supported state power) 'necessary' and 'tolerable', on the one hand, and 'avoidable' and 'blatantly unjust' forms of violence, on the other. The state today becomes the prime agency entrusted for preserving 'public law and order'. It enjoys wide latitude in practice, resulting in situations in which unauthorized and unjust use of force is employed. Yet there is no easy or proven modern formula for controlling such a consequence, as this century has repeatedly shown. Similarly, modernity and violence also enter into a highly variable and difficult relationship. Modernity may be found cultivating, tolerating, and rationalizing violence 'under law' or by expedient need or circumstance.

Anthropology, a product of modern intellectual temper and values, also faces a similar dilemma, but at another level. It must, so to speak, step out of itself to evaluate its own descriptive and analytical bias for modern social 'order' over traditional disorder, cultural complexity, and ambiguity. But the discipline has often tried to remain either 'neutral' (preserving scholarly distance) or 'silent' toward modern violence and its consequences. It has generally neglected to study violent social events or conditions closer home, focusing instead on those socially distant and unfamiliar. However, as some recent studies have begun showing, such disciplinary assumptions need critical examination within a regional and a truly global human background. We need to give attention to that whole range of social forces, political languages, and modern technologies of violence that produces in today's world new and hidden modes of exploitation and social suffering, especially among the weak and the poor (Desjarlias et al. 1995; Scheper-Hughes 1992).

A spectrum of modern forces makes social violence a fertile ground for expanding domains of victimization, scapegoating, and pain and suffering. Societies tend to overlook their own suppressive and repressive power structures for both traditional and modern reasons (Girard 1982; Kearney 1995). Here, internal conflicts within traditional power structures may be as much to blame as those found in modern institutions and their exercise of power.[1] Ironically, while trying to control violence, many modern institutions engender violence, especially when the politics of vested and dominant political interests accentuates. Under the circumstances, conflicting religions and traditions, along with the state, produce a powerful, if unintended, nexus that variously produces, ignores, and abets social violence, increasing the suffering of the common person.

Under such conditions, victims of violence and their human rights get socially buried even deeper, making the quest all the more difficult. However, more contentious issues appear when the global and local issues of human rights are juxtaposed in a specific context or dispute. For instance, should not the cost of all violence and human suffering, particularly at the end of this modern 'humanizing' century, be *equal* for *all* human victims all over the globe (instead of being, as under the current Tort, one cost for victims of the North and another for the South)? The issue was particularly evident as the courts in the US initially followed the 1984 Bhopal industrial accident (see Anderson 1995; Baxi and Dhanda 1990; and Baxi and Paul 1985; for an ethnographic discussion, see Section V below). In some ways the North/South economic divide and its discourse politics came into clear view, where the loss of life, suffering and pain of the Bhopal gas victims somehow cost—and hence meant—less than those affected by the same company's plant in West Virginia in the US. For such issues, even the recent 'globalization' debate, which is at its core a product of international corporate economics, does little more than parody the old geopolitical divisions of the world. The implications of such a situation should be particularly sobering for any truly *global* movement for human and civil rights, particularly when the poor and the weak are the worst victims of inequity, injustice, and violence.

Besides such issues of inequity, modern violence raises the question of comprehending its ever wider and deeper reach within the human self. Anthropology and history must face the crucial conceptual question whether this century has not produced, as some have already posited, unique and unprecedented experiences, expressions, consequences, and meanings of violence (e.g., as evident in the recent Cambodian, Bosnian, and

Rwandan atrocities; see Langer 1996).[2] It is as if this new reach of violence demands a new language and a cultural sensitivity more than ever before. Strikingly, if the traditions are said to have tyrants, modernity has also had its share of infamous ideologists and revolutionaries during this century. They, as Feuer (1975: 191) pithily observed, 'have led to the fires of the Nazi crematoria, and to the Arctic wastes of the Soviet labor camps. Men's visions have been warped by ideology; their hatreds have been exacerbated; and every anointed elite has felt itself anointed to misuse human beings'. Nandy (1990: 89) makes a similar point on the misuse of power in the Indian colonial context.

Contemporary India, placed in such a frame, has produced its own record-setting episodes of mass violence (e.g., the Indian partition, the long-term regional [Kashmiri and Assamese] conflicts, to violence at Amritsar and Ayodhya). Whether local, regional, or national, no social domain, moral positions, or power arenas are today beyond violence. Violence evoked to solve a problem, as is well known, only produces more violence, making victims despair, distrust neighbors and lose hope. Narratives of traumatic experience, loss, and suffering under such conditions are born everyday, but they are pushed aside by the claims of conflicting authorities, government inquiries, expert reports, and even unscrupulous and exploitative local 'sympathizers'. On the other hand, villagers, city dwellers, babus, and even 'enlightened and powerful modern sahibs and leaders' weave a network of silence or collusion when violence serves a major selfish group or party interest. Women and children barely register anywhere on such a skewed screen of power and influence, while, their narratives, voices and rights are, ironically, ever more talked about rather than listened to and recognized.

Against such a background, I consider below some selected violent events, actors and conditions to show how today's India, traditional and modern, constructs notions of victimhood and victimization and then 'interrelates' these with violent occurrences, perpetrators and bystanders or spectators (*tamaashbin*). Viewed another way, it is a powerful commentary on the surrounding popular and public cultural ethos, and on hopes to 'implement' human rights over the length and breadth of India. But despite such hopelessness, it is remarkable that the Indian victim, not unlike any other human being, yearns for nothing so much as to obtain justice and fair play in life. My examples, incorporating some ethnographic situations, comments and observations, concern examples of violence that are culturally 'given' (female infanticide), traditionally extolled (the Sati custom), community-produced (communalism), or alien (the Bhopal Union Carbide gas disaster).

II 'A Fire-fighting State': An Ethnographic Evaluation

Diverse Indian traditions, popular culture, the Indian *sarkar* and uneven 'public debate' appear in all such forms of violence, but all these forces enter and exit each form at different points and with different cultural messages and consequences for the suf-ferer. Violence narratives now increasingly concern themselves with contested meanings. It is a distinct sign of the times, in which traditional authority faces contemporary skepticism, questions and uncertainties, and practical loss and gain overtakes human suffering. Victims may thus recall the same events differently, if it means some practical or political advantage. My examples of vio-lence are therefore selected to show an interplay of such concerns against that wide social background where the state as well as one or more major Indian tradition fight their old as well as new bat-tles. Still, where violence narratives are concerned, they are mostly about a struggle to recognize, recollect, express, and, when nec-essary, report one's own story for others' judgment. In such an effort, victims seldom make sufficiently explicit references to how they see perpetrators, spectators, and public authorities. Mostly, all this remains buried.

Though popular and social science commentaries are now available on some of the issues surrounding victims' narratives, direct ethnographic field discussions and assessments of such de-velopments are still rare. What do the people of one's own locality think, for example, when the issues (or specific cases) of female infanticide, wife-burning and Sati are brought up? In India this in-variably entails a discussion of these issues before people of dif-ferent castes and communities against the background of most major episodes of local, regional, or national violence. The early and mid-1990s were no stranger to the Sikh–Hindu problems and to the Ayodhya temple–mosque conflict. These readily attracted people from the upper castes, Dalits, Sikhs, and Muslims in a large and politically active city like Lucknow. The group that had assembled in a neighborhood at my request was diverse and vocal. Some had even directly suffered as either Dalits, Sikhs, or Muslims. Some others were close relatives of victims. Some had 'seen the violence with my own two eyes on a train', but they themselves had escaped major physical injury. Many had privately hurled abuse at 'the offending community'. All of this was so much a part of the late 1980s and early 1990s that few were entirely above the fray (in thought and word) when 6 December 1992 (the day of the Ayodhya riots) came.

Lacking space for detailed reportage, I will restrict myself to a few perspectival comments as these people remarked on 'the tangle (*gutthi* or *paycheeda maslaa*) and the trouble (*jhanjhat*) our leaders, preachers, sadhus, and *sarkar* make when violence is concerned. Everybody wants to use violence for a personal or political goal; nobody thinks of ordinary people's suffering and pain at the time'. My field-discussion group was vocal and it viewed itself as one of 'observant Indians, including some victims'. They viewed and commented on diverse violent events in generally three distinct time frames: (*a*) during the crisis; (*b*) immediate aftermath; and (*c*) 'when things cooled down'. Not only did social divisions, emotions, and suspicion run highest during the event (e.g., between Hindu and Sikh in 1984, and Hindu and Muslim during 1991–92), but the *sarkar* and its leaders also came under the heaviest criticism during the same period. Those recently victimized or still suffering were sometimes a part of my field discussions. Generally, these sat mostly silent and shocked, letting others speak on their behalf. Some others tried to speak but soon broke down and had to be taken away. However, the same victims had much more to say after a cooling period.

The Hindu–Sikh conflicts and the Deorala Sati case of the 1980s, for example, evoked largely predictable responses from Lucknow upper castes, Sikhs, and Dalits. Lucknow Sikhs particularly blamed the selfish upper-caste politicians in New Delhi and Punjab for 'a bloody separation of the two [Hindu and Sikh] communities long joined by marriage, overlapping faith, and daily peaceful social life'. In the Sikh crisis, on the other hand, Dalit reformers saw their

208 ◄ Cultural Diversity and Social Discontent

fears of upper-caste power politics confirmed. They commented, 'There is a hard lesson here about a long and difficult struggle still ahead of us.' Upper-caste Hindus, however, squarely blamed all these problems on 'the exploitative and violent party politics of corrupt and power hungry leaders. These now pose real danger to the unity of India'. Some Muslims had a 'we-have-seen-it-all' message for Sikhs and Dalits as minorities. They thought that Sikhs were getting the first taste of being a minority like themselves.

If the Deorala Sati case was geographically distant for my dis-cussants, it was religiously, culturally, and psychologically much closer. The Hindu, Sikh, and Dalit (except some radical reform-ers), while reflecting subtle differences, viewed Sati cases (in gen-eral) as a manifestation of feminine spiritual force, whose moral authority and temporal authenticity, as a religious principle, could never be questioned. 'We will see a Sati as long as India remains India', was the remark of an old upper-caste Hindu woman. Mus-lims, on the other hand, simply took themselves out of the debate, but after remarking, 'Sati is a specific matter of Hindu religion and faith (*mazhab aur imaan*). We may doubt it, so what? [But still] it is an ideal of chastity for Hindu women. They may not want us to meddle in their affairs such as we do not want them in ours.'

These discussions, however, clearly showed the centrality of the Indian state (*sarkar*)[3] in such matters. But if legal provisions and public speeches conjure up its one face, actual weaknesses and practices show another. For instance, female infanticide, a prac-tice known as illegal to even remote villagers, cannot get swift and decisive justice because, as my informants said, 'even policemen know in their hearts that girls, only a bundle of unending anxiety for parents, are still dispensable at birth.' But when it came to en-countering an actual case, my Lucknow informants, especially those with rural connections, loudly denied 'ever seeing such a thing'. Yet nobody could rule out 'such a thing from happening as long as people viewed girls as a social burden and a possible threat to one's honor...'. Those involved, they agreed, observed strict secrecy and even bribed the police to hush up the matter. The same collusion between the local police and doctors holds sway when aborting a female foetus in a large city after using such medical technologies as the ultrasound and amniocentesis.

Overall, the state's legal, administrative, and political authority remains strikingly 'toothless' in such matters, my informants repeatedly stressed. There was little concern here for the victim, 'unless one was a relative or a friend of a big man'. 'Who would care to hear the story of an ordinary victim,' they asked, 'when the police seldom write what we tell them...? But, when some prominent person is involved, they immediately know what they must write. What can we do, we are helpless? What we can do is just agree. They have the might [*lathi*] while we feel helpless. It is everyday reality.'

As my Hindu, Muslim, Dalit, and Sikh discussants reviewed such a situation, they found fault not only with political leaders, administrators, and the police, but also with a general social indifference toward human suffering. It has made traditions hollow, religions callous, and the Indian *sarkar*, even after 50 years of Indian independence, little more than an ad hoc (and inadequate) fire-fighting squad. The episodes of major social violence repeatedly make the state an after-the-event visitor, 'rounding up miscreants', awarding token compensations, making a flurry of largely symbolic political announcements, and passing ineffective legislative initiatives. Misreading of major events continues. The Sati case at Deorala, for instance, had ironically 'surprised' the politicians as well as the public media at the speed and depth with which it became an all-India 'public affair'.

Viewed sociologically, all such issues and response patterns are interrelated, representing India's most recent struggle to forge a new post-independence (i.e., a post-Gandhi and post-Nehru) cultural identity that must somehow learn to manage caste *realpolitik*, religious conflicts, and people's pragmatic needs and democratic demands in interdependent terms.[4] But where are, at present, the victims and their narratives within such an exercise? Literally nowhere. Where are the concerns for ordinary people's human rights, amidst the claims and counter-claims of only those politically significant? Again, the answer has to be: nowhere. But social awareness has certainly increased in local communities, as our brief ethnographic excursion showed, and the people increasingly demand, if still from the sidelines, removal of social oppression and injustice. Some now claim and demand fairness every day from those who dominate and control (see Chapter 6). Unfortunately, such battle lines, though multiplying, often become too costly for the majority of Indians after a while, prohibiting prolonged committed pursuit. Let us see how these forces and other related issues are reflected in the available accounts of, and commentaries on female infanticide, the Deorala Sati case, communal violence, and the Bhopal gas disaster.

III Female Infanticide: Hide-and-Seek Customary Violence

Female infanticide is a strikingly low legal and political liability (yet a serious social and demographic) issue in India. In popular cultural terms, 'it still occurs because it means a continuing preference to beget sons over daughters'. But, as my diverse Lucknow informants vigorously agreed, it is nevertheless 'a moral blot on modern India'. Its practice is secretive, crude, and cruel, though socially unattributed. The cases are hard to investigate unless one is lucky enough to win the confidence of one or two of those who have 'seen' (or have been a part of) a case. However, carefully recorded stories often highlight an utter helplessness and psychological caging of a mother, even if she was complicit or silent during the act. The customary moral and social calculus is such that it makes a mother complicit. Her consent may in fact be customarily assumed.

Sociologically, female infanticide in India occurs because of a combination of factors such as the absence of a son or sons, abject poverty, the protection of male honor, and a mother's helpless family position (for a British colonial reference, see Crooke 1972 [1906]; a recent study, Pakrasi 1972; and a woman journalist's investigation, Bumiller 1991).[5] A mother usually faces a combination of such social forces. Experientially, a mother, in the words of a Rajasthani woman, 'finds her insides ripped apart' after such an act. 'A part of me died every time I lost a daughter', said another Rajasthani woman to me in 1993, who 'had to give up two daughters to my mother-in-law to put them to sleep'.[6] Such mothers' narratives, with all their moral, social, and emotional anguish, give us a picture rarely presented in the literature on the subject. These stories also poignantly comment on the travesty of human rights not only of the infant killed but of the mother silenced. We cannot assume the mother to be always the culprit in female infanticide. The issue needs careful examination. Similarly, the cumulative social and demographic effects of such a practice are also widely overlooked, and even neglected.[7]

The narratives of such violence I collected reveal certain clear strands: An intense cultural politics surrounds the issue, where perpetrators, aides and abettors, and survivors spend enormous time and effort to hush up the matter, to not let 'our enemies report it to police'. The affected mother, routinely assumed as complicit, receives little attention for her true feelings, grief, psychological wounding, and compensatory mourning. When followed up, a killer (and the mother) are found to suffer from moral (karmic) guilt. They fear supernatural punishment. Some reported that the dead soul of the girl haunted them; others attributed their mishaps and mental and physical illnesses to such an act, 'until the dead soul of the child was properly pacified' (for similar feelings expressed in Tamil Nadu, see Bumiller 1991: 108–9).

Modern educated Indians, however, find the practice 'cruel', 'abhorrent', 'horrifying', and 'immoral', with little patience for the mother's narratives or standard sociological explanations. But the importance of begetting a son still remains paramount even for most of these members of the urban middle (and upper middle) class. Despite the legal ban, they are also known to seek help from modern medical technology (amniocentesis and ultrasound) to abort a female foetus. But, once again, even the mothers of this class, over time, suffer from remorse, guilt, fear, and self-doubt (also Bumiller 1991: 101–24).

However, no one can deny the fact that in both rural and urban India some groups or families, irrespective of their education, income and status, still resort to female infanticide and justify it in religious, economic, and social terms. The silence of urban educated Indians, men and women, on the subject is striking. No confessional accounts come forth from those who 'saw' such things among their relatives or in their neighborhoods. The subject hardly attracts sustained attention from women activists. Under the circumstances, the ineffective 'laws on paper' continue. They have been there ever since the British enacted the first law against this practice in 1795, while the latest one is only a decade old. The corrosive customary violence continues, nevertheless. An exasperated Elisabeth Bumiller thus, for example, had to put her faith in the feminist-led political action dedicated 'to change the system from the outside' for 'raising people's consciousness'.

IV Sati: Cultural Ambiguity and Ineffective Reforms

The famous Sati custom provides another example of corrosive customary violence. Again, hard to overlook and hard to socially weed out, the practice evokes sharp indignation from the educated Indian elite, while people 'encounter' such cases every few years. The issue may genuinely represent, an anthropologist might argue, deep people-subscribed civilizational ambiguity. It may be paraded to defend or condemn a certain 'custom' which just does not go away, despite a century of reform legislation. The Sati narratives, not unlike those of female infanticide, quickly trigger a dispute about 'what really took place', 'who were the main culprits', 'who or what is to blame', and 'who is really telling the truth?'.

For relating a recent Sati episode, I here rely on two non-academic narratives to help me sketch the overall storyline of a recent Sati case and of a wife-burning family. One is produced by the erstwhile British (BBC) commentator, Mark Tully, and the other by Elisabeth Bumiller, an American woman journalist. Mark Tully's study is useful because he explicates the story of Deorala Sati from different positions (and without any obvious academic or political agenda of his own; see Tully 1991: 210–36). He wants to find out what happened one day in early September 1987, in Deorala. The crucial question in this case was: Did Roop Kanwar, a teenage bride of only eight months, *voluntarily* become Sati? Or was she forcibly murdered by her Rajput in-laws to reassert their Rajput male honor, and thus also to maintain their local social and religious supremacy in contemporary India? The public adulation of a Sati inevitably throws the spotlight on the Sati's husband's family and awards a religious aura to all her relatives, the community, and the region. After all, Rajasthan reports such occurrences much more frequently. It has produced, for example, 28 such incidents since 1947, India's year of independence (Tully 1991: 224).[8]

The three versions of the Deorala incident (by her and her husband's relatives, by the police, and by national and regional newspapers) competed to present 'the truth' soon after the event. Women activists from several cities and universities vociferously joined the fray a little later, seeking the state's sternest criminal punishment for murdering a girl. But the relatives literally deified Roop Kanwar in public ceremonies. They immediately worshipped her (and her husband's) cremation spot, organized a huge gathering on the 12th-day *chunari* (head cover) ceremony, and planned the construction of a Sati temple on the spot, with the provision for an annual pilgrimage and fair. By no means traditionally uncommon, such a response, as Tully also noted, clearly fit the traditional upper-caste—Brahman, Rajput, and Bania (Marwari)—interests of status purity, male social honor, and local business interests. The local and state political leaders also went along such a 'public response', with their own political calculations, until some persistent and vociferous women activists took the case before the state chief minister. Still several days passed. The state police, politicians, national journalists, and even the country's prime minister, Rajiv Gandhi, remained silent, sizing up the political fallout from 'an unfolding situation'. The roles of the public media, regional opinion and rural popular sentiments came into play, nudging the state to act hesitatingly, while the traditional opposition solidified its stand.

Thus, it is not surprising that several contradictory versions of 'what really happened to Roop Kanwar' remain current to this day. The local community did not come forward to let the police determine 'the truth'. The two major sides—the relatives of Roop Kanwar (who eventually mobilized 100,000 people and formed a 'Committee for the Protection of Religion') and the 'Westernized elite and "independent" women'—clashed, while many political leaders and social reformers remained inactive, and paralyzed the judiciary. Thus a recent Sati incident in India, even after a century of British and Indian legislative initiatives, still remains trapped among the conflicting forces of Hindu tradition, the modern 'secular' state laws and judiciary, and feeble civic or public culture.

Most recently, such a situation resulted in what *India Today* called 'Legal Embarrassment' (Mitta 1996). On 11 October 1996, the Rajasthan Sessions Court acquitted the 32 accused in the case because the prosecution could not prove that Roop Kanwar's death was a case of murder, rather than the lesser charge of abetment of suicide. In legal terms, since the first could not be proved, the second could also not automatically apply. However, the 1988 Sati Prevention Act does help erase this legal difficulty, allowing the lesser charge to apply automatically and thus, as Mitta (1996: 89) hopes, 'to prevent the perpetrators of Sati from taking refuge in religious and cultural arguments'.

In a modern political and intellectual accounting, Sati events still evoke deep misgiving toward religious and traditional forces, but the modern temper has seldom produced an intensive, objective, and systematic account of such events. Nor has it produced reliable, undistorted narratives of those surrounding the Sati (or the victim, depending on one's perspective), particularly of her parents and brothers (for a recent sociological interpretation and criticism, see Veena Das 1995: 12–15, 107–14; Nandy 1995a). But such studies have to be done long after the event, when the dominant tradition's immediate control of the storyline relaxes and differing vantage points can emerge.

Traditionally, the Sati event celebrates a verity of eternal cosmic morality (*sanatan dharma*)—a rededication of women to uphold this-worldly and otherworldly order. To view the same event in preponderantly modern legal or human rights terms is still a distant goal where ordinary people are concerned. Modernity's score so far, as we have already indicated, has not been very promising. On the other hand, if a Sati event hides from the law a violent killing or a suicide of a woman, then the tradition, paradoxically, degrades itself to seek social reinforcement and glory. It sacrifices a woman to close its social, ritual, economic, and political ranks for rejuvenation. However, if these stories are seldom that simple, perhaps we still do not know how to reach the truth in such events, and the modern century has not helped here much.

Even before self-immolation, tradition awards a Sati superhuman properties, identifying her above all personal pain and suffering as she performs a divinely inspired blissful act of cosmic sacrifice. As a public test of her genuine Sati-hood, Roop Kanwar is said to have cured an old sick woman just before alighting her husband's pyre. Practically a goddess *during* the act, Tully writes, she had demanded circumambulation from the surrounding chanting crowd. In contrast, in the police and in some later news reports, the same Roop Kanwar was depicted as an adulterous, drugged, confused, and terrified woman, who was forcibly pushed on to her impotent husband's pyre in Deorala. The two versions of the same event could not have contrasted more greatly.

Violent Sati incidents, known since the 10th century, seem to have always had such a dual face, one extolled and the other reviled. While the modern period has introduced new meanings into violence against women, including politicization and legal measures for its control, the practice has neither spread uncontrolled, nor has it ever totally disappeared. The prevailing local and regional caste and religious factors, however, play a crucial role in creating and sustaining support for Sati events.

These events, in today's popular cultural conception, are neither totally above moral skepticism, social suspicion and debate nor, despite all the modern legal legislation and education, a public-accepted crime.[9] My field interviews on the subject led me to such a conclusion in the summer of 1988. Both male and female, and upper castes and lower-caste people (including Dalits) in Lucknow, subscribed to the notions that, though a genuine Sati is extremely rare, 'such events do—and must—occur because it is India, a land of sacrifice'. 'A Sati sanctifies and maintains this creation; it is an ideal that generations of married women look up to', a woman had maintained during the discussion. However, only one person in the group interviewed had visited a Sati's sacred spot (*sati sthala*). But the subject immediately led people to say what they heard and remembered. 'We can but only very rarely find such a soul passing before us.' Yet no parent, however orthodox and devout, wanted to see his/her daughter become a Sati, 'for even the goddess Sati's mother did not. You cannot wish it; it just happens'. In life, one thus expects a Sati case to occur in somebody else's house, not one's own. Such practical rationality appears among the same ordinary Hindus who, as mothers and grandmothers, routinely tell little girls stories of Sati in mythologies, medieval tales, and even recent times.

Such a view is of course supposed to be the polar opposite of the pure greed, social exploitation, and torture the cases of wife-burning for dowry today represent (for an evaluation of Sati and wife-burning as modern cultural and historical issues, see Nandy 1995a: 32–52). Yet, as a sign of the changing times, many urban Hindus today express doubt about a Sati event, especially after the Roop Kanwar controversy had reverberated in the country for months. 'Who knows what really happened', is the frequent question, and 'how can one distinguish between a genuine and false (or forced) Sati, when a bride's powerful in-laws conspire for local name and political gains, and the weaker parents are forcibly silenced?' All over India, the issue of the genuine and the fake (*asli-nakli*) is crucial in religious personages, places, actions, things, and events. The fake makes the genuine all the more desirable, but difficult. Such a moral and political suspicion, as women's activist groups had also argued in the Roop Kanwar case, works to confound the issue. It can quickly, first, eliminate the distance between a recent Sati event and a wife-killing case, and second make ordinary people either more gullible or vigilant against fraud under violent coercion. As a skeptical Lucknow parent had remarked, 'Whenever I hear of a Sati case, I glance toward my unmarried daughters with concern. Who knows what is hidden behind a Sati story *these days*? Nobody tells the truth'.

The foregoing discussion, based on fieldwork, reflects the continuing dilemma before the modern Indian intellectual: How does one bridge the yawning gap between what the ordinary Indian thinks about Sati and what the modern state's laws want to achieve (see also Nandy 1995a: 49). Modern intellectuals and academics still do not know how to reconcile the secular and the modern rational with the prevalent ambivalent Hindu cultural reasoning, in which one venerates Sati yet locally keeps its occurrences limited by closely 'knowing' what really went on. A modern thinker is, however, often reluctant to recognize the ordinary Hindus' controlling role in such events, when, in fact, the modern Indian laws against the Sati custom have repeatedly failed, and when social violence against women has also multiplied during this modern century, despite such laws.

Or, to put the matter another way, Sati events expose the weakness of both modern and traditional forces. If the local Hindu tradition has sometimes engineered and exploited the event for selfishness, local caste and lineage honor, the Indian (colonial and postcolonial) state has also repeatedly failed to prove itself effective where social violence against women is concerned. Indian modernity, or modernity more generally, therefore, cannot be an effective judge and jury where Sati cases are concerned.

V Narratives Recalled, Masked, or Lost

Ranging between moral ideals, cultural ambiguity, and political expediency, Indian popular culture today locally produces more, diverse, and therapeutically necessary violence narratives. But most are either lost or recalled in masked form to meet practical constraints. Such stories usually expose weaknesses of the traditional world alongside the foibles and failures of the legislative, administrative, and judicial branches of the modern state. Violence narratives of ordinary people are often about a social helplessness that actually also reflects governmental neglect, political agendas, and weak public memories. Simultaneously, such narratives expose a core weakness of major Indian traditions—an erosion in their social consensus and moral certitude.

Communal Violence

To illustrate differences in the state's and the victim's worlds in a clear way, let us consider here briefly two forms of social violence in contemporary India: first, community-inflicted (particularly customary and communal) violence and second, technology-generated violence, death, and suffering. To begin with, what types (and range) of narratives does Indian communal violence produce? We still hardly know the full range. Anthropology, history, sociology, and psychology have to collaborate on the subject much more than they have done so far. Some perceptive accounts already show, however, the complexity 'Indian communal violence' reflects. In one approach, driven by distinct colonial and postcolonial forces of political dominance and of contentious centers of religious power, it is a form of social violence in which antagonists locally remember and maintain 'ledgers' of past victimization, 'unanswered violence' and accumulating social insult and injustice (see Veena Das 1990a; Kakar 1995; and Pandey 1990).

The wounds of such violence are as distinctly bodily as religious, social, and psychological. Hence they remain open much longer, and easily 'fester'. Though British colonial history has also influenced the accounts of (and accountability for) female infanticide and Sati cases, communal violence received, as we now know, increasing attention (and concern) for a variety of administrative, political, and religious reasons. It has continued to receive only more, if hackneyed, attention and interpretation after independence, ranging from 'riots', 'irrational mob behavior', to 'bigoted violence'. Hazy notions of modernist collective guilt and shame, rather than acute investigations of actual people's narratives, experiences, and explanations, usually surround this form of violence.

The scope, purpose, and meaning of communal violence particularly widened with the Sikh–Hindu conflicts of the 1980s. It occurred as if to repudiate whatever the modern educated Indian had laid as the foundation for shaping secular India and the Indian state (see Veena Das 1990a: 1–36; Nandy 1990: 69–91). But again, discussions of such developments most often remain either administrative, policy-oriented, or analytical, where those who became a rape, trauma, torture, or arson statistic usually remain absent, silent, or passive. The victims' stories largely remain untold. Even more rarely, victims themselves are heard in their own 'broken language', in the background of their own violated selves. Given its social history, the Hindu–Sikh violence might be particularly poignant and deep for such narratives. Ever since the mid-1980s, so many stories remained untold every day. This may have been unlike any other communal event in recent times in India, since their kinship and brotherhood first gave way to communal violence, and it later graduated into 'terrorism', while, on the other hand, state power lost its bearings and degraded into brute for e (see Colvard 1996: 3–8).

In such violence, perpetrators (and unjust state power) reveal as well as hide their tracks. Those opposed bitterly attribute blame as well as mourn for the events. However, the languages of victory and defeat and of insult and revenge become hollow after a while, since the loss is found deeper than both, touching the soul of both communities. The overall message is that Indian communal violence is becoming increasingly inward-oriented. Dalits, tribals, migrants, and the exploited stand as the next internal frontiers for Indian 'communal' violence.

Uninvited Violence and Suffering

Now let us juxtapose the violent calamity the 1984 Bhopal industrial accident represented. Here the all-India secular governmental policies, decisions, and forces essentially shaped the cause and course of this calamity of historic proportions, in contrast to the Deorala Sati case and varieties of recent communal (including now the Dalit, Sikh, and regional Kashmiri Muslim) violence and religious riots.

At the Bhopal disaster's core still stand tens of thousands of women and children as the worst faceless victims and unattended sufferers. To recapitulate briefly, a multinational corporation, two national governments (the US and India) and a host of national and international tort, criminal, and constitutional (and human rights) experts wrestled with one another for legal and economic liability for years, while tens of thousands of victims waited for the aid crucial to survive from one day to the next. But as is now well known, all forces dramatically deadlocked before the labyrinthine case-clogged courts, leaving those bereaved, incapacitated, and destitute, to fend for themselves—many are in the same situation even today (see Anderson 1995: 154–71).[10]

These victims endured a distinct type of violence. It was brought to them by 'strangers and outsiders'. It erupted suddenly, 'spreading a dense muddy cloud of choking gas' in a cold night from a chemical factory rather than from a known hostile community shouting slogans and wielding knives, swords, and guns. In interviews with the survivors just across the Union Carbide factory in Bhopal in the summer of 1986, one coughing Muslim had remarked, 'Whether [it flows] from the chimney of the factory or a sword, violence is like the weevil in a granary. It slowly eats away the whole crop—what we call a human being or a society—leaving only a hollow shell'. Yet he considered

> violence necessary for life…. For all life feeds only on life. But that is nature. A human becomes human only by learning to control all forms of violence, including when it is justifiable. The Union Carbide plant, a man-made factory, became an earth-shaking disaster for us, killing and maiming hundreds of thousands. Nobody but these merchants of poison must be squarely blamed for it.

The factory typified to him 'modern man's unlimited avarice…. And the resulting violence is worse than a few people running amok [as in a communal riot]. It can strangle all of us humans the next time'.

The same informant also commented on the traditional Indian approach to stemming social violence. He stressed that it lay not in human selfishness and greed but in doing one's duty toward others. Again, in his words,

> In India for centuries common man lived by taking care of his family, kin, community and strangers. This produced social

harmony. But greed, anger and selfishness today make people blind. To be selfish, as many people these days are, is to multiply others' [social suffering].... The government officers pocketed money while we suffered in Bhopal. Everybody [still] is blind to our pain.

The Bhopal accident was no exception, however, in shutting out such victims' narratives for many months. Immediately after the accident, all, including the physicians, hospital staff, and community healers, were too numbed and traumatized to say much. For weeks they were overwhelmed by the sheer size of the calamity and the lack of even primary care at local hospitals, jammed with hysterical or dying patients and their dazed relatives. Those less severely sick seemingly merited only a flying visit by a politician, a government official, a social reformer, or a news reporter. Everybody wanted to snatch a few quotable words from a sufferer and take 'a dramatic picture of human misery', to peddle their own stories. Those suffering incapacitating pain felt the worst exploited, for government officers, media, lawyers, and even aid agencies and social activists mobbed and caged them for their own purposes, rather than giving help. Beleaguered yet silenced, these sufferers had no one to comfort them for months. Whatever ultimately did come out about them was often masked, distorted, subverted, or doctored. Such stories from Bhopal provide another benchmark of the silent violation of human rights, often by those government officials supposed to be their protectors.

Yet, personal stories of pain and suffering, but also help and care, trickled out from the victims after a few months. Local private relief workers, along with friends and relatives, listened to victims and survivors. Issues of medical care, employment, and complex legal claims produced an endless paper chase, vexing most survivors (Khare 1987b; 1990). At the core of the survivor stories were often desperate efforts for bare survival. In the summer of 1986, one had a bittersweet memory:

God bless that doctor who gave me medicine to let me breathe from one hour to the next, from one day to the next. I had lost my whole family to the disaster. Once I could breathe on my own, I searched for food and a roof over my head. My relatives and a friend helped, not government. I lived for months on the

hope of receiving government help. But remember, I am a Bhopal gas victim; I still beg and borrow to see the next day.

Sociologically, caste, religion, urban administrative connections,
and local political conflicts and patronage had sorted out tens of
thousands of Bhopal victims from the beginning. While those socially 'connected' received attention, most others hoped to be
similarly included some day, with government promises remain-
ing empty and distant. The suffering deepened and widened with
time, making people increasingly bitter. One activist survivor's
comment was, 'The city has been totally ruined by the factory for
generations to come. It is just as the Big [atom] Bomb did in Japan'.
The graffiti on the ghost factory's walls in 1986 repeatedly drew
such a parallel.

To summarize, we need to examine a whole spectrum of victims
and victims' narratives for learning about the current notions of
victimhood, victimization, scapegoating, and political and legal
blame. Victims hold at least one precious corner of such experience. But as we have seen, their narratives are rarely directly,
fully, and readily accessible in modern surroundings. Many hurdles stand in the way. They are first drowned in trauma, and then
are emotionally blocked or masked for a long period. Only a patient and careful treatment of victims allows a sort of recovery possible, but in many difficult cases, recovery remains woefully
painful and incomplete. Some experiences are blocked and lost
forever. Whether customary, religiously cosmological, self-induced
or imposed, severe, traumatizing violence invariably produces
far-reaching consequences deep within the victims and in their
view of the surrounding world. Behind every traumatic event,
equally surely, the worst victims hide *multiple stories*, but these
are hardest to reach. Similarly, those illiterate, weak, dependent,
and marginal, often suffering first and longest, hide many more
untold stories. These often get assumed as 'the ignorant sufferers'
and are either bypassed or are heard yet not really heard.

But the fact is that all victims, as humans, once in a state to tell,
seek attention and understanding in their social surrounding.
Missing that, and fearing social distrust, neglect, and ridicule, victims either withhold or mask their stories. They suffer inside, develop self-doubt and withdraw within themselves. They even
begin to doubt their memory and experience, wondering if what

they know is really the truth. Yet, over time, victims must relentlessly search for the truth and authenticity in what they recall. These are the necessary foundations to rebuild their shattered selves and the broken world around them (on some Indian women as victims, see Veena Das 1990b: 345–98).

Where women victims are concerned, sex and gender issues immediately surround them in Indian culture. Their narratives run through a whole range of moral framing produced by the customary male dominance. Their stories most often reflect the male-approved facts and certainties. The events thus have a 'genuine' and a 'false' face, as the Sati and female infanticide issues repeatedly show. Women's own sense of justice and fairness rarely expresses itself under such conditions. It remains buried under 'self-doubts' and social contradictions. As such hopelessness and helplessness deepens in women (particularly those old and illiterate), the will to tell (but not the need) is lost. Such victims' suffering becomes silent (as my Rajasthani rural women informants had stressed), but the non-verbal languages of the body, sensoria, and 'heart–mind' (*man*) intensify. How should an ethnographer adequately record them? An unwilling Indian mother losing several daughters to female infanticide, a mother losing her only son and husband to communal violence, and an old asthmatic Bhopal survivor of a family of seven repeatedly posed such a question to me (for a comparison of women from other societies, on Brazil, see Scheper–Hughes 1992: 19–20, 216–67; for a 'view from below' on Haiti, see Farmer 1996: 261–81).

Recalling in the same context the ordinary Bhopal survivors, especially the poor women and children, we find that both customary and modern Indian social forces, paradoxically, conspired against the Bhopal survivors' pain and suffering. After the first few days of the tragedy, traditional indifference toward suffering women and children quickly returned. The most severely affected neighborhoods became increasingly emotionally and socially distant to the remainder of the city. This happened despite the initially impressive and sustained volunteer help of many Bhopal citizens. All volunteer victims' aid committees and rehabilitative camps slowly disappeared, leaving the work to the *sarkar*. In the victims' own words, 'it was ultimately the *sarkar* that failed us most', whether it was in the local hospitals, in government offices, during political leaders' rounds, or in the courts up and down the

PATN.

New York–Delhi–Bhopal corridor of power and politics. If international lawyers, relief agencies, and multinational businesses and corporations came first, and left first, without doing much, people did not expect much from them. But how could one's own *sarkar* be so callous, they wondered. Their disillusion deepened as little happened even years after to break the cycle of continued disease, poverty, pain, and suffering. Worst of all, the uneducated, incapacitated, and behind-the-purdah Bhopal women, living just across from the ghost of that infamous Union Carbide plant, had nobody to listen to them. These still remain the worst sufferers. The *sarkar*, they thought, had let them down the most. They are still in search of a normal life ever since that fateful December 1984.

Such unmitigated social suffering somehow 'routinizes' trauma, making victims seem like ordinary people, though for them it means 'losing themselves, the ownership of their bodies to the random forces and institutionalized violence of the modern, even democratizing, state' (Scheper–Hughes 1992: 19–20). What Veena Das (1990a: 1–36) calls 'governmentality' in such a context, the Bhopali sufferers called, rather derisively, '*nirdayi sarkari khopari*' or 'the cruel government's [or government officer's] mind'. Some had argued at length in 1987 that such a 'mind' could be by itself a much worse source of people's suffering than any bad social or religious custom. Those 'awakened' by the Bhopal disaster found such 'government mind' at work elsewhere, whether it was a communal riot, a police station, a hospital, or a market place.

But such violence and injustice, though ever more unjust, vicious, and unmanageable on a daily basis, remains mostly underrepresented or marginalized in governmental reports and statistics. Despite swelling social protests, it still remains the forgotten social event, where narratives seldom find the time or psychological space to be born. They are far too routine, and are far too many, while powerful governments busy themselves with balkanizing wars, inter-tribal mass killings, genocide, terrorism, and 'ethnic cleansing'. These capture the news headlines. To find this century so violence-prone should be sobering. But simply 'to be horror-struck', as Langer recently remarked, 'is a frugal form of charity' (Langer 1996: 47). If anything, today's epidemic of violence is set to gather even more force, especially as it rides on the wings of unprecedented technologies of rapid radio and electronic messages, mass media communication, cyberspace, suicide bombers, and weapons of mass destruction (e.g., see Chirot 1995: 141–66).

Still, unfortunately, the same technology seldom turns up to help the victims of violence and their narratives. This source of human perception, insight and knowledge, remains unrecovered, while center stage is occupied by the modern state and its power structures.[11] But to reduce human suffering and to plough the ground for human rights to take root, ordinary suffering people, as my Bhopal gas victims insisted, must be heard, and the experts must stop to listen to and learn from them. Victims' stories are about much more than just an occasion to prick a conscience or horrify one aesthetically. They reveal, in uniquely felt language, all those exploitative forces of power, dominance, and control that conspire against human rights. If some of these forces come from religions and traditions, modern state institutions are hardly beyond blame. Today both tradition and modernity stand indicted for sheltering or promoting violence at the end of the century. Far from being an apotheosis of human life, each side increasingly employs violence to gain advantage and control. Each side openly seeks to control people's attention. In such a race, however, since it is the state that today most often amasses the organized coercive power, it has the ever greater responsibility to learn when, how, and to what degree to counter violence with violence, and when 'no-response response' might be best. Unfair state responses now provoke not only unfair retaliation, but also unleash a spiralling terrorist violence, eroding state authority and legitimacy (for a concise statement, see Colvard 1996: 3–8).

In such a situation, no wonder that numerous 'contested' narratives of violence are now appearing, juxtaposing 'our' version against 'theirs', justifying 'our' response against 'their' unjust cruelty and tyranny. Thus human rights in India also face ever greater hurdles, politically masked and unmasked. A recent several-nation study, for example, reached an anthropologically obvious conclusion: 'the process of overcoming the subordination of whole communities entails recognition of their collective right to order their own affairs' (Mendelsohn and Baxi 1994: 7). But to make a beginning, it is high time that the state exercise its power only under publicly-earned social consensus and transparent democratic legitimacy. Actually, the last may be the best first step to move toward respecting people's human rights.

_____

◄ NOTES

1. Behind such formulations still stands the culturally comprehensive but now rather old-style contrast between 'tradition' and 'modernity'. The contrast itself does not become anthropologically outdated, provided it is used with awareness of the internal heterogeneities and inconsistencies within each, and for the diverse power relationships that the two today culturally and historically forge, sometimes against each other and sometimes together, to shape the late 20th century society. Other prevalent markers (e.g., 'Western' and 'non-Western', 'North' and 'South', 'developed' and 'developing', 'local' and 'global', 'dominant' and 'subaltern', and 'colonial' and 'postcolonial') are distinctly slanted toward power-and-control but are culturally limiting and often biased against the tradition. I will accordingly use the earlier terminology but with full awareness of what the two *now* culturally and historically connote.

2. See Lawrence L. Langer (1996: 47–65). He makes the crucial point about human violence and suffering that 'the familiar verbal modes for approaching [violence and suffering] have been exhausted by centuries of repetition' (p. 47).

3. *Sarkar* is a widely used cultural term in India for master, ruler, and ruling authority or government. Extremely useful to the ethnographer, popular usage readily includes the Indian state and its various powerful officers, leaders, and functionaries. It is culturally reified in everyday use, attracting daily criticism from the ordinary Indian for its nurturing and protective or uncaring and unjust governance.

4. Though beyond the scope of this discussion, 'caste realpolitik' and 'pragmatic nationalism' deserve separate discussion. The first emphasizes the politicization of castes by regional forces for forging competing, protesting, and co-opting power grids. Shifting coalitions produce a qualitatively different political map than the local factional politics of the 1950s or caste voting blocs of the 1980s. The pragmatic state, on the other hand, realizes its limitations in solving Indian problems and allows others to try.

5. Though female infanticide, like the Sati custom, early received the attention of British administrators, and the issue has cropped up every now and then during this century, comprehensive studies and sustained reform movements are strikingly few. Ironically, even women's rights movements agitate more about Sati than female infanticide.

6. My brief but planned field inquiries on the subject in the rural areas around Lucknow and Jaipur faced well-recognized initial resistance. 'Nobody here knows about these things' was the standard reply, often by men. Everybody knew the practice to be illegal, while the women remained aloof and silent (or were silenced before me). Yet 'the practice' would gradually come into view, when the investigator was found not to be a trouble maker.

7. Indian demographic data show a distinctly widening gap between the female–male sex ratio. It has declined during every decade since 1901, sliding from 972 women for every 1,000 men to 929 in 1991. One of my educated informants in Rajasthan had mentioned these figures. See also Pakrasi (1972). Though female infanticide alone may not be responsible for such a sharp decline, it still cannot be easily overlooked. Given the surrounding social secrecy (and the complicit or unconcerned local authorities), the actual prevalence of the practice is hardly known in either cities or villages.

8. 'The standard procedure' the police followed on such occasions was to register the case under the Indian Penal Code, and disallow worship of the Sati and any collection of donations. The publicity of the Roop Kanwar case, however, did not allow the police to do so until much later.

9. The following discussion is based on my field interviews with 20 upper- and lower-caste, male and female, Hindus in Lucknow during the summer of 1988. Those interviewed, educated and illiterate, however, still avidly discussed the Roop Kanwar case for its religious meaning and message, and for the situation 'if your sister or daughter were to be a Sati'.

10. The literature on the Union Carbide Bhopal industrial accident has been quite vast and varied. The legal and court proceedings have dragged out interminably, with the suffering victims at the bottom still mostly unheard. For more discussions on the Bhopal accident, see Baxi and Paul (1985) and Baxi and Dhanda (1990).

11. This situation now attracts widely differing commentaries. Some see the roots of 'modern tyranny' in faulty or incomplete modernization, some in the structure of modern ideology, some in traditional or religious resurgence, and some in missing or misunderstanding the modern ideology itself. For example, see Chirot (1995).

8

Hindu Cultural Reasoning Under Challenge: Politicizing Traditions, Modern Commentaries, and Social Mistrust

Prologue

This chapter is a sequel to my earlier work (Khare 1993c: 191–212), where distinct forms of Hindu philosophical, mythological, and popular cultural reasoning were outlined and related to some popular cultural ideas, relations, and explanatory schemes. I had identified three major forms of reasoning—axiomatic, performative, and judgmental, arguing that, despite the mounting cultural diversity and social conflicts within the society, there is still significant evidence of sociocultural sharing in everyday thinking and living among those called 'Hindus'.[1] While writing the 1993 paper, I decided to focus on my ethnography of the mostly upper-caste urban Hindus (both men and women), explicating how this cultural majority reasoned in everyday life and how the strands of such reasoning linked up with various Indian philosophies and perspectives concerned with issues of 'the one and the many'. However, the account also hinted that the main reasoning patterns, while reflecting textual formulations, were a part of the ordinary Indian's struggles. These included those who called themselves 'Hindus' and sometimes non-Hindus.[2] If they were integral to people's practical problems as well as for religious authorities and storytellers, they also experienced the new challenges a changing India posed.

I Cultural Classifications under Social Conflict

The 'general logic' of cultural classifications in lived social situations shows a continuing presence of the culturally normative but not without social divisions and contested cultural claims and counter-claims. People negotiate through social contingencies to reach desired moral goals and practical results. But since modern sociological classifications often rest on the dominant normative social order, it needs to be shown how people's knowledge, cultural rules, and practical logic modify and work under social challenge. In such a context, earlier sociological formulations of Durkheim and Mauss remain helpful in a most general sense, where logical hierarchy is seen as 'only another aspect of social hierarchy, and the unity of knowledge is nothing else than the very unity of the collectivity, extended to the universe' (1963: 84).

Similarly, anthropological interpretations of social classifications as either archetypes, logical binary oppositions, gradations, 'family resemblances', 'polythetic classifications', or models of unity behind multiplicity, guide us only up to a point, since contextual forces and their contingencies intervene in both thought and practice (for anthropological literature on normative social classifications, see Berlin and Kay 1969; Dumont 1980; Durkheim and Mauss 1963; Ellen and Reason 1979; and Needham 1983). As templates of people's cultural reasoning, however, the same classifications also attract—and symbolize—cultural conflicts and social contingencies, posing moral, political, and practical dilemmas (for such exercises, see Geertz 1983; Parkin 1982b; and Overing 1985). On India, anthropologists have similarly studied traditional caste classifications not only as forms of ideal cultural reasoning but also as contested this-worldly (locational, ritual, transactional, and emotional) and otherworldly formations, including protests and counter-representations (Daniel 1984; Khare 1983a; 1984; Madan 1987b; Raheja 1988; and Trawick 1990).

Such exercises on classifications relate to mine, allowing me to extend my two previous exercises on Indian cultural classifications.[3] The first, 'the one and the many', proposed that philosophical ideals, logical rules, symbolic interpretations, and life experiences, all together, made up Hindu classifications (Khare 1983a). The second exercise first explicated a range of philosophical, textual, and mythological formulations and then presented their practical reformulations and social use to convey how Hindu classifications work in life by becoming a contextually sensitive 'multiform'—axiomatic, performative, and judgmental—reasoning (Khare 1993c). The present attempt extends the same interpretive argument one more step, showing how Hindu classifiers and their multiform reasoning[4] today face social criticisms, disputation, and counter-representation from within, and from without.

But in an anthropological account of contemporary India, it is equally important that one neither reads too little or too much into all sorts of social conflicts or the long-standing civilizational and institutional structures. Given such a caution, one could look for a spectrum of moral positions and social consensus that people follow in life. Under these conditions, the dominant reasoning, whether attacked or supported, is still that of the highly varied learned, vernacular, and 'popular' Hindu culture. Popular cultural commentaries now widely discuss the strengths and weaknesses of this dominant system.[5]

With appropriate examples (including some anomalies), dispersed across the learned and popular cultural domains, we will see the roles the contesting cultural 'emplotments' play in challenging aspects of Hindu cultural reasoning.[6] But we start the exercise by reminding ourselves that the Indian grounds for making or not making distinctions differ from those of modern Western culture, where such dichotomies as ideals and practice, reason and emotion, mind and body, and individual and collective, structure the argument. In anthropological terms, Indian distinctions play on both what Evens (1983: 121–23) calls 'orthodox logic' and the 'cultural logic'.[7] Compared to recent structuralist and post-structuralist debates (Lévi–Strauss 1966; Manganaro 1990b; and Sahlins 1976; 1995), people in India pursue a cultural reasoning that simultaneously problematizes their conflicted social reality as well as some long-standing cultural and civilizational verities. Considered comparatively, in one view (Dumont 1980, had posited),

India provided a needed 'external' critique to modern Western reasoning.

At the local level, ethnography becomes a crucial tool for conducting and grounding such an exercise. It helps ascertain what (and how) Indians (Hindus and non-Hindus) think and do as they live their lives, and what (and how) some modern writers, including anthropologists, historians, and social commentators, reason about such entangled subjects as social dissent against caste and gender rules, and against religious violence and the questionable uses of power by the modern state. Thanks to mass media communication, critical social conflicts, as we will see, today quickly travel back and forth between urban localities, regions, and the country.

Anthropologists (and historical anthropologists) engaged in studying such events quickly realize that their own cultural locations and social involvement cannot but frame their writing and analysis, including an explication of theoretically overarching perspectives. They also realize that they must grapple with changing power equations of cultural otherness, including the different languages of accountability available (e.g., colonial, modern, national, and subaltern) and their moral and political dilemmas (e.g., for remarks on domination, social violence, and Indian nationalism, see Chatterjee 1994: 1–49; Pandey 1994). As the violent conflicts of power and domination attract ever more attention, investigators concern themselves with wide-ranging issues: the reason and unreason behind violence; the documentation of victims, perpetrators and the ethos of 'victimage' to learn the 'truth'; morality and the management of 'everyday violence'; and the roles of religion, colonial history and the state power behind what are called the 'law and order issues' (on India, see Veena Das 1990b: 345–98; Pandey 1990: 188–221; and Spencer 1992; and for a comparative account of social violence and the state in Europe, see della Porta 1995).

Anthropologists often contribute to such discussions by showing that dissent, violence, and social dominance cannot be adequately understood through simple ideological dichotomies, essentialized traditions, or historical vantage points limited to specific aspects. Instead, a people's social past and present must be treated as an interrelated cultural continuum, radiating a range of people's social values, hopes, failures, and concerns. Win or lose, they try again, accepting what is, and claiming what is necessary and what seems just and fair (for a wide-ranging and successful study of this kind on Brazil, see Scheper–Hughes 1992).[8] Modern technology, anthropologists note, also plays a culturally crucial but 'double-edged' (but still largely unexamined) role here vis-à-vis strong and weak traditions *and* nation-states. If it is often an ally of state power against 'social disorder', it is also now employed with significant effect by traditions and religions. Similarly, traditions and the modern state use for their countervailing goals not only modern mass-communication media but also medical technology, weapons of violence, and globalizing transportation of humans, commodities, and information (Chirot 1995; Robertson 1992).

II Contesting Emplotments and their Reasoning Patterns

Just as Hindu distinctions base themselves on distinct cultural ideals as well as specific social and temporal 'emplotments', giving us a better sense of the distinctive *forms* of Hindu reasoning, the 'alternative' cultural reasoning that challenges or controverts the dominant cultural system also develops its historically and culturally distinct emplotments.[9] Since such challenges to Hindu reasoning are today diverse, both from within and without, and since some are more elaborate than others, we will take a sociological perspective from a position where multiple cultural centers, margins, and alternative locations remain in mutual, practically evident, tension.

Dalit Cultural Logic

Current 'Dalit reasoning', especially as it is expressed in the recent Dalit social reform and political literature, illustrates an ideology under formation (see Bhagwan Das and Massey 1995).[10] For my purposes, Dalit publications from Lucknow or those closely related are particularly suitable, since they complement my field interviews and observations, often of some central reformers, writers, critics, editors, etc. Besides *Dalit Solidarity*, I will rely on certain issues of *Dalit Asia Today*, a Lucknow monthly Hindi magazine with an English name, and *Dalit Voice*, a major similar publication from Bangalore.[11]

Following the logic that to identify oneself better one must clearly identify one's social opponents and others, both publications converge on the crucial question: 'Who or what really are the caste Hindus, twice-born Hindus, and particularly Brahmans?' The current Dalit argument wants to establish how really politically unrepresentative, socially residual, and morally untenable the position of Brahmans and caste Hindus is. In this view, Indian traditions cannot be equated with (much less subordinated to) Hinduism, and least of all with Brahmanism. According to a recent 'activist scholarly' formulation, Dalit politics must (*a*) challenge 'the Aryan/Vedic/Sanskritic/Brahmanic core'; (*b*) spread this theme to all those exploited, weakened and marginalized by caste, including women, peasants, and tribals; and (*c*) mount a new concerted political and economic challenge for Dalits to (re)gain their rightful place in India (see Omvedt 1995: 87, 96).

More temperate Dalit arguments start with the question of how the dominant others (e.g., caste Hindus, rulers, national leaders, and governments) have historically subordinated Untouchables by variously naming and classifying them socially. But the Dalit goal now is to launch an authentic initiative to name and represent themselves accurately and fully within Indian history and polity (Bhagwan Das 1995; Massey 1995: 3–33).[12] In such a pursuit, to recall a list of derogatory or patronizing names is to justify one's moral right for accurate self-representation. Since the society has perpetually misnamed Untouchables, Bhagwan Das actually goes through a whole list of unacceptable popular or political names: 'Pariahs', 'Jamadars', 'Halalkhor', 'Menials', 'Depressed Classes', 'Scheduled Castes', including Gandhi's 'Harijans' (banned by the government for official use since 1978). The official term 'Scheduled Castes' is found least objectionable, while 'Dalit' wins increasing acceptance among urban Untouchables (Bhagwan Das 1995).[13]

The customary social classification of Dalits, however, remains caste-based, if regionally distinct and locally varied, reflecting the continuing problems of social divisions, economic dependence, and political disunity. For instance, as Bhagwan Das (1995: 41) notes, the official Scheduled Castes list between 1936 and 1950 expanded from 429 to 900, with many more still trying to get on the government roster. But their religious overlap (i.e., a pursuit of more than one religion in life), strikingly enough, obstructed their inclusion in the Scheduled Caste list, forcing many to declare that they belonged to only one religion. One's proclaimed religion thus had to meet the officially recognized criteria of 'total' religious differences among the Hindu, Sikh, Buddhist, Muslim, and Christian. A vestige from the last phases of British colonial rule, it ironically pushed people toward religious intolerance. To get government protection, a Buddhist, for example, had to proclaim that he did not practice any Hindu customs or worship any gods and goddesses. However, more political 'adjustments' followed after independence; for example, Untouchables in Punjab were counted with Sikhs, and in Maharashtra the converted Buddhists and 'Christians of Untouchable origin' were given government protection. But Untouchables were not attracted to the Muslims because of their caste structure and their 'general [social] backwardness', Bhagwan Das notes (1995).

But despite all such governmental need to 'list' Dalits in distinct single-caste and religious columns, and the Dalit reformers' efforts to overthrow caste distinctions, the Dalit reasoning in life continues to reflect caste-based social inclusion/exclusion, and feels the force of ritual–pollution-based social inequality and exploitation. Here we still find intact that ideological conflict between Dalits and caste Hindus that had prompted B.R. Ambedkar to argue for 'the annihilation of caste' as the only cure of the disease. 'Today every fifth man in India is an Untouchable of some kind or the other', says Bhagwan Das (1995: 46), while the social and material position of these Dalits, ever since Indian antiquity, has hardly changed. The British came and went but, in B.R. Ambedkar's words, they also faithfully preserved 'in the manner of the Chinese tailor who, when given an old coat as a pattern, produced with pride an exact replica, rents, patches and all' (quoted in Bhagwan Das 1995: 48). Bhagwan Das argues that, all the social (including Gandhian) reform and state support notwithstanding, between the end of the last century and the close of this one, the situation for Untouchables in remote rural areas has not improved much.

Building essentially on Ambedkar's critical formulations, Bhagwan Das reasons as follows:

1. 'A Hindu does not carry in mind only the fear of pollution but also the feeling of hostility and prejudice against a man or woman of Untouchable origin.'

234 ◀ Cultural Diversity and Social Discontent

2. Untouchability, as Ambedkar said in 1954, is 'a kind of disease of the Hindus ... it is a mental twist.... I do not know how my friend is going to untwist the twist which the Hindus have got for thousands of years unless they are all sent to some kind of hospital' (quoted in Bhagwan Das 1995: 53).
3. There is in India a conflict between the 'divine laws' and man-made laws, where the latter fail because the witnesses turn hostile, plaintiffs retreat out of fear, pressure, or greed, and the courts take years to decide.
4. The continuing internal casteism (e.g., Mahars being still with 12 and one-half castes and Chamars with more than 60) is the worst enemy of the Dalit. But, 'why do people cling to their castes? Caste, they know, divides them; caste weakens them.... Perhaps the only answer we can give is that caste gives them security ... [giving them a] feeling of belonging.... [Yet] the Dalit has to break the shackles of his slavery ... to get out of the cage....' (Bhagwan Das 1995: 69).
5. The solution lies with the Dalits in empowering themselves by directly electing their own representatives, while securing a proportionate representation in the executive. Such political power should (*a*) create a 'sweeper-less' society; (*b*) free the land-bonded labor in villages to establish, as Ambedkar had suggested, separate villages of Untouchables, with rights to till the land; (*c*) free Dalit women from social oppression, prostitution, and harassment, and (*d*) contain and control the 'atrocities', old and new, against Scheduled Castes and Tribes in different states.

The preceding two profiles of Dalit reasoning, one more moderate than the other, illustrate the increasing distance and differences between Dalit and Hindu cultural reasoning. Sociologically, these differences may still be 'included' within caste-based everyday life, but not without new political awareness and social self-assertion. Recent anthropological overviews, based on ethnographic studies from different regions of India, however, tend either to shy away from such changes in the name of institutional caste continuities (see Fuller 1992), or to explicate their full anthropological implications for contemporary India (Veena Das 1995). Either way, the current 'multiform' social reasoning appears throughout both the caste Hindu and Dalit communities while rooted in a larger civilizational ground, on the one hand,[14] and, on the other, grappling with increasing violent social conflicts. The recent violence between upper castes and Dalits only further tests—and erodes—customary cultural continuities. The answer to how long such continuities might last, may depend on what the two sides do to contain and counter the real causes of such conflicts.

The Muslim Paradox: Controlled Cultural Assimilation

As the largest minority in India (14 per cent of 934 million Indians),[15] Muslims, in certain ways, present a more ideologically contrasting but socially no less complicated cultural picture vis-à-vis the Hindu. In religious ideology and polar political rhetoric, the two become unambiguously distinct. Recently this was once again made evident when, for example, Syed Shahabuddin (1996: 297), a member of the Indian Parliament, wrote to the BJP leader (and Indian Prime Minister for the shortest duration) Atal Behari Vajpayee to take exception to Mr Vajpayee's characterization of Indians as those who 'do not limit [themselves] to one God or one Prophet or a single Book ... we believe in the equality of all religious faiths'. Shahabuddin rejoined, 'It appears to me that "we" does not represent all Indians because there are people among us who do limit themselves to one God or one Prophet or a single Book'. A little later on, Shahabuddin observes, 'All this implies articulation, perhaps unconsciously, as a leader or spokesman of the Hindu community and not as a leader of the Indian people'.[16]

When considering Muslim cultural reasoning in the India of the 1990s, a discussion of the 1992 Ayodhya temple–mosque riots becomes unavoidable. Though a subject of innumerable news accounts, citizen and government inquiry reports, and academic documentation and debates, my concern here is limited to a few sociological observations about any 'swing' in the local Hindu–Muslim reasoning and relationship before and after 6 December 1992, the day the Hindu *karsevaks* (literally 'doer of service' but effectively a militant brigade) demolished the Babri Mosque and went on a rampage afterward, looting and burning property and killing Muslims in Ayodhya (for further discussion, see Section IV).

Our present illustrative purposes are well served by a recent study, based on a series of 'field visits', independent opinion surveys and interviews with many Hindu and Muslim Ayodhya residents, with local accounts of the event (including people's experiences) both before and after the Mosque demolition (Nandy et al. 1995).[17]

For example, if one Munnu Mia (Ilias Ansar Hussain), 'a builder and a manager of Ram temple called Sunder Bhavan', represented the pre-riot Ayodhya, the 75-year-old Nawab Tahir Husain Sahib (with his over 300-year-old local ancestry), who was 'reduced to ashes' in front of his house during the *karsevak* rampage, spoke about another reality in pre-riot Ayodhya. Simultaneously, we also find a Sheetal who saves the lives of several of his neighbors like a hero but is 'dubbed a traitor' by Hindus (Nandy et al. 1995: 170–75, 199–200). In pre-1992 Ayodhya, we read that local Muslims, not unlike many other Indians, attributed all the trouble to politicians' battles for 'votes and notes', but after the riot, they saw a new and much deeper divide between the two communities. 'They are afraid and angry, many of them feel let down by the local Hindus', remark the authors (Nandy et al. 1995: 204). The residents of Sehnawa, a village nearby Ayodhya, worried about their safety and survival after the Ayodhya violence, since it was alleged to be the place of the Mosque's builder's (Mir Baqi) descendants (Nandy et al. 1995: 205–6). Even the small boys in Ayodhya were found talking about guns and fighting for survival 'like the Palestinians'. Such a picture leads the authors to remark:

The community at Ayodhya was always an imperfect one but it was a community all the same, whereas it has become now a place haunted by the private demons of two separated groups, fearful, suspicious and on guard. Hindu nationalism and its foot-soldiers have done their job (Nandy et al. 1995: 203).

Simultaneously, Muslim cultural reasoning in India, while recognizing such a sobering development, also faces the challenge of evolving an engaged social role for the community. It must neither dilute their distinct religious identity nor give up on the generations-old social cooperation with local Hindus and all other Indian communities. Sociologically, the issue concerns the question of minorities culturally integrating themselves in the larger society, but without losing their distinct religious and social identities. Muslims face the issue of 'controlled cultural assimilation' in several other nations. In China, for instance, Muslims constitute 12 per cent of the population, in Europe, 6.1 per cent, and in the Americas and Oceania, less than 2 per cent. The question before such Muslim communities is: 'How—and how far—does one absorb the majority culture, without losing one's either distinct religious identity or the practical effectiveness?' (Ahmed 1996: 333).

Although it may be a crucial question for the local and national Muslim communities (and the *ummah*), its relevance in India should be obvious to both Muslim and Hindu communities. In history, population distribution, politics and cultural influence, the two sides, in spite of the Ayodhya riot, remain so intertwined that any major challenge to one side also translates into a distinct challenge to the other. Thus even the traumatizing Ayodhya temple–mosque conflict, as succeeding local and national events show, has had declining public support and diminishing political 'vote and note' dividends. Politicians of all stripes know that Ayodhya is not a cost-free 'political trigger' any more for any party. But simultaneously, Indian Muslims, commensurate with their 'most visible minority status', feel the need to raise an alarm against, as well as integrate with the Hindu majority.

The preceding discussion of Dalit and Muslim cultural reasoning depicts only a segment of the prevailing cultural dynamics in contemporary India. Here Indian Dalits, Muslims, and Hindus, among others, routinely try to set the terms for an interdependent, practically working, Indian cultural and political identity. Thus, in social practice, despite all the distinct ideological oppositions and political pronouncements, cultural sharing and selective group and community interdependence make up daily life. Such practical social sharing and cooperation for everyday survival gets shaken (even disrupted for a period) whenever partisan political rhetoric translates into actual violence and the resulting social mistrust. At the height of a conflict, sharp, ideological divisions reappear, where each side may reiterate some self-evident (axiomatic) grounds for being opposed and inimical to the other side (e.g., karma and dharma for the Hindu, and the Prophet and the Koran for the Muslim). But the real social cost under such situations is increasing mutual suspicion; one routinely suspects the other side's motive and actions, whether it is for social inclusion or tolerance.[18]

But the Hindu, Muslim, and Dalit (along with smaller ethnic groups) must return to share socially as a fact of practical necessity. The three communities depend on one another for goods and services, while widely sharing some general customary social attitudes and practices due to their own structurally similar caste organizations. Politically, the three communities, despite their religious distinctness, occasional intolerant social behavior, communal violence and social suspicion, continue to try coalition politics toward a socially better, safe, and just life for their children.

We now turn our attention to a few popular social commentaries that help us explicate further how people from different communities, genders, and age groups today deal with the issues where religious ideals, social practice, and the modern state form a stressful triangle of inconsistent reasoning, practical difficulties, and social dilemmas. They are particularly useful to our discussion since they direct social criticism toward, blame or challenge the dominant Hindu ideas, ideals and practices as the pervasive social backdrop.

III Popular Commentaries on Modern Challenges

Given the continued strength of Indian castes, no one can miss the 'axiomatic reasoning' that such groups exemplify: The all-important caste status comes by birth. At the center of the Hindu formulation of the same reasoning is the powerful conceptual chain of karma—'womb'—rebirth (until a soul realizes liberation or the creation-cycle ends). The 'womb' here means many things—from simple birth of any creature to the female sex organ, feminine reproductive power, the goddess, and the karma–caste–rebirth complex. Quoting from my earlier work (Khare 1993c: 191–212), the womb, as a Hindu conceptual category, 'represents (a) the creation and a cycle of rebirth (saṃsāra), (b) a birth to experience one's accumulated past karmas (prārabdha), (c) a human birth to strive for one's spiritual uplift until liberated, (d) an opportunity to worship the divine, and (e) a chance to serve humankind (paropakāra)'.

But such normative meanings of 'womb' give little clue of the customary gender discrimination the majority of Hindus practice as soon as a girl is born (if not sooner, given the dubious new use of medical technology). The issue is of course related to the notions of a woman's bodily and ritual impurity and her consequent low status, costly marriage and lifelong social dependence. Again, while starting from their differing religious ideals, Hindus and Muslims, under caste practice, show similar attitudes toward women. A subject of vigorous modern criticism, let us see how some Hindi commentators take up the moral and social challenge the traditional ways explicitly or implicitly pose.

A clutch of Indian commentators, female and male, Hindu and Muslim, for example, recently wrote on the subject in Hindi in a book called *Striyon ke liye Jagah* (Place for Women), published for a series called 'Today's Issues'.[19] Relating to their own different social backgrounds and experiences, their discussions reflect, in an ethnographically welcome fashion, everyday social experiences and observations, highlighting, on the one hand, the social ironies, dilemmas, suffering and most of all *a continued subjugation of women by 'the womb'*, and, on the other, an open but ambiguous battle between Indian traditional and modern social forces.[20]

The following discussion of popular commentaries begins by illustrating the Hindu–Muslim overlap in women's discrimination in India, moves next to women's (including feminist) views of changing—or unchanging—Indian womanhood, to men's views on such changes, and finishes with what was termed as an 'alarming puzzle'. Each commentary reveals not only the cultural otherness of the Indian woman, but also a continued categorization of women as lifelong social dependents.

Shamsul Islam (1994: 65–71), a Delhi resident activist academic, dramatist, and journalist, finds that, despite bitter ideological confrontation between the Hindu and Muslim positions, they showed 'powerful similarity and unity' (*zabardast samanta aur ekata*) where women are concerned (Islam 1994: 70). Similarly, he highlights the hollowness of the modern Indian state and its penal code in not fulfilling the promises of women's equality, justice, and individual freedom. He argues that both Hindu and Islamic cultures, in their religious, mythological, and popular writings, continue to disregard, vilify, and downgrade women. Striking popular sayings ('a woman's intellect is in her heels' or 'she is the biggest cause of quarrels, and her real medicine is beating') reveal the same. The violence against, or even the death of, a woman still produces, he points out, little (or only ambiguous) response, 'when compared to a road accident by a motorist'.

The author finds the structure of traditional reasoning not only intact but actually reinforced and popularized by certain religious publications: 'There is a spate of books concerning women from both Hindu and Muslim publishing houses' (Islam 1994: 67). He regards them as a major source of perpetuating social domination and injustice against Indian women.[21]

The popularized Hindu tradition, for instance, still instructs that women, 'innately weak', need a male 'watchman' (*pahredar*) throughout their lives. On the division of paternal money and property, the main cause of family quarrels and enmity, women are advised to maintain their 'traditional disinterest' in such matters. Such an attitude helped them, the Hindu religious teachers argued, in upholding 'their dharma, purity and family roles', whether they were with their parents, husbands, or sons. Women were told, 'Money and the related materials are not of consequence [as far as you are concerned]. They are the matters of [male] transactions [*vyavahāra*]' (Islam 1994: 68, quoting the Hindu religious writer, Hanuman Prasad Poddar). Strikingly, on dowry, Shamsul Islam again quotes Poddar, 'In the [authoritative religious texts] there is provision only on giving a dowry, not on receiving it' (Islam 1994: 68). Such a formulation approves dowry-giving but apparently without its 'acceptance' or 'use'. This notion is indeed a socially unknown and impractical goal, regardless of its lofty idealism.

On the other hand, says the author, Islam regards women as 'agricultural soil', giving men full rights and control over 'its use' for procreation. It has such handbooks as 'The Rights of Husband and Wife' and 'Muslim Wife' to popularize its own ideology. Such literature, says the author, is as ideologically direct and easily available as the traditional Hindu's (Islam 1994: 69–70). For example: A woman 'must regard herself a slave (*ghulam*) and the husband her master (*aaqaa*). And suppose the master sometimes becomes violent, then one must endure the provider's violence (*annadata ki himsā*) with patience.' Again, as an anomaly for a secular and modern India, he notes that book hawkers openly sell such religious publications even within the precincts of the Indian Supreme Court. 'The reality is', he concludes, 'that to end this anomaly not one but hundreds of Taslima Nasrins will have to be born on this Indian subcontinent' (Islam 1994: 71).[22]

Stark social behavioral expectations, differences and dividers mark a woman's world all her life, notes another woman journalist, writing in an autobiographical mode. Gender discrimination starts very early indeed in India: 'My brothers' schools, their education, their sports, and convenience—all allured me. [But they were not for me.] I felt, I do not count, definitely not in comparison to my brothers' (Vajpai 1994: 11). But, as a 10-year-old girl, she was expected to achieve much more—'something extra'—with far less, and from within a highly restricted social life. A young girl learns very early to decipher and cope with this traditional Hindu social calculus. With her preferences repeatedly overruled in education, she, a bright student, sighs by the time she reaches high school: 'No decision of this life is my own' (Vajpai 1994: 9–20).

A male author corroborates the Indian women's dependent world-view by another strikingly simple example: 'There would hardly be any reader reading this article who has seen any woman lying [alone] on a bench in a park'. In north India, it would still be impossible to see a girl strolling alone in a public park. 'When I recall this way I still see many scenes of my childhood's little town replicated [right here] in Delhi.... [But] I could think only years later that how cruel mockery this was of girls' lives, that they were not free to experience the routine happiness of childhood' (Krishna Kumar 1994: 114–18, 116).

Another woman author, Sumita (1994: 154–57), more hopeful of the eventual beneficial impact of modern forces, searches for a 'new grammar of relationships'. The woman freed from the house searches for a new social configuration, and such a quest, argues Sumita [a Germaine–Greer-citing Hindi author], is 'really not against man, [it is only] against the situation' (1994: 154). Her strategy is to neutralize the traditional male opposition without frontally attacking it. She reminds her reader that women's-rights struggles often fizzle out when, as the Western feminist movement knows, men feel threatened and close ranks in defense. The modern reasoning that brought women out of the house, often against men's wishes, had also yielded only mixed results. Men at work become her competitors and opponents, increasing her loneliness and social and mental stress. To Sumita, 'The [working] woman has increasingly become isolated within the family, and the main reason, to an extent, is man's ego' (1994: 156). The move toward modernity thus has its own costs and women must be prepared to accept them largely on their own.

But a male writer (Shukla 1994: 149–53) here finds the creativity of the recent Indian culture reassuring. Some recent prominent Indian women (e.g., Kiran Bedi, Medha Patekar, Sonal Mansingh, Madhvi Mudgal, and Madhu Kishwar) already show how to change at their own pace, and influence the social surrounding in their favor, largely outside 'of the feminist's protest marches'. And he adds, '...we simply want to say that if there is now a counter-current [of woman's reform] starting to flow, we should not regard it simply as a result of some Western magic'. A woman, surveying the lives of her grandmother and aunts, on the other hand, wants to locate (and justify) for her daughter a 'cost-free balance' between the traditional and modern forces affecting Indian women (Saravgi 1994: 142–48).

Yet, despite the wish for a favorable social outcome of modern changes, Kathkali Bagchi and Mini Philip (1994) raise the darkest question: 'Why are the women disappearing [from India]?' The continuing decline in the women's ratio in Indian population (from 972 per 1,000 men in 1901 to 929 in 1991) 'is a hard social fact'. Any study of Indian women's social position cannot ignore such information. Rajkishore, editor of *Place for Women*, blames the situation (as I have also discussed it elsewhere; see Chapter 7) on 'the murderous customs and despicable selfishness' of modern medicine (since the ultrasound and amniocentesis increased the abortion of female foetus). Increasing rape is another striking indicator of the continued decline in Indian women's position. If such a situation strongly underscores a continuing custom-bound interpretation of the traditional Hindu preferences (including those for begetting a son), it remains so after 50 years of political power and legal reform by the Indian state. The condition raises a sobering question for Indian protagonists of both traditional and modern values. Neither side can be held blameless. Such premeditated violence as female infanticide has to have many hidden social allies, violent gender interactions, cold practical necessities, and several 'triggering' advisors, actors, and events. There is no simple blame game available for such practices.

In anthropological terms, the preceding commentaries show how—and why—'the womb' still remains an all-too-powerful

Indian (and not only a Hindu or Dalit) cultural paradigm. Its social power remains practically unchallenged for the Hindus, since all the crucial supporting notions are still in place—karma, 'seed', 'blood', body, purity, dharma, and rebirth (see Khare 1993c). A Hindu female, whether a foetus, an infant or a woman, finds social odds quickly compounding against her as men, caste order, and the divine surround and dominate her. In such matters of gender, Dalits socially differ from caste Hindus in giving relatively more social freedom to their women. Yet they (and even the radical Buddhist reformers) tend to fall within the same basic karma–womb–rebirth paradigm, with male domination of women in moral and material matters (for a view of the debate between Hindu and Dalit Buddhist thinkers, including Ambedkar, see Jigyasu 1969). Though guided by Islamic laws, Muslims, as already indicated, in social life also end up producing a similar social situation for their women. Even a Westernized secular Indian is seldom entirely free of such social influences.

IV Judgmatic Reasoning: Different Locations

Despite what the preceding discussion of the woman's position suggests, situations in contemporary India put people in those social situations where they must make a judgment, accepting its costs and consequences. This is true for all Indians, whether Hindus, Muslims, or others. They increasingly encounter social and emotional conditions which test their own sense of what is morally right, unjust, or wrong. Such decisions have to be a part of the social reality which, on the one hand, is overwhelmed by multiple social divisions and selfish politics, and, on the other, demands everyday cultural sharing under a resilient common and practical sense for social survival. If the 'unprincipled' politics of power and patronage now brings ordinary Indians to despair, their only reliable daily guide is their own intuitively shared sense of right and wrong for social survival. Such moral, social, and practical pressures also result in what I have elsewhere termed as 'temporization' (tāl-matol; see Introduction) among Indians. It includes a conscious decision to postpone, hedge or hide one's decision, or to decide to remain undecided until a strategic future time. People often express ambivalence and dilemma when a matter is too complicated or risky to decide; it is usually when they can neither totally accept nor reject some condition, action, or meaning.

In the following sections, I discuss different faces of such Indian judgmatic reasoning in different situations. First, I will briefly remark on the ways upper-caste Hindus, Dalits, and Muslims now challenge the status quo and demand recognition from one another in daily life and under major violent crises. Next, we will see how anthropologists, modern commentators, and journalists approach and explicate critical violent events. This way we will get the picture from both sides—those studied and those who study or comment on Indian social situations, while evaluating their assumptions and views on the dominant Hindu—and Indian—world.

Social Discrimination to Communal Violence

Though more systematic ethnography is needed than I currently have available to me on the upper-caste Hindus, Dalits, and Muslims from Lucknow, there is enough with me to make some preliminary remarks and observations on the judgmatic reasoning of some major castes and communities. For instance, during the 1990, all the three communities in a large city tend to remark about the social pressure they feel from each other for recognizing each others' interests. The upper castes cannot assume unquestioned social dominance any more; rather, they must remain 'on guard', particularly, as my informants would say, 'in the Mandal-Commission India'. Some politically active upper-caste Hindu informants had very sharp comments on the point. For example:

- 'The Mandal reservation policy and its threats sowed the seeds of the Ayodhya incident (*Ayodhya kand*).'
- 'You cannot snatch bread from one's mouth, give it to another, and call it justice. You simply must have more to give before doing so.'
- 'If the Ayodhya riots scared Muslims, the Mandal Commission, several years before, scared Hindus. What were we to do? Just sit and let our children immolate themselves on the street?'
- 'India will be a land where nobody will get things free, whether Dalits or us or Muslims. Everybody will get only what one deserves after hard work.'

Muslims and Dalits, in turn, also know that they can cry wolf only so often at the slightest pretext to make the government or politicians come to their rescue. Politically, however, the charges and counter-charges of favoritism or unjust discrimination are a part of daily social life. One side may charge the other of outright political persecution, as, for example, *Dalit Asia Today* (December 1994: 9), had recently declared in a headline: 'Dalit Bureaucracy a Target of Upper Caste Bureaucracy'. In response, those in power, whether upper castes, Dalits or Muslims, must shield themselves against any such charges, or rebut them. Often, therefore, these days one has to distinguish the reasoning for the public arena from that of private (caste and family) life.

Within the public arena, which mostly means the political, people and their leaders make a further distinction among the domains of public speeches, the formal office, and smaller and informal 'drawing room' or private back-room conclaves. The first two represent the 'public face' of political and administrative work while the third concerns the hidden and suspect dealings, including clandestine (*luka-chipi*) caste and communal alliances and discrimination. Whenever someone breaks the secret informal pact or understanding, the supporters become opponents and they complain of 'overt' (*khullamkhulla*) discrimination of favoritism. All Indian communities now know these as the facts of everyday life, and thus try to adapt to them. As is often popularly recognized, including by my field informants, those who cannot change this way lose and suffer. Sociologically, this is the 'other—practical—side' of all the religious principles and political ideologies that varied Indian castes and communities (Hindu, Dalit, Sikh, Muslim, etc.) must work with. But equally important, though often missed or bypassed in social science studies, people of different communities, when necessary (including in national elections), 'see through' such practical social divisions, exploitative conclaves and differences to maintain a sense of larger moral consciousness and emotional togetherness. In a major social crisis or external political threat, it gives the content and form to regional or Indian nationality and nationalism (i.e., the notion of *desh*, *vatan*, *rashtra*, etc.). Even ordinary illiterate people in a city like Lucknow now carry a vague sense of nation and nationalism while struggling to meet daily practical interests (i.e., of work, wages, schools, and *sarkar* or government).

Though the Hindu–Muslim and Hindu–Sikh communal violence has recently tested as well as sharpened such a sense, people exercise their moral and practical judgment before openly blaming an opponent, or in deciding to postpone or hide it. As reports repeatedly show, local people well know who is to blame most for the harm, atrocities, and injustice caused, and also know those who had saved the lives of members of the opposed community. The majority, either way, tends to return to a socially moderate and fair position, even if the past painful memories remain hard to forget.[23] The 1992 Ayodhya violence had clearly left some such wounds and scars on the public memory: '[Muslims of Ayodhya] are now convinced that, in at least some cases, their neighbors have been willing partners in the atrocities committed against them. It is this sense of betrayal rather than the death of more than a thousand people in riots all over India after December 6 that seems to occupy their mind' (Nandy et al. 1995: 204).

However, the people, particularly victims, also know that as the stakes in such violence increase, they cannot let the conflicts run their lives. To survive in a practical world, they must weigh their past painful memories against what their daily life demands of them in order to survive. Willingly or unwillingly, they learn to forgive and/or forget, just to live. All such actions reflect a necessity to 'fine tune' their judgmatic reasoning (i.e., their capacity for reaching, balancing, recovering judicious and fair positions in life).

On the other hand, with repeated communal violence, and especially when perpetrators go unpunished, these coping devices of victims undergo severe strain and demoralization. The deeply-felt religious and traditional animosities quickly build up, and the suffering increases under unjust political domination and exploitation at the hands of those considered guilty. As recent historiography tells us, such perpetrating agents of dominance and violence deeply color the social perception, memory, documentation, and politics of the whole society. Even more generally, those dominant set the rules of writing and representation, while victims and the weak wait to be written about. Most archives, museums, memorials, and legal judgments most often record and extend the same storyline, until, as a historian recently remarked, historical reading and writing are done 'at variance' (see Amin 1995; also Pandey 1990).[24]

The Anthropologist's Stance

When anthropologists narrate and explicate a violent event from the victim's position, they face the general human issue of how to judge and relate with such human experiences vis-à-vis their own self-location and circumstance. Their judgmatic reasoning, often standing behind the screen of scholarly distance, informs their writing and representation. However, when violent events hit home, even those near and dear, the anthropologist's human vulnerability surfaces. This is as it should be. Some recent events of Indian communal violence, especially the Delhi violence against Sikhs, the Bhopal gas disaster, and the Ayodhya conflict confronted some Indian anthropologists with a similar situation (e.g., Das 1990b; Khare 1987b; see also Chapter 7 of this book; Dube 1994, see below).

An example of how an anthropologist may approach a recent major episode of Indian violence appears in a short but insightful essay by Professor S.C. Dube (1994: 56–62), written for a publication in Hindi called 'Ayodhya and Afterwards' (*Ayodhya aur ussey aagey*). He probed the Indian 'national future' by sketching three possible post-Ayodhya scenarios, while asking himself whether India will still have a government of a secular majority, or a government sharing regional power with the Bhartiya Janata Party (BJP), or a government heavily dependent on coalition. Considered against the actual subsequent political developments, Dube's remarks have proved to be strikingly on target. The succeeding Indian governments have already enacted his last two scenarios, with all the entailed social and political costs. But Dube, showing his analytical balance, did not condemn outright the possibility of a BJP government as totally inadmissible or unacceptable. Instead, he kept an open mind on the subject. But for the other contributors to the same volume, such an option was simply unmentionable, since it contradicted modern secularism.

Veena Das (1990b; 1995; 1996) is another anthropologist who has been writing with acuity on Indian violence and its victims (particularly women). Her comments on the Ayodhya temple–mosque dispute essentially share, in my view, Professor Dube's 'balanced' cultural sensibilities, although she more directly engages herself with the contesting languages Hindu and Muslim religious traditions, modern intellectuals, and the Indian state generate, underscoring 'a destruction of certainty as the only condition for the production of knowledge about Indian society' (1995: 54). She finds the Ayodhya conflict showing how Hinduism, community, the nation-state, minorities, and secularism 'juxtaposed as alterities' to one another, with many open-ended, still-forming social messages (Veena Das 1995: 41–47).

On the larger issue of violence from the victim's position, Veena Das (1990b: 345–98; 1996: 67–91) focuses on the victim-based experience and meaning of violence, including those living 'at the limits of human endurance'. Given the victim-selecting nature of Indian communal violence, she explicates the reasons why writing about it and its victims cannot be easy. Victims' experiences require, as I argue elsewhere (see Chapters 5 and 7), that we must be able to recognize our own locational biases and reset our 'normal' sensorial and experiential thresholds. Only thus can one better hear the victim's voice and story and can decipher the surrounding culture of victimization. Writing in 1996, Das plumbs the subject with greater acuity, moving away from her 1990 efforts to intellectually clothe violence somehow by varied sociological theorizations (Veena Das 1990b: 345–98).[25]

In 1996, she opens her argument by saying:

> In repeatedly trying to write the meaning(s) of violence against women in Indian society, I find that the languages of pain through which social sciences could gaze at, touch, or become textual bodies on which this pain is written often elude me.

And she remarks in conclusion: 'In the register of the imaginary, the pain of the other not only asks for a home in language but also seeks a home in the body' (Veena Das 1996: 67, 88). Such sensitivity, much more than empathy, has its own trajectory of development and expression once an investigator finds a way to tune into the ever-shifting narration and meaning of the victim.[26] At such a point, the victim and the listener, once sufficiently in tune with each other, jointly enter a shared domain of aesthetics, judgmatic reasoning, and shared expressions. The usual intellectual scaffolds, favorite theoretical filters, and supportive disciplinary canons unobtrusively recede to let humanness enrich communication. It becomes unavoidable since the listener, attentive to the victim's sensoria and self-location vis-à-vis his/her own, discovers the limits of scholarly turns of images, tropes, and meanings.

A similar victim-based study of the 1992 Ayodhya violence is in order, where the cultural history of victimization and violent ethos is dealt with much more inclusively than by selected victims of only the two major (Hindu and Muslim) local communities. With the continuing regional, national, and international repercussions, the Ayodhya conflict and the resulting episodes of counter-violence interweave a much larger tapestry of historical, political, and socio-psychological forces. Its victims provide us with one side of the story, while the actual 'perpetrators' of violence and their world bring in another, just as the local Ayodhya-resident 'spectators' (from religious heads to ordinary persons on the street) would have theirs. In sociological language, these narrative domains may also help translate violence-prone social and political circumstances and the 'crowd behavior', along with surging symbols of threat, aggression, and fear, on the one hand, and of state inaction, on the other. Here a social scientist, properly armed with scholarly distance, may also be now as inquisitive to learn from 'the voices of the *perpetrators* of violence' as from the victims (Spencer 1992: 261–79).

A Journalist's Position

As I have done before, I again juxtapose a social scientist's quest for 'what had actually happened' with that of a journalist. The purpose in doing so is to underscore the significance of the 'framing' each engages in while searching for an answer to the same question. In India, communal violence particularly attracts diverse interpretations. An Indian journalist, M.J. Akbar (1991), approached a range of Indian social violence from his personal and professional standpoint. His comments reflect his graphic on-the-spot 'experiences and investigations'. Expressing open disgust for the warring Hindus and Muslims, and writing without any claim of social science objectivity, he takes to task all those local and state agencies who mistreated the victims, mismanaged the investigations, and let the cruelty, injustice, and neglect linger years afterwards. He describes *his* 'standard' approach to a scene of communal violence this way:

One prepares. Of course, one prepares. There is a certain mental drill which one goes through while traveling toward a communal riot. One must be normal. There is now a spectrum of familiar expectation.... There will be dead bodies, with ants crawling over them, sometimes with the filth of a gutter embalming the corpse, sometimes placed surgically beside each other in the stench of a filthy morgue. Train yourself to get used to it. Train yourself to hear the bitter accusations.... When you get down to the business of the actual business of reporting and writing these conversations, you sift and trim. All that is normal (Akbar 1991: 160).

Akbar reasons as follows while grappling with the still unfolding violence in the Ayodhya temple–mosque dispute:

Death has been an instrument of politics through every age of history.... When the target is power, the last vestiges of human emotion, compassion, are the first to be destroyed.

And again:

Religion is the privilege of human beings. Beasts do not belong to any religion. Murderers of children do not represent any faith, they are manifestations of deep and sordid evil that lies in some dark cesspool of the human psyche, turning men into maniacs for the while that this mood seizes control of human behavior (Akbar 1991: 159, 166).

How does one make anthropological sense of Indian communal violence, captured above in a range of frames of description, narration, and analysis? Accounts of such violence in India still all too clearly reflect analysts' preferred interpretive locations, including their analytical biases and blindspots. For example, if some find Indian traditions unjustifiably held accountable for a violence that the colonial divide-and-rule policies accentuated (Nandy 1990: 69–93), others argue that one should not regard British colonialism (and hence modernity) 'as the source of all political ills' (Spencer 1992: 278)

V Whither Hindu Reasoning: A Challenging Mistrust

In sociological and historical terms, Hindu reasoning today faces major challenges from several different directions, even as it might socially adapt as well as occasionally reassert itself. The first major challenge arises as the customary, religious, or traditional domains of unquestioned certainty and authority face erosion of social consensus. The traditional Hindu approach to women's status, for example, clearly faces social opposition and resistance when the issues of female infanticide, girl neglect, and dowry deaths are concerned. The second threat appears as upper-caste Hindus, Dalits, and Muslims enter into new prolonged violent conflicts for political power and dominance, challenging their traditional as well as modern democratic ways of shared existence. The more they do so, the more they distrust each other's motives, methods, and goals. The third challenge was most directly manifest during and after the 1992 Ayodhya riots. Much has been written but far more still remains anthropologically uninvestigated and unknown. Beyond and beneath the radar of the politicians, its paradigmatic implications are still unfolding for the Indian society and polity (justifying our repeated discussion of the issue).

Though still under formation and with uncertain social consequences, increasing social conflicts encourage polar ideological positions. To illustrate both the pro-Hindu and anti-Hindu positions, I conclude here by briefly alluding to at least one example from each side.

Those championing the cause of Dalits from the political left castigate *Hindutva* (now often meaning 'militant Hinduism' or 'Hindu nationalism'). They render Hindu traditions 'unapproachable', and want to banish any serious consideration of them from the Dalit discourse. Here the Nehruvian and Gandhian notions of the 'Indian' also become highly suspect, since these reformist versions implicitly identify '"Hindu" with "Bhartiya", [and] Hinduism with the tradition of India' (Omvedt 1995: 4). Omvedt further remarks:

> The dalit movement … has in recent times brought forward most strongly this ideological challenge, this contesting of Hinduism. Indeed the impetus to challenge the hegemony and the *validity* of Hinduism is part of the very logic of dalit politics (Omvedt 1995: 5).

In contrast, let us examine the Hindu nationalist position. Sud-heendra Kulkarni, a newspaper critic and commentator, recently bemoaned the silence of English-language media on the first death anniversary of the erstwhile chief of the Rashtriya Swayam-sevak Sangh (RSS), Balasaheb Deoras. Correcting the imbalance, Kulkarni published his piece in *The Pioneer*, an English daily, highlighting Deoras' lifelong concern with promoting *samarasatā* (translated as 'harmony') within Hindu society. In Kulkarni's words: 'Just one sentence of Deoras—"If untouchability is not a crime, then nothing in this world is a crime"—should suffice to show the intensity of his concern for social reform in the Hindu society.' While admitting that Hindus still had a long way to go, he argues that the RSS had begun 'a serious and honest re-appraisal of [Dr B.R.] Ambedkar. The process has progressed so far that, to-day, the RSS considers the great champion of social justice to be *prataḥsmaraṇīya* (worthy of being reverentially remembered every morning)' (Kulkarni 1996: 6).

In today's political debate, Kulkarni and Omvedt would clearly represent two opposite poles that distrust and dispute each side's motive, historical, and sociological assumptions, and argument and evidence. Their languages of representation, the messengers and the messages contrast. To a Dalit protagonist, the RSS position engages verily in euphemisms and symbolic gestures, underesti-mating the gathering (and hardening) politics of Dalit challenge.[27] The RSS gesture responding to such a threat, for example, still fol-lows what a Hindi writer recently succinctly characterized as the Hindu's usual approach to opposition, 'You either capture [the opposed forces] or digest [them]; or alternatively, defang them by disregard or worship' (Keshari 1994: 75, 72–76). The Dalit side, however, claims to be all too familiar with such strategies, limiting their effectiveness.

Such a polarization poses new political and social challenges to Hindu reasoning, especially for continuing its practices of social exclusion and control in the name of dharma. These also weaken the customarily intuitive and commonsensical cultural resilience of the ordinary Hindu, increasing social mistrust among victim-ized castes and other religious communities. Contemporary India amply betrays such an ethos. However, we are in a social phase in which India still ultimately relies on the massive majority of or-dinary Indians who, with 'cussed' cultural resilience, everyday morality, and practical common sense, combat mounting social mistrust as much as they can. But it can only be a losing battle if the social inequalities and unjust social suppression and exploitation continue unabated. This much was repeatedly clear to my groups of informants and discussants in Lucknow during the summer of 1995. They emphasized another point: Ordinary Indians, men and women, do *not* view every aspect of social life as a tussle of (and for) power and dominance. They 'depoliticize' the surrounding violence, and tackle it locally by helping and consoling the victims. They find, after a cooling period, moral and religious grounds to forgive and forget, to let regular life slowly overcome the feelings of trauma, suffering, and revenge. Their success varies, but they know how to suffer patiently and recover without rancor. 'It is a way of everyday Indian life,' as most of my Lucknow informants—upper-caste Hindu, Dalit, and Muslims—emphasized.

Though these ordinary Indians (men and women) still perform an enormous balancing act in India (compensating for their leaders' and elite's many petty foibles and follies), they no longer dismiss the seriousness of major social conflicts and partisan political exploitation of people's religious faiths, overarching mythic reality, memory, and customary moral–ritual complexes. Social conflicts are becoming too persistent and sharp to let the nebulous Hindu culture 'digest', 'disregard', or 'worship' the opposed quickly enough. The *realpolitik* of caste coalitions now clashes with the gathering 'anti-caste' Dalit movement and anti-Hindu Muslim politics (see Omvedt 1994; 1995). The post-Ambedkar anti-caste Dalit movement, not averse to cooperating with Muslims for political gains, makes the Hindu/Indian identity (not Hindu–Muslim conflicts) its central battleground.

In Dalit ideology, Hindus have only a hollow moral–cultural core and an oppressive–exploitative Brahmanic, patrilineal social order, with little justifiable claim to a broad and pluralistic historical identity of pan-Indian proportions (Omvedt 1995: 94–103). Such a cultural ideology works by proposing new ethnic divisions and subdivisions and their transient political coalitions within its own community, and among others. Yet an overall moral sense of the just and the unjust concerns all the Indian communities, and whenever injustice mounts, there also appears a darkening shadow of moral and social mistrust, as we saw with the Ayodhya violence.[28]

There is another change. Today traditions, Hindu and non-Hindu, do not automatically recede before modernity; they dig in their heels by issue and oppose one another and the constraining nation-state to reassert their moral authority. In evidence, we encounter new and unfamiliar political rhetoric. Thus if the RSS euphemistically renders Dr B.R. Ambedkar *prataḥsmarṇīya* (worthy of being recalled in the morning) as a gesture of 'genuine reform', then an erstwhile state chief minister (Mayawati) is found making derogatory remarks against Mahatma Gandhi within the state legislature, and a Dalit folk poet cries in rage, 'We will burn, but we will light the earth!' (Zelliot 1996: 286).

But, to put things in perspective, India nevertheless remains a civilization much more inclusive than all these contemporary predicaments suggest. At its heart is the vast Indian (Hindu and non-Hindu) majority that still lives by that whole range of 'multi-form' reasoning that still manages through all the different pressures of cultural diversity and discord (Khare 1993c). India's vast reservoirs of myths, local pasts, and a workaday yet caring social life are still shaped by such a reasoning. It still conjures up hope when injustices weigh India down. Such reasoning does not find that diversity and multiplicity just have only one solution—the violent politics of counter-exclusion and annihilation of opposition. There is also that distinct way which my Lucknow informants insisted on, in which life is *not* for always seeing everything only in political and power terms.

So even as we outdate Manu, criticize Gandhi, find fault with Nehruvian socialism, and rediscover Jotiba Phule and B.R. Ambedkar for a socially inclusive society, we find a generally shared thread running through them that sees India as a culturally deeply grounded civilization. It is undoubtedly internally conflicted, even sometimes with overwhelming violence, but not without that majority that defies simple pictures of both violence and non-violence, disorder and order, and injustice and justice. But foremost, as the educated Indians know and suffering Indians demand, it has to forge a genuinely just social order. There is no other way.

≺ NOTES

1. For further discussion of this issue and on the definitional politics of the term 'Hindu', see the Introduction.

2. This anthropological view of Indian culture stresses actual and active cultural similarities and differences in people's daily lives, including various extant religious and ethnic conflicts. If the communities, otherwise socially sharing, tend to pull away under religious or communal violence, then they also most often revert to their 'normal life'. But as the politics of Hindu and non-Hindu distinction intensifies, the question 'who is a Hindu' gains importance. Those non-Hindu (besides Muslims, Christians, tribals, etc.) may now call themselves Sikhs, Dalits, non-caste Hindus, or 'the Hindus opposed to the twice-born castes', and so on.

3. Though minority politics now objects when one means 'Indian' by the term 'Hindu', our reference here is primarily cultural, stressing shared cultural sensibilities and social practices among both Hindus and 'non-Hindus'.

4. In popular culture, if 'reason' glosses for such Sanskrit, Hindi and Urdu terms like *tarka*, *yukti*, and *dalila*, it also refers to *hetu* and *kāraṇa* of the learned. The term *tarka* includes such meanings as supposition, speculation, discussion, wish, desire, and even free-thinking (Apte 1965: 470). In everyday life, 'reason' and 'reasoning' also reflect, let us not forget, knowledge as well as contention, including debate and argumentation (*bahas*) and quarrel (*larai*).

5. For an anthropologist, 'popular cultural commentaries', once written and published, become a part of the documentary social data. To an ethnographer, if these commentaries concern some ongoing social events, they remain a part of people's open-ended oral history and social memory. Since such documents and social memories comment on everyday social life and its debates, they help capture people's different cultural locations.

   An ethnographer may also sometimes find it useful to take the published scholarly commentaries to his/her field for further commentary by informants. This may provide another reading of a major regional or national issue, as with the Deorala Sati case and the Ayodhya temple–mosque violence. For a generally similar approach to popular writings, see Nandy (1995a).

6. See note 9 below for my use of this concept from narrative history.

7. As I have noted earlier (Khare 1993c), the Hindu cultural logic admits much more than formal logic, including alternative postulations, debates, and dissent, with room for intuition, experience, and insight for augmenting (or in certain schools overruling) 'the logical' (e.g., Kunjunni Raja 1963; for an overview, Staal 1988: 1–56).

8. Such a discussion also helps anthropology better review its disciplinary 'canons' and conundrums, particularly those grounded in relativism, holism, and empirical studies of the social order. Reflecting a need to discuss such matters, the American Ethnological Society, for example, decided to hold its 1997 annual meetings on 'Anthropology and the Canon', perhaps as a corrective step after postmodern self-doubts.

9. I retain here the notion of 'emplotment' from Hayden White (1978: 83; for an anthropological use, see Khare 1993c). The concept helps me emphasize the social contingency that society and history inevitably retain by their 'emplot-

ments' or 'encodation' of facts and knowledge. Here, the classical Indian notion that true knowledge comes only from an established tradition (*parampara*) is juxtaposed with counter-claims. My present usage also emphasizes the point that karmas, destiny, and the divine not only introduce multiple—seen and unseen—emplotments, but that they also, in practice, include dealing with ambiguity, irony, and sometimes even dissent and protest.

10. For two recent comprehensive statements on the Dalit position, justifying largely Amedkerite cultural and historical emplotments, see Das and Massey (1995: 3–93). However, James Massey, representing The Indian Society for Promoting Christian Knowledge (ISPCK), is not without his own proselitizing agenda.

11. The magazine, it seems, changes its name from time to time. In 1994, for example, it was known as *Dalit Asia Today* but in June 1995 it was *Dalit Liberation Today*. It is published by a reform-minded government officer currently with the Indian Administrative (Police) Service.

From Bangalore, on the other hand, appears *Dalit Voice: The Voice of the Persecuted Nationalities Denied Human Rights*, edited and published by V.T. Rajshekhar in six editions with a circulation of several thousand copies. For recent international coverage of its viewpoint, see Cooper (1996: A16).

12. I will increasingly switch to 'Dalit' in this discussion. Untouchables increasingly prefer to clearly juxtapose themselves with both Hindus and Hindu culture. However, some Lucknow reformers felt that 'Dalit' (a historical, socioeconomic, and political label for all those oppressed) reflected more the 'left-wing' political agenda, diluting their long moral and civilizational battle against caste Hindus.

13. The credit for popularizing 'Dalit' as a term goes to the more radical 'Dalit Panthers' of Maharashtra. For these and other related points on the name, see Bhagwan Das (1995: 34–93).

The following discussion, among other sources, is based on Bhagwan Das' article, since it broadly gives cultural and historical content to what I here call 'Dalit cultural reasoning'.

14. My reference point here is to civilizational time and space. Underneath all the conflicting political and economic agendas, the Indic cultures (i.e., Hindus, Buddhists, Sikhs, and Jains), for example, may still be found engaging in a cultural language of civilizational assumptions, cognitive markers, and relations. They may, for instance, variously debate and dispute (*a*) the seen and the unseen (*dṛṣṭa* and *adṛṣṭa*) reality; (*b*) the relations of contact (*saṃyoga*), joining (*yoga*), conjunction (*saṃyogan*), and dissolution (*pralaya*) or nothingness; (*c*) states of experience (*anubhava*) and their relationships to forms of knowledge and truth; and (*d*) tendencies toward inwardness (*antarmukhatā*) and outwardness (*vahirmukhatā*).

15. These figures roughly compare with other recent claims, including those by the Indian Muslims themselves. For example, see Ahmed (1996: 333); and also as reported in an article in the *Washington Post* (Cooper 1996: A16) on 'India's Majority Lower Castes'. Despite mutual suspicion, Dalit activists regard Muslims as occasional collaborators in opposing the caste Hindu dominance.

16. This is according to the account excerpted in the magazine *Muslim India*, edited by Syed Shahabuddin, and subtitled 'Monthly Journal of Reference Research and Documentation'.

17. Despite the use of the editorial 'we' in so many ways, the book is particularly useful to my study because, as the authors themselves observe in their 'preface', it is a narration retaining not only the imprint of its four—'independent and self-willed'—authors, but also of a social profile of actual hopes, frustrations, fears, and social mistrust of many victims, sufferers, and unsung local heroes. We thus find recorded a rather rare cultural language and logic surrounding the event. Unfortunately, the experiential accounts are most often the first to be excluded by a government inquiry report, and often also by 'scientific' accounts primarily interested in proving a certain empirical hypothesis or a favorite theory.

18. Those who suspect one another are as concerned about being socially or politically excluded as about being included into something. The hidden motives of the other side come under maximum scrutiny under such circumstances. When asked, many circumspect Hindus, Muslims, and now Sikhs today make sure that they tailor their comments to suit the occasion and the audience.

19. Among the 18 contributors to the volume, seven were women, and all, as far as I could decipher, from the upper- or middle-Hindu or Muslim castes. On the other hand, to the volume's credit, male authors not only observed and commented on women, they also reflected on their own male viewpoints, often biographically, and also as 'the guilty other'.

20. All the quotations in the following discussion are my translations from Hindi, done primarily for the authors' cultural sense and interpretation.

21. In evidence he cites some Hindi and Urdu publications which were already familiar to me, particularly religious authors, Hanuman Prasad Poddar and Swami Rama Sukh Das of the Gita Press, Gorakhpur.

22. The author is referring to the controversial Bangladeshi writer of the famous book *Shame* (or *Lajja*) on women's status in her country (see Nasrin 1994).

23. Even during the worst communal riots, examples of individual people's courage and care in saving 'the enemy' from death or physical harm repeatedly occur in the accounts of communal riots. For several examples, see Akbar 1991; Veena Das 1990b; and Nandy et al. 1995.

24. In addition, an Indian psychiatrist recently found ways to 'read' Indian violence via colors in both social and psychological terms. See Kakar 1995.

25. We all search for a more adequate and meaningful 'language' under the circumstances, and only sometimes does one succeed, when violence and victim stare each other in the face. Though Das was of course well aware of the general issue earlier as well (see Veena Das 1990b: 33), her quest to give an expression to women's pain and suffering is much more evident in 1996. She shows how she struggles to compose a language much more reflective of the depth of human suffering.

26. My observations on the subject rest on a Rockefeller Foundation project on violence, culture, and survival, focused on the Cambodian refugees in Washington DC, and the northern Virginia area in the US. See also Chapter 7. The

project, started in 1995, still continues in collaboration with Dr Roberta Culbertson of the Virginia Foundation for the Humanities.

27. The Dalit movement, though still too badly divided to pose a serious grass-roots social challenge to caste Hindu dominance, today nevertheless publicly (and effectively) challenges the political majority of the caste Hindu. The latter generally evades a direct collective response. For a balanced and critical study of the Ambedkar movement, see Zelliot 1996.

28. 'Mistrust' refers to much more than a transient social distrust. It concerns the self and the other, doubting each other's motives, action, and judgment. Not only that: the moral grounds of truth, validity, and effective action are also doubted or suspected. Eventually, mistrust confuses right from (and as) wrong, creating dangerous cul de sacs particularly for narrow-minded, selfish leaders entrusted with public power and their followers.

References

AGAR, MICHAEL H. 1982. 'Toward an Ethnographic Language', *American Anthropologist*, 84, 4: 779–95.

AGGER, BEN. 1991. 'Critical Theory, Poststructuralism and Postmodernism: Their Sociological Relevance', *Annual Review of Sociology*, 17: 105–31.

AHMAD, IMTIAZ. 1972. 'For a Sociology of India', *Contributions to Indian Sociology*, n.s., 6: 172–78.

AHMED, MUNIR D. 1996. 'Review of *World Muslim Minorities*. Karachi: WMC', *Muslim India*, 163: 333.

AKBAR, M.J. 1991. *Riot After Riot: Reports on Caste and Communal Violence in India* (Revised updated edition). New Delhi: Penguin Books.

AMBEDKAR, B.R. 1945. *Annihilation of Caste, With a Reply to Mahatma Gandhi*. Bombay: Thacker.

AMIN, SHAHID. 1995. *Event, Metaphor and Memory: Chauri Chaura 1922–1992*. Delhi: Oxford University Press.

ANAND, MULK RAJ and ELEANOR ZELLIOT (eds). 1992. *An Anthology of Dalit Literature*. Delhi: Gyan Publishing House.

ANDERSON, MICHAEL. 1995. 'Public Interest Perspectives on the Bhopal Case: Tort, Crime or Violation of Human Rights', in Robinson, D. and J. Dunkley (eds), *Public Interest Perspectives in Environmental Law*. London: Wily Chancery.

APPADURAI, ARJUN. 1986. 'Is Homo Hierarchicus?', *American Ethnologist*, 13: 745–61.

APTE, V.S. 1965. *The Practical Sanskrit English Dictionary*. Delhi: Motilal Banarsidass.

ARDENER, EDWIN. 1985. 'Social Anthropology and the Decline of Modernism', in Overing, Joanna (ed.), *Reason and Morality*. London: Tavistock Publications.

ASAD, TALAL. (ed.). 1973. *Anthropology and the Colonial Encounter*. San Jose, CA: Humanities Press.

———. 1975. *Anthropology and the Colonial Encounter*. New York: Humanities Press.

ASAD, TALAL. 1982. 'A Comment on the Idea of Non-Western Anthropology', in Fahim, Hussein (ed.), *Indigenous Anthropology in Non-Western Countries.* Durham: Carolina Academic Press.

BABB, LAWRENCE A. 1987. *Redemptive Encounters: Three Modern Styles in the Hindu Tradition.* Delhi: Oxford University Press.

BAGCHI, KATHKALI and MINI PHILIP. 1994. '*Striyan lupta kyon ho rahin hain?* [Why are women disappearing?], in Kishore, Raj (ed.), *Place for Women.* New Delhi: Vani Prakashan.

BAILEY, F.G. 1959. 'For a Sociology of India', *Contributions to Indian Sociology,* 3: 88–101.

BASHAM, A.L. 1964. *Studies in Ancient Indian History and Culture.* Calcutta: Sambodhi Publications.

BAXI, UPENDRA. 1987. *The Right to be Human.* New Delhi: Lancer International.

———. 1992. 'Emancipation as Justice: Babasaheb Ambedkar's Legacy and Vision', in *Ambedkar and Social Justice,* Vol. 1. New Delhi: Publications Division, Government of India.

———. 1994a. *Inhuman Wrongs and Human Rights: Unconventional Essays.* Delhi: Har-Anand Publications.

———. 1994b. 'Human Rights Education: The Promise of the Third Millennium?'. American University: Washington College of Law. Typescript.

———. 1996. 'The Unreason of Globalization and the Reason of Human Rights'. The A.R. Desai Memorial Lecture, 1996. Typescript.

———. n.d. 'State and Human Rights Movements in India'. Typescript.

BAXI, UPENDRA and A. DHANDA (eds). 1990. *Valiant Victims and Lethal Litigation: The Bhopal Case.* Bombay: Tripathi.

BAXI, UPENDRA and T. PAUL (eds). 1985. *Mass Disasters and Multinational Liability: The Bhopal Case.* Bombay: Tripathi.

BEATTIE, JOHN. 1964. *Other Cultures.* New York: Free Press.

BEIDELMAN, T.O. 1989. 'Review of *The Predicament of Culture* (by James Clifford), *Anthropos,* 89: 263–67.

BERLIN, BRENT and PAUL KAY. 1969. *Basic Color Terms: Their Universality and Evolution.* Berkeley: University of California Press.

BERNSTEIN, RICHARD. 1995. 'Cook Was (a) a God or (b) Not a God', *The New York Times,* Wednesday, May 24.

BERREMAN, GERALD. 1973. 'The Social Responsibility of the Anthropologist, Anthropology, and Moral Accountability', in Weaver, T. (ed.), *To See Ourselves: Anthropology and Modern Issues.* Glenview: Scott, Foresman.

———. 1980. 'Are Human Rights Merely a Political Luxury in the World Today?', *Anthropological Humanism Quarterly,* 5: 2–13.

BHAVE REPORT. 1974. *Inquiry Commission Report on Bilaspur, Mungeli Clashes between Hindus and Harijans in 1968* (Hindi). Bhopal: Government Publications.

BHAVE, SUMITRA. 1988. *Pan on Fire: Eight Dalit Women Tell Their Story.* New Delhi: Indian Social Institute.

BIARDEAU, MADELEINE. 1981. *L'Hindouisme: Anthropologie d'une Civilization.* Paris: Flammarion (English version 1989: *Hinduism: The Anthropology of a Civilization.* Delhi: Oxford University Press).

BONDURANT, JOAN V. 1971. *Conquest of Violence: The Gandhian Philosophy of Conquest*. Berkeley: University of California Press.

BOURDIEU, PIERRE and LOÏC J.D. WACQUANT. 1992. *An Invitation to Reflexive Sociology*. Chicago: University of Chicago Press.

BOWIE, MALCOLM. 1979. 'Jacques Lacan', in Sturrock, John (ed.), *Structuralism and Since*. London: Oxford University Press.

BRECKENRIDGE, CAROL A. and PETER VAN DER VEER (eds). 1993. *Orientalism and the Postcolonial Predicament: Perspectives on South Asia*. Philadelphia: University of Pennsylvania Press.

BROWN, MICHAEL F. 1996. 'On Resisting Resistance', *American Anthropologist*, 98: 729–35.

BUMILLER, ELISABETH. 1991. *May You Be the Mother of a Hundred Sons: A Journey among Women in India*. New Delhi: Penguin Books India.

BURGHART, RICHARD. 1990. 'Ethnographers and Their Local Counterparts in India', in Fardon, Richard (ed.), *Localizing Strategies: Regional Traditions of Ethnographic Writing*. Washington D.C.: Smithsonian Press.

CARRITHERS, MICHAEL. 1983. *The Forest Monks of Sri Lanka: An Anthropological and Historical Study*. Delhi: Oxford University Press.

CHATTERJEE, PARTHA. 1989. 'Colonialism, Nationalism, and the Colonized Women: The Contest in India', *American Ethnologist*, 16: 622–33.

————. 1994. 'Claims of the Past: The Genealogy of Modern Historiography in Bengal', in David, Arnold and David Hardiman (eds), *Subaltern Studies VIII: Essays in Honour of Ranajit Guha*. Delhi: Oxford University Press.

CHIROT, DANIEL. 1995. 'Modernism without Liberalism: The Ideological Roots of Modern Tyranny', *Contention: Debates in Society, Culture and Science*, 5: 141–66.

CHOUSALKAR, ASHOK S. 1986. *Social and Political Implications of Concepts of Justice and Dharma*. Delhi: Mittal Publications.

CLIFFORD, JAMES. 1981. 'On Ethnographic Surrealism', *Comparative Studies in Society and History*, 23: 4.

————. 1988. *The Predicament of Culture: Twentieth-Century Ethnography, Literature, and Art*. Cambridge, Mass.: Harvard University Press.

CLIFFORD, JAMES and GEORGE E. MARCUS (eds). 1986. *Writing Culture: The Poetics and Politics of Ethnography*. Berkeley: University of California Press.

COHN, BERNARD S. 1987a. 'History and Anthropology: The State of Play', in Cohn, Bernard (ed.), *An Anthropologist among the Historians and Other Essays*. Delhi: Oxford University Press.

————. 1987b. 'Representing Authority in Victorian India', in Cohn, Bernard (ed.), *An Anthropologist among the Historians and Other Essays*. Delhi: Oxford University Press.

————. 1987c. (ed.) *An Anthropologist among the Historians and Other Essays*. Delhi: Oxford University Press.

COLSON, ELIZABETH. 1982. 'Anthropological Dilemmas in the Late Twentieth Century', in Fahim, Hussein (ed.), *Indigenous Anthropology in Non-Western Countries*. Durham: Carolina Academic Press.

COLVARD, KAREN. 1996. 'What We Already Know about Terrorism: Violent Challenges to the State and State Response', *The HFG Review*, 1: 3–8.

COMAROFF, JOHN and JEAN COMAROFF. 1992. *Ethnography and the Historical Imagination*. Boulder, Colo.: Westview Press.

CONTUSI, JANET A. 1989. 'Militant Hindus and Buddhist Dalits: Hegemony and Resistance in an Indian Slum', *American Ethnologist*, 16: 441–57.
COOPER, FREDERICK and ANN L. STOLER. 1989. 'Tensions of Empire: Colonial Control and Visions of Rule', *American Ethnologist*, 16: 609–21.
COOPER, KENNETH J. 1996. 'India's Majority Lower Castes Are Minor Voice in Newspapers', *The Washington Post*, September 5: A16.
CRAIN, MARY M. 1994. 'Opening the Pandora's Box: A Plea for Discursive Heteroglossia', *American Ethnologist*, 21: 201–10.
CRAPANZANO, VINCENT. 1980. *Tuhami: Portait of a Moroccan*. Chicago: University of Chicago Press.
CROOKE, WILLIAM. 1972 [original 1906]. *Things Indian*. New Delhi: Oriental Books Reprint Corporation.
Dalit Asia Today, December 1994. Lucknow: Ved Kumar Publisher.
DANDEKAR, G.N. 1988. 'The Last Kirtan of Gadge Baba', in Zelliot, Eleanor and Maxine Berntsen (eds), *The Experience of Hinduism: Essays on Religion in Maharashtra*. Albany: The State University of New York Press.
DANIEL, E. VALENTINE. 1984. *Fluid Signs: Being a Person the Tamil Way*. Berkeley: University of California Press.
———. 1996. *Charred Lullabies: Chapters in Anthropography of Violence*. Princeton: Princeton University Press.
DAS, BHAGWAN. 1963. *Selected Speeches of Dr. Baba Saheb B.R. Ambedkar*. Jullandhar: Bheem Patrika Publications.
———. 1995. 'Socioeconomic Problems of Dalits', in *Dalit Solidarity*. Delhi: ISPCK.
DAS, BHAGWAN and JAMES MASSEY (eds). 1995. *Dalit Solidarity*. New Delhi: The Indian Society for Promoting Christian Knowledge (ISPCK).
DAS, VEENA. 1982. *Structure and Cognition: Aspects of Hindu Caste and Ritual*. Delhi: Oxford University Press.
———. (ed.). 1986. *The Word and the World: Fantasy, Symbol and Record*. New Delhi: Sage.
———. 1989. 'Subaltern as Perspective', in Guha, Ranajit (ed.), *Subaltern Studies VI*. Delhi: Oxford University Press.
———. 1990a. 'Introduction', in Das, Veena (ed.), *Mirrors of Violence*. Delhi: Oxford University Press.
———. 1990b. 'Our Work to Cry: Your Work to Listen', in Das, Veena (ed.), *Mirrors of Violence: Communities, Riots and Survivors in South Asia*. Delhi: Oxford University Press.
———. (ed.) 1990c. *Mirrors of Violence: Communities, Riots and Survivors in South Asia*. Delhi: Oxford University Press.
———. 1994. 'The Anthropological Discourse on India: Reason and Its Other', in Borofsky, Robert (ed.), *Assessing Cultural Anthropology*. New York: McGraw-Hill.
———. 1995. *Critical Events: An Anthropological Perspective on Contemporary India*. Delhi: Oxford University Press.
———. 1996. 'Language and Body: Transactions in the Construction of Pain', *Daedalus*, 125: 67–91.
DELLA PORTA, DONATELLA. 1995. *Social Movements, Political Violence, and the State*. Cambridge: Cambridge University Press.

DERRIDA, JACQUES. 1972. *Speech and Phenomenon*. Evanston: Northwestern University Press.

———. 1977. *Of Grammatology*. Baltimore: Johns Hopkins University Press.

DESJARLIAS, ROBERT, LEON EISENBERG, BYRON GOOD and ARTHUR KLEINMAN. 1995. *World Mental Health: Problems and Priorities in Low-Income Countries*. New York: Oxford University Press.

DIRKS, NICHOLAS B. 1987. *The Hollow Crown: Ethnohistory of an Indian Kingdom*. Cambridge: Cambridge University Press.

———. 1992. *Colonialism and Culture*. Ann Arbor: University of Michigan Press.

DOMINGUEZ, VIRGINIA R. 1994. 'Differentiating Women/Bodies of Knowledge', *American Anthropologist*, 96: 127–30.

DONIGER, WENDY. 1991. *The Laws of Manu*. New York: Penguin Classics.

DOUGLAS, MARY. 1980. *Evans–Pritchard*. Glasgow: Fontana Paperbacks.

DREYFUS, HUBERT and PAUL RABINOW (eds). 1982. *Michel Foucault: Beyond Structuralism and Hermeneutics*. Chicago: University of Chicago Press.

DUBE, S.C. 1994. 'After Ayodhya: Three Visible Plans', in Kishore, Raj (ed.), *Ayodhya and Afterwards*. New Delhi: Vani Prakashan.

DUMONT, JEAN-PAUL. 1978. *The Headman and I: Ambiguity and Ambivalence in the Fieldwork Experience*. Austin: University of Texas Press.

DUMONT, LOUIS. 1966. 'A Fundamental Problem in the Sociology of Caste', *Contributions to Indian Sociology*, 9: 17–32.

———. 1975. 'Preface to the French Edition of the Nuer' (tr. Mary and James Douglas), in Beattie, J.H.M. and R.G. Lienhardt (eds), *Studies in Social Anthropology*. Oxford: Clarendon Press.

———. 1977. *From Mandeville to Marx: The Genesis and Triumph of Economic Ideology*. Chicago: The University of Chicago Press.

———. 1979. 'The Anthropological Community and Ideology', *Social Science Information*, 18: 785–817.

———. 1980. *Homo Hierarchicus: The Caste System and Its Implications* (complete revised English edition). Chicago: University of Chicago Press.

———. 1986a. *Essays on Individualism: Modern Ideology in Anthropological Perspective*. Chicago: University of Chicago Press.

———. 1986b. 'The Anthropological Community and Ideology', in Dumont, Louis (ed.), *Essays on Individualism*. Chicago: University of Chicago Press.

DUMONT, LOUIS and DAVID POCOCK. 1957. 'For a Sociology of India', *Contributions to Indian Sociology*, 1: 7–22.

———. 1960. 'For a Sociology of India', *Contributions to Indian Sociology*, 4: 82–89.

DURKHEIM, EMILE and M. MAUSS. 1963. *Primitive Classification* (tr. Rodney Needham). Chicago: University of Chicago Press.

ECO, UMBERTO, JONATHAN CULLER, R. RORTY and C. BROOK–ROSE. 1992. *Interpretation and Overinterpretation*. Cambridge: Cambridge University Press.

ELLEN, R.F. and D. REASON. 1979. *Classifications in Their Social Context*. London: Cohen and West.

ENGINEER, ASHGAR ALI (ed.). 1984. *Communal Riots in Post-Independence India*. New Delhi: Sangam Books.

ERICKSON, ERIK. 1974. *Dimensions of a New Identity*. New York: Norton.

264 ◀ Cultural Diversity and Social Discontent

EVENS, T.M.S. 1983. 'Mind, Logic and the Efficacy of the Nuer Incest Prohibition', *Man*, 18, 1: 118–33.

FABIAN, JOHANNES. 1983. *Time and the Other: How Anthropology Makes Its Object*, New York: Columbia University Press.

———. 1990. 'Presence and Representation: The Other and Anthropological Writing', *Critical Inquiry*, 16: 753–72.

———. 1995. 'Ethnographic Misunderstanding and the Perils of Context', *American Anthropologist*, 97: 41–50.

FAGAN, BRIAN. 1995. 'The Capt. Cook Debate, Cont'd.', *The Washington Post*, August 3: C3.

FAHEEM, HUSSEIN (ed.). 1982. *Indigenous Anthropology in Non-Western Countries*. Durham, N.C.: Carolina Academic Press.

FARMER, PAUL. 1996. 'On Suffering and Structural Violence', *Daedalus*, 125: 261–83.

FEUER, LEWIS S. 1975. *Ideology and the Ideologists*. Oxford: Basic Blackwell.

FIRTH, RAYMOND. 1938. *Human Types*. London: T. Nelson and Sons.

FOUCAULT, MICHEL. 1965. *Madness and Civilization: A History of Insanity in the Age of Reason*. New York: Pantheon Books.

———. 1973. *The Birth of the Clinic*. London: Tavistock.

———. 1977. *Discipline and Punish*. New York: Pantheon Books.

———. 1982. 'Subject and Power', in Dreyfus, Hubert and Paul Rabinow (eds), *Michel Foucault: Beyond Structuralism and Hermeneutics*. Chicago: University of Chicago Press.

———. 1984a. 'The Great Confinement', in Rabinow, Paul (ed.), *The Foucault Reader*. New York: Pantheon Books.

———. 1984b. *The Foucault Reader* (ed. Paul Rabinow). New York: Pantheon Books.

FOX, RICHARD G. 1991. *Recapturing Anthropology: Working in the Present*. Santa Fe, N. Mex.: School of American Research Press.

FULLER, C.J. 1992. *The Camphor Flame: Popular Hinduism and Society in India*. Princeton: Princeton University Press.

FULLER, C.J. and JONATHAN SPENCER. 1990. 'South Asian Anthropology in the 1980s', *South Asia Research*, 10: 85–105.

GALANTER, MARC. 1984. *Competing Inequalities: Law and the Backward Classes in India*. Berkeley: University of California Press.

GALSTON, WILLIAM A. 1980. *Justice and the Human Good*. Chicago: University of Chicago Press.

GEERTZ, CLIFFORD. 1973. *The Interpretation of Cultures*. New York: Basic Books.

———. 1983. *Local Knowledge: Further Essays in Interpretive Anthropology*. New York: Basic Books.

———. 1988. *Works and Lives: The Anthropologist as Author*. Stanford: Stanford University Press.

———. 1992. '"Local Knowledge" and Its Limits: Some *Obiter Dicta*', *The Yale Journal of Criticism*, 5: 129–35.

———. 1994. *After the Fact: Two Countries, Four Decades, One Anthropologist*. Cambridge, Mass.: Harvard University Press.

GELLNER, DAVID N. 1992. *Monk, Householder and Tantric Priest: Newar Buddhism and its Hierarchy of Ritual*. Cambridge: Cambridge University Press.

GIRARD, RENÉ. 1972. *Violence and the Sacred*. Baltimore: Johns Hopkins University Press.
———. 1978. *Things Hidden Since the Foundation of the World*. London: Athlone Press.
———. 1982. *The Scapegoat*. Baltimore: Johns Hopkins University Press.
GOOD, ANTHONY. 1982. 'The Actor and the Act: Categories of Prestation in South India', *Man*, 17: 23–41.
GOPAL, S. 1991. *Anatomy of a Confrontation: The Babri Masjid–Ramajanmabhumi Dispute*. New Delhi: Viking.
GORDON, DEBORAH. 1990. 'The Politics of Ethnographic Authority: Race and Writing in the Ethnography of Margaret Mead and Zora Neal Hurston', in Manganaro, Marc (ed.), *Modernist Anthropology: From Fieldwork to Text*. Princeton: Princeton University Press.
GOUGH, KATHLEEN. 1963. 'Indian Nationalism and Ethnic Freedom', in Bidney, David (ed.), *The Concept of Freedom in Anthropology*. The Hague: Mouton.
GUHA, RANAJIT (ed.). 1989. *Subaltern Studies IV: Writings on South Asian History and Society*. Delhi: Oxford University Press.
GUHA, RANAJIT and GAYATRI C. SPIVAK (eds). 1988. *Selected Subaltern Studies*. New York: Oxford University Press.
HALBFASS, WILHELM. 1988. *India and Europe: An Essay in Understanding*. Albany, N.Y.: State University of New York Press.
HATCH, ELVIN. 1983. *Culture and Morality: The Relativity of Values in Anthropology*. New York: Columbia University Press.
HEESTERMAN, J.C. 1985. *The Inner Conflict of Tradition: Essays in Indian Ritual, Kingship, and Society*. Chicago: University of Chicago Press.
———. 1993. *The Broken World of Sacrifice: An Essay in Ancient Indian Ritual*. Chicago: University of Chicago Press.
HEILBRONER, ROBERT. 1974. *Reflections on the Human Prospect*. New York: Norton.
HERMAN, JUDITH L. 1992. *Trauma and Recovery*. New York: Basic Books.
HIRSCHKIND, LYNN. 1994. 'Bedeviled Ethnography', *American Ethnologist*, 21: 210–15.
HOLLIS, MARTIN. 1982. 'The Social Destruction of Reality', in Hollis, Martin and Steven Lukes (eds), *Rationality and Relativism*. Oxford: Basil Blackwell.
HOLLIS, MARTIN and STEVEN LUKES (eds). 1982. *Rationality and Relativism*. Oxford: Basil Blackwell.
HOLMSTRÖM, LAKSHMI (ed.) 1991. *The Inner Courtyard: Stories by Indian Women*. Delhi: Rupa & Co.
HUME, ROBERT ERNEST. 1985. *The Thirteen Principal Upanishads* (second revised edition). Delhi: Oxford University Press.
ISLAM, SHAMSUL. 1994. '*Kyonki aurten tumhari kheti hain*' [Because Women Are Your Crop], in Kishore, Raj (ed.), *Place for Women*. New Delhi: Vani Prakashan.
ISPCK, Delhi. 1989. *Three Oppressions*. Delhi: Indian Society for Promoting Christian Knowledge.
JAER, OYVIND. 1987. 'The Ideological Constitution of the Individual: Some Critical Comments on Louis Dumont's Comparative Anthropology', *Contributions to Indian Sociology*, n.s., 21: 353–62.
JAIN, GIRILAL. 1994. *The Hindu Phenomenon*. New Delhi: UBSPD Publications.

JARVIE, I.C. 1967. 'On the Theory of Fieldwork and the Scientific Character of Social Anthropology', *Philosophy of Science*, 34: 223–43.
———. 1983. 'The Problem of the Ethnographic Real', *Current Anthropology*, 24, 3: 313–24.
JIGYASU, CHANDRIKA PRASAD. 1969. '*Nari-jivan ki kahani* [Story of Woman's Life] (Hindi Pamphlet). Lucknow: Bahujan Kalyan Prakashan.
———. 1984. 'The Story of Woman's Life', in Shrivardhan, Shri (ed. and tr.), *The Rise and Fall of Hindu Woman* (Hindi, 3rd edition). Lucknow: Bahujan Kalyan Prakashan.
———. March 1972. Interview in Lucknow.
JUERGENSMEYER, MARK. 1993. *The Cold War? Religious Nationalism Confronts the Secular State*. Berkeley: University of California Press.
KAKAR, SUDHIR. 1995. *The Colors of Violence*. New Delhi: Penguin India.
KANTOWSKY, D. 1969. 'A Critical Note on the Sociology of Developing Societies', *Contributions to Indian Sociology*, n.s., 3: 128–31.
KARLEKAR, MALAVIKA. 1993. *Voices from Within*. Delhi: Oxford University Press.
KARVE, IRAWATI. 1988 [1972]. '"Boy Friend": An Essay', in Zelliot, Eleanor and Maxine Berntsen (eds), *The Experience of Hinduism*. Albany, N.Y.: State University of New York Press.
KEARNEY, RICHARD. 1995. 'Myths and Scapegoats: The Case of René Girard', *Theory, Culture and Society*, 12: 1–14.
KEER, DHANANJAY. 1954. *Dr. Babasaheb Ambedkar: Life and Mission*. Bombay: Popular Prakashan.
———. 1971. 3rd edition. *Dr. Ambedkar: Life and Mission*. Bombay: Popular Prakashan.
KESHARI, SUMAN. 1994. '*Naam mein kya rakkha hai* [What's in a name?], in Kishore, Raj (ed.), *Place for Women*. New Delhi: Vani Prakashan.
KHARE, R.S. 1976. *Culture and Reality: Essays on the Hindu System of Managing Food*. Simla: Indian Institute of Advanced Study.
———. 1983a. *Normative Culture and Kinship: Essays on Hindu Categories, Processes and Perspectives*. Delhi: Vikas.
———. 1983b. 'Between Being Near and Distant: Reflections on the Initial Approaches and Experiences of an Indian Anthropologist', in Lawless, Robert and Vinson H. Sutlive, Jr. (eds), *Fieldwork: The Human Experience*. New York: Gordon and Breach.
———. 1984. *The Untouchable as Himself: Ideology, Identity and Pragmatism among the Lucknow Chamars*. New York: Cambridge University Press.
———. 1985. *Culture and Democracy: Anthropological Reflections on Modern India*. Baltimore: University Press of America.
———. 1986. *Parts and the Whole: Cultural Reasoning in Indian Classifications* (mimeo.). Charlottesville: University of Virginia.
———. 1987a. 'The Bhopal Accident: Anthropological and Civic Issues', *Anthropology Today*, 3: 3–4.
———. 1987b. *Issues in Compensatory Justice: The Bhopal Accident*. (Working Paper 2). Charlottesville, VA: Center for Advanced Studies, University of Virginia.
———. 1988. 'India's Modernity: Some Preliminary Notes and Comments', *South Asian Anthropologist*, 9: 163–70.

References ➤ 267

KHARE, R.S. 1989. 'Review of Louis Dumont, J.P.S. Uberoi and Joanna Overing', *American Ethnologist*, 16: 177–79.
————. 1990. 'The Bhopal Tragedy: Labrynthine Law and Unending Politics', *Anthropology Today*, 6: 12–14.
————. 1991. 'The Issue of Right to Food among the Hindus: Notes and Comments', *Human Rights to Food: Religious Promise and Practice*. Lecture Series: Brown University.
————. 1992. 'Cultural Clues and Stories in Denial and Deprivation: The Cambodian Refugee Experience'. Paper read at the American Anthropological Association Meetings. San Francisco.
————. 1993a. 'Issues of Social Justice and Human Rights among the Dispossessed: Untouchable Women in Changing India'. Typescript.
————. 1993b. 'Pain, Suffering and the Saint-Awarded Memory: The Case of Untouchable "Kitchen Poetess"'. Typescript.
————. 1993c. 'The Seen and the Unseen: Hindu Distinctions, Experiences and Cultural Reasoning', *Contributions to Indian Sociology*, n.s., 27: 191–212.
KISHORE, RAJ (ed.). 1994. *Striyon ke liye jagah* [Place for Women, Hindi]. Today's Issues No. 7. New Delhi: Vani Prakashan.
KLEINMAN, ARTHUR and JOAN KLEINMAN. 1996. 'The Appeal of Experience, the Dismay of Images: Cultural Appropriations of Suffering in Our Times', *Daedalus*, 125: 1–23.
KLUCKHOHN, CLYDE. 1949. *Mirror for Man*. New York: Whittlesey House.
KODIAN, P.K. 1978. *Atrocities on Harijans and Weaker Sections*. New Delhi: Communist Party Publications.
KOHLI, ATUL. 1990. *Democracy and Discontent: India's Growing Crisis of Governability*. Cambridge: Cambridge University Press.
KONDO, DORINNE K. 1990. *Crafting Selves: Power, Gender, and Discourses of Identity on a Japanese Workplace*. Chicago: University of Chicago Press.
KOTHARI, RAJNI. 1970. *Politics in India*. New Delhi: Orient Longman.
————. 1976. *Democratic Polity and Social Change*. Bombay: Allied Publishers.
————. 1986. 'Masses, Classes and the State', *Alternatives*, 11, 2: 210–16.
————. 1996. 'Call of 1996: A New Debate on Governance', *Biblio: A Review of Books*, II, 5: 4–5.
KOTHARI, SMITU and HARSH SETHI. 1989. *Rethinking Human Rights: Challenges for Theory and Action*. New York: New Horizon Press.
KRISHNA IYER, JUSTICE V.R. 1976. *Ambedkar Memorial Lectures 1976*. New Delhi: Jawaharlal Nehru University.
KRISHNA, DAYA. 1991. *Indian Philosophy—A Counter Perspective*. Delhi: Oxford University Press.
KRYSTAL, H. 1969. *Massive Psychic Trauma*. New York: International University Press.
KULKARNI, SUDHEENDRA. 1996. 'RSS and Its Role in Reforming Hinduism', *The Pioneer*, 13 August: 6.
KUMAR, KRISHNA. 1994. '*Stri kitna daraye gi*' [How much will woman frighten us?], in *Place for Women*. New Delhi: Vani Prakashan.
KUMAR, NITA (ed.). 1994. *Women as Subjects: South Asian Histories*. Charlottesville: University Press of Virginia.
KUNDERA, MILAN. 1992. *Immortality* (tr. Peter Kussi). New York: Harper Perennial.

KUNJUNNI RAJA, K. 1963. *Indian Theories of Meaning*. Madras: The Adyar Library and Research Center.

LACAN, JACQUES. 1977a. 'The Mirror Stage', in *Écrits: A Selection* (tr. Alan Sheridan). New York: Norton.

———. 1977b. *The Four Fundamental Concepts of Psychoanalysis* (ed. Jacques-Alain Miller, tr. Alan Sheridan). New York: Norton.

LANGER, LAWRENCE. 1996. 'The Alarmed Vision: Social Suffering and Holocaust Atrocity', *Daedalus*, 125: 47–65.

LARSON, GERALD JAMES and ELIOT DEUTSCH (eds). 1988. *Interpreting Across Boundaries: New Essays in Comparative Philosophy*. Princeton: Princeton University Press.

LEACH, EDMUND. 1989. 'Writing Anthropology', *American Ethnologist*, 16: 137–41.

LEARS, JACKSON. 1981. *No Place of Grace: Antimodernism and the Transformation of American Culture*. New York: Pantheon.

LÉVI–STRAUSS, CLAUDE. 1966. *The Savage Mind*. Chicago: University of Chicago Press.

———. 1976. *Structural Anthropology*, Vol. 2. New York: Basic Books.

LIFTON, ROBERT J. 1967. *Death in Life: Survivors of Hiroshima*. New York: Random House.

LORIGGIO, FRANCESCO. 1990. 'Anthropology, Literary Theory, and the Traditions of Modernism', in Manganaro, Marc (ed.), *Modernist Anthropology, From Fieldwork to Text*. Princeton: Princeton University Press.

MACINTYRE, ALASDAIR. 1981. *After Virtue: A Study in Moral Theory*. Notre Dame: University of Notre Dame Press.

MADAN, T.N. 1966. 'For a Sociology of India', *Contributions to Indian Sociology*, 9: 9–16.

———. 1978. 'A Review Symposium on M.N. Srinivas's *The Remembered Village*', *Contributions to Indian Sociology*, n.s., 12, 1.

———. 1981. 'For a Sociology of India', *Contributions to Indian Sociology*, n.s., 15: 405–18.

———. 1987a. 'Secularism in Its Place', *Journal of Asian Studies*, 46: 747–58.

———. 1987b. *Non-renunciation: Themes and Interpretation of Hindu Culture*. Delhi: Oxford University Press.

———. 1994. *Pathways: Approaches to the Study of Society in India*. Delhi: Oxford University Press.

MANGANARO, MARC. 1990a. 'Introduction', in Manganaro, Marc (ed.), *Modernist Anthropology: From Fieldwork to Text*. Princeton: Princeton University Press.

———. (ed.). 1990b. *Modernist Anthropology: From Fieldwork to Text*. Princeton: Princeton University Press.

MARANHAO, TULLIO (ed.). 1990. *The Interpretation of Dialogue*. Chicago: University of Chicago Press.

MARCUS, GEORGE E. 1980. 'Rhetoric and the Ethnographic Genre in Anthropological Research', *Current Anthropology*, 21, 4: 507–10.

MARCUS, GEORGE E. and MICHAEL M.J. FISCHER. 1986. *Anthropology as Cultural Critique*. Chicago: University of Chicago Press.

MARK, LILLA. (ed.). 1994. *New French Thought: Political Philosophy*. Princeton: Princeton University Press.

MARRIOTT, McKIM (ed.). 1955. *Village India: Studies in the Little Community*. Chicago: University of Chicago Press.

———. 1959. 'Interactional and Attributional Theories of Caste Ranking', *Man in India*, 39: 92–107.

———. 1966. 'The Feast of Love', in Singer, Milton (ed.), *Krishna: Myths, Rites and Attitudes*. Honolulu: University of Hawaii Press.

———. 1968. 'Caste Ranking and Food Transactions, a Matrix Analysis', in Singer, Milton and Bernard S. Cohn (eds), *Structure and Change in Indian Society*. Chicago: Aldine.

———. 1969. 'Review of Homo Hierarchicus', *American Anthropologist*, 71: 1166–75.

———. 1976a. 'Hindu Transactions: Diversity without Dualism', in Kapferer, Bruce (ed.), *Transactions and Meaning: Directions in the Anthropology of Exchange and Symbolic Behavior*. Philadelphia: Institute for the Study of Human Issues.

———. 1976b. 'Interpreting Indian Society: A Monistic Alternative to Dumont's Dualism', *Journal of Asian Studies*, 36: 189–95.

———. 1987. *A Description of Samsara: A Realization of Rural Hindu Life*. The College: University of Chicago.

———. 1989. 'Constructing an Indian Ethnosociology', *Contributions to Indian Sociology*, n.s., 23, 1: 1–39.

———. 1991. 'On Constructing an Indian Ethnosociology', *Contributions to Indian Sociology*, n.s., 25: 295–308.

MARRIOTT, McKIM and RONALD INDEN. 1977. 'Toward an Ethnosociology of South Asian Caste Systems', in David, Kenneth (ed.), *The New Wind*. The Hague: Mouton.

MASSEY, JAMES. 1995. 'History and Dalit Identity', in *Dalit Solidarity*. Delhi: ISPCK.

MATHEW, JUSTICE K.K. 1978. *Democracy, Equality and Freedom* (ed. Upendra Baxi). Lucknow: Eastern Book Company.

MATILAL, BIMAL KRISHNA. 1971. *Epistemology, Logic and Grammar in Indian Philosophical Analysis*. The Hague: Mouton.

———. 1977. *The Logical Illumination of Indian Mysticism* (lecture). Oxford: The Clarendon Press.

———. 1985. *Language, Logic and Reality*. Delhi: Motilal Banarsidass.

McGILVARY, D.B. (ed.). 1982. *Caste Ideology and Interaction*. New York: Cambridge University Press.

McGRANE, BERNARD. 1989. *Beyond Anthropology: Society and the Other*. New York: Columbia University Press.

MEGILL, ALLAN. 1989. 'Recounting the Past: "Description", Explanation, and Narrative in Historiography', *American Historical Review*, 94: 627–53.

MENDELSOHN, OLIVER and UPENDRA BAXI (eds). 1994. *The Rights of Subordinated Peoples*. Delhi: Oxford University Press.

MESSER, ELLEN. 1993a. 'Anthropology, Human Rights and Social Transformation', in Moran, E. (ed.), *A Transforming World: Roles for Anthropologists*. N.y.: Gordon and Breach.

———. 1993b. 'Anthropology and Human Rights', *Annual Reviews in Anthropology*, 1993: 221–49.

MILNER, MURRAY, JR. 1994. *Status and Sacredness: A General Theory of Status and Analysis of Indian Culture*. New York: Oxford University Press.
MINES, DIANE PAULL. 1989. 'Hindu Periods of Death Impurity', *Contributions to Indian Sociology*, n.s., 23: 103–30.
MITTA, MANOJ. 1996. 'Roop Kanwar Case: Legal Embarrassment', *India Today*, November 15: 89.
MOFFATT, MICHAEL. 1990. 'Hard Times for Culture Theory in South Asia', *Reviews in Anthropology*, 14: 257–66.
MOHANTY, CHANDRA TALPADE. 1984. 'Under Western Eyes: Feminist Scholarship and Colonial Discourses', *Boundary*, 12: 333–58.
MOHANTY, S.P. 1989. 'Us and Them: On the Philosophical Bases of Political Criticism', *Yale Journal of Criticism*, 2: 1–32.
MOORE, MELINDA A. 1989. 'The Kerala House as a Hindu Cosmos', *Contributions to Indian Sociology*, n.s., 23: 169–202.
MORENO, MANUEL and McKIM MARRIOTT. 1989. 'Humoral Transactions in Two Tamil Cults', *Contributions to Indian Sociology*, n.s., 23: 149–67.
MUKERJI, D.P. 1958. *Diversities*. New Delhi: People's Publishing House.
NAGAR, AMRITLAL. 1992. *The Face Behind Seven Veils* (a novel) (tr. Jai Ratan). Delhi: B.K. Publishing Corporation.
NANDY, ASHIS. 1980. *At the Edge of Psychology*. Delhi: Oxford University Press.
———. 1983. *The Intimate Enemy: Loss and Recovery of Self under Colonialism*. Delhi: Oxford University Press.
———. 1987. *Traditions, Tyranny and Utopias: Essays in the Politics of Awareness*. Delhi: Oxford University Press.
———. 1990. 'The Politics of Secularism and the Recovery of Religious Tolerance', in Das, Veena (ed.), *Mirrors of Violence: Communities, Riots and Survivors in South Asia*. New Delhi: Oxford University Press.
———. 1995a. *The Savage Freud and Other Essays on Possible and Retrievable Selves*. Princeton: Princeton University Press.
———. 1995b. 'History's Forgotten Doubles', *History and Theory*, 34: 44–66.
NANDY, ASHIS, SHIKHA TRIVEDI, SHAIL MAYARAM and ACHYUT YAGNIK. 1995. *Creating a Nationality: The Ramjanmabhumi Movement and the Fear of Self*. Delhi: Oxford University Press.
NARAYAN, KIRIN. 1993. 'How Native is a "Native" Anthropologist?', *American Anthropologist*, 95: 671–86.
———. 1994. *Love, Stars and All That*. New Delhi, New York: Penguin Books.
NASRIN, TASLIMA. 1994. *Lajja* [Shame] (tr. from Bengali by Tutul Gupta). New Delhi: Penguin Books.
NEEDHAM, RODNEY. 1983. *Against the Tranquillity of Axioms*. Berkeley: University of California Press.
NEHRU, JAWAHARLAL. 1946. *The Discovery of India*. New York: John Day.
NOZICK, ROBERT. 1974. *Anarchy, State, and Utopia*. New York: Basic Books.
O'FLAHERTY, WENDY. 1980. *Karma and Rebirth in Classical Indian Traditions*. Berkeley: University of California Press.
O'MEARA, J. TIM. 1989. 'Anthropology as Empirical Science', *American Anthropologist*, 91: 354–69.
OBEYESEKERE, GANANATH. 1992. *The Apotheosis of James Cook: European Mythmaking in the Pacific*. Princeton, N.J.: Princeton University Press.

OMVEDT, GAIL. 1994. *Dalits and the Democratic Revolution: Dr. Ambedkar and the Dalit Movement in Colonial India.* New Delhi: Sage Publications.

———. 1995. *Dalit Visions* (Tracts for the Times/8). New Delhi: Orient Longman.

ORTNER, SHERRY B. 1984. 'Theory in Anthropology Since the Sixties', *Comparative Studies in Society and History*, 26: 126–66.

———. 1995. 'Resistance and the Problem of Ethnographic Refusal', *Comparative Studies in Society and History*, 37: 173–93.

OVERING, JOANNA (ed.). 1985. *Reason and Morality.* London: Tavistock Publications.

PAKRASI, KANTI B. 1972. *Female Infanticide in India.* Delhi: Munshiram and Manoharlal.

PANDEY, GYANENDRA. 1990. *The Construction of Communalism in Colonial North India.* Delhi: Oxford University Press.

———. 1994. 'The Prose of Otherness', in Arnold, David and David Hardiman (eds), *Subaltern Studies VIII: Essays in Honour of Ranajit Guha.* Delhi: Oxford University Press.

PANTHAM, THOMAS. 1988. 'Interpreting Indian Politics: Rajni Kothari and His Critics', *Contributions to Indian Sociology*, n.s., 22: 229–46.

PARKIN, DAVID. 1982a. 'Introduction', in Parkin, David (ed.), *Semantic Anthropology.* London: Academic Press.

———. (ed.). 1982b. *Semantic Anthropology.* London: Academic Press.

———. 1985. 'Reason, Emotion and the Embodiment of Power', in Overing, Joanna (ed.), *Reason and Morality.* London: Tavistock Publications.

PARRY, JONATHAN. 1985. 'The Aghori Ascetics of Banaras', in Burghart, Richard and Audrey Cantile (eds), *Indian Religion.* London: Curzon Press.

PAZ, OCTAVIO. 1982. *Conjunctions and Disjunctions* (tr. Helen Lane). New York: Arcade Publishing.

POCOCK, DAVID. 1971. *Social Anthropology.* London: Sheed & Ward.

POTTER, KARL H. 1965. *Presuppositions of India's Philosophies.* New Delhi. Prentice-Hall.

———. 1980. 'The Karma Theory and Its Interpretation in Some Indian Philosophical Systems', in O'Flaherty, Wendy (ed.), *Karma and Rebirth in Classical Indian Traditions.* Berkeley: University of California Press.

RABINOW, PAUL. 1977. *Reflections on Fieldwork in Morocco.* Berkeley: University of California Press.

———. (ed.). 1984. *The Foucault Reader.* New York: Pantheon Books.

RAHEJA, GLORIA G. 1988. *The Poison in the Gift: Ritual, Prestation, and the Dominant Caste in a North Indian Village.* Chicago: University of Chicago Press.

RAHEJA, GLORIA G. and ANN G. GOLD. 1994. *Listen to the Heron's Words: Reimagining Gender & Kinship in North India.* Berkeley: University of California Press.

RAMANUJAN, A.K. 1989. 'Is There an Indian Way of Thinking? An Informal Essay', *Contributions to Indian Sociology*, n.s., 23: 41–58.

REGE, M.P. 1985. *Concepts of Justice and Equality in the Indian Tradition.* Pune: Gokhale Institute of Politics and Economics.

ROBERTSON, ROLAND. 1992. *Globalization: Social Theory and Global Culture.* London: Sage.

RORTY, RICHARD. 1980. *Philosophy and the Mirror of Nature.* Oxford: Basil Blackwell.

RORTY, RICHARD. 1989a. 'Review of *Interpreting across Boundaries: New Essays in Comparative Philosophy* (ed. Gerald James Larson and Eliot Deutsch)'. Princeton: Princeton University Press. Typescript.
———. 1989b. 'Comment on Mark Taylor's "Paralectics"'. University of Virginia: Center for Advanced Studies. Typescript.
RÜSEN, JÖRN. 1987. 'Historical Narration: Foundation, Types, Reason', *History and Theory*, 26: 87–97.
RYLE, GILBERT. 1954. *Dilemmas* (The Tarner Lectures). Cambridge: Cambridge University Press.
SABERWAL, SATISH. 1983. 'Uncertain Transplants: Anthropology and Sociology in India', *Contributions to Indian Sociology*, n.s., 17: 301–15.
———. 1986. *India: The Roots of Crisis*. Delhi: Oxford University Press.
SAHLINS, MARSHALL. 1976. *Culture and Practical Reason*. Chicago: University of Chicago Press.
———. 1995. *How 'Natives' Think: About Captain Cook, for Example*. Chicago: University of Chicago Press.
SAID, EDWARD W. 1978. *Orientalism*. New York: Vintage Books.
———. 1983. *The World, the Text, and the Critic*. Cambridge: Harvard University Press.
SALMOND, ANNE. 1985. 'Maori Epistemologies', in Overing, Joanna (ed.), *Reason and Morality*. London: Tavistock Publications.
SAMKARACHARYA. 1932. *Vivēkacudāmaṇi* (tr. in Hindi by Munnilal). Gorakhpur: Gita Press.
SANGARI, KUMKUM and SUDESH VAID. 1989. *Recasting Women: Essays in Colonial History*. New Delhi: Kali for Women.
SAPTARSHI, KUMAR. 1988. 'Orthodoxy and Human Rights: The Story of a Clash', in Zelliot, Eleanor and Maxine Berntsen (eds), *The Experience of Hinduism: Essays on Religion in Maharashtra*. Albany: State University of New York Press.
SARAN, A.K. 1962. 'A Review of *Contributions to Indian Sociology*, No. IV', *Eastern Anthropologist*, 15: 25–31.
———. 1963. 'Hinduism and Economic Development in India', *Achives de sociologie des religions*, 15: 87–94.
———. 1989. 'Gandhian Concept of Politics: Toward a Normal Society', *Gandhi Marg.*, 1: 675–727.
SARAVGI, ALKA. 1994. '*Apni beti ke liye* [For my daughter]', in Kishore, Raj (ed.), *Place for Woman*. New Delhi: Vani Prakashan.
SATPRAKASHANANDA, SWAMI. 1965. *Methods of Knowledge*. London: George Allen and Unwin.
SCARRY, ELAINE. 1985. *The Body in Pain*. New York: Oxford University Press.
SCHEPER–HUGHES, NANCY. 1992. *Death Without Weeping: The Violence of Everyday Life in Brazil*. Berkeley: University of California.
———. 1995. 'The End of Anthropology: Clifford Geertz Reflects on a Much Reduced Science', The *New York Times* Book Review, May 7: 22–23.
SCHREMPP, GREGORY. 1989. 'Aristotle's Other Self: On the Boundless Subject of Anthropological Discourse', in Stocking, George W. Jr. (ed.), *Romantic Motives: Essays on Anthropological Sensibility*. Madison: University of Wisconsin Press.
SCOTT, JAMES C. 1990. *Domination and the Arts of Resistance: Hidden Transcripts*. New Haven: Yale University Press.

References ⊳ 273

SHAHABUDDIN, SYED. 1993. 'Massive Disenfranchisement of Muslims', *Muslim India.* 127 (July): 290–92.
———. 1996. 'Letter to BJP Leader A.B. Vajpayee', *Muslim India.* 163: 297.
SHUKLA, PRAYAG. 1994. '*Rasta idhar se hai* [Path is This Way]'. in Kishore, Raj (ed.), *Place for Women.* New Delhi: Vani Prakashan.
SHYAM SUNDER, B. 1987. *They Burn: The 160,000,000 Untouchables of India.* Bangalore: Dalit Sahitya Akademy.
SINGER, MILTON. 1972. *When a Great Tradition Modernizes: An Anthropological Approach to Indian Civilization.* New York: Praeger.
———. 1984. *Man's Glassy Essence: Explorations in Semiotic Anthropology.* Bloomington: Indiana University Press.
SINGH, PARIYAR LALAYI. 1966. *Vir Sant Maya Balidan* [The sacrifice of valiant Saint Maya] (in Hindi). Jhinjhak, Kanpur: Lalayi Singh Charitable Trust.
———. 1983. 'Publisher's Preface', in *Dharma kya hai?* [What is moral order?] (in Hindi). Jhinjhak, Kanpur: Lalayi Singh Charitable Trust.
SINGH, RAJENDRA. 1992. 'Steps Away from an Indian Ethnosociology: A Reply to Marriott', *Contributions to Indian Sociology,* n.s., 26: 143–49.
SINGH, YOGENDRA. 1983. *Image of Man: Ideology and Theory in Indian Sociology.* Delhi: Chanakya Publications.
———. 1986. *Indian Sociology.* New Delhi: Vistaar Publications.
SMITH, BARBARA H. 1988. *Contingencies of Value: Alternative Perspectives for Critical Theory.* Cambridge: Harvard University Press.
SPENCER, JONATHAN. 1990. 'Writing Within: Anthropology, Nationalism and Culture in Sri Lanka', *Current Anthropology,* 31: 283–91.
———. 1992. 'Problems in the Analysis of Communal Violence', *Contributions to Indian Sociology,* n.s., 26: 261–79.
SPIVAK, GAYATRI CHAKARVORTY. 1988. *In Other Worlds: Essays in Cultural Politics.* New York: Routledge.
SRINIVAS, M.N. 1952. *Religion and Society among the Coorgs of South India.* Oxford: Clarendon Press.
———. 1964. *Social Change in Modern India.* Berkeley: University of California Press.
——— (ed.). 1966. *Caste: Its Twentieth Century Avatar.* New Delhi: Penguin Books.
———. 1975. 'The Indian Village: Myth and Reality', in Beattie, J.H.M. and R.G. Lienhardt (eds), *Studies in Social Anthropology.* Oxford: Clarendon Press.
———. 1976. *The Remembered Village.* Berkeley: University of California Press.
———. 1996. *Indian Society, through Personal Writings.* Delhi: Oxford University Press.
SRINIVAS, M.N. and PANINI, M.N. 1973. 'The Development of Sociology and Social Anthropology in India', *Sociological Bulletin,* 22: 179–215.
SRIVASTAVA, RAHUL. 1995. 'Anthropology as Cultural Criticism' (Review of Veena Das 1995), *Economic and Political Weekly,* 312–14.
STAAL, FRITS. 1988. *Universals: Studies in Indian Logic and Linguistics.* Chicago: University of Chicago Press.
STRATHERN, MARILYN. 1990. 'Out of Context: The Persuasive Fictions of Anthropology' (with Comments by I.C. Jarvie, Stephen A. Tyler, and George E. Marcus),

in Manganaro, Marc (ed.), *Modernist Anthropology*. Princeton: Princeton University Press.

SUMITA. 1994. '*Sambandhon ka naya vyakāraṇ*' [New Grammar of Relationships], in Kishore, Raj (ed.), *Place for Women*. New Delhi: Vani Prakashan.

TALWAR, VIR BHARAT. 1989. 'Feminist Consciousness in Women's Journals in Hindi: 1910–1920', in Sangari, K. and S. Vaid (eds), *Recasting Women: Essays in Colonial History*. New Delhi: Kali for Women.

TAMBIAH, STANLEY J. 1986. *Sri Lanka: Ethnic Fratricide and the Dismantling of Democracy*. Chicago: University of Chicago Press.

———. 1996. *Leveling Crowds: Ethno-Nationalist Conflicts and Collective Violence in South Asia*. Princeton: Princeton University Press.

TAYLOR, MARK. 1989. 'Paralectics. Symposium on Hermeneutics of the Other'. Charlottesville: Committee on Individual and Society, University of Virginia.

THAPAN, MEENAKSHI. 1988. '*Contributions* and the "Sociology of India"', *Contributions to Indian Sociology*, n.s., 22: 259–72.

The Pioneer, Lucknow (India). 1995. 'Mahasabha Plans Stir against "Manuvaad"', July 17: 1, 4.

TARKUNDE, V.M. 1993. 'Speech of the Month', *Muslim India*, 127 (July): 312–13.

TRAUTMANN, THOMAS R. 1980. 'Review of Marriage and Rank in Bengali Culture by Ronald B. Inden', *Journal of Asian Studies*, 39: 519–24.

TRAWICK, MARGARET. 1986. *Truth Tales: Contemporary Writing by Indian Women*. New Delhi: Kali for Women.

———. 1988. 'Spirits and Voices in Tamil Songs', *American Ethnologist*, 15: 193–215.

———. 1990. *Notes on Love in a Tamil Family*. Berkeley: University of California Press.

TULLY, MARK. 1991. *No Full Stops in India*. New Delhi: Penguin Books India.

TYLER, STEPHEN. 1986. 'Post-Modern Ethnography: From Document of the Occult to Occult Document', in Clifford, James and George Marcus (eds), *Writing Culture*. Berkeley: University of California Press.

UBEROI, J.P.S. 1968. 'Science and Swaraj', *Contributions to Indian Sociology*, n.s., 2: 119–23.

———. 1978. *Science and Culture*. Delhi: Oxford University Press.

———. 1984. *The Other Mind of Europe: Goethe as Scientist*. Delhi: Oxford University Press.

VAJPAI, PURNIMA. 1994. '*70 se '94 tak*' [From '70 to '94] in Kishore, Raj (ed.), *Place for Women*. New Delhi: Vani Prakashan.

VENUGOPAL, C.N. 1986. 'G.S. Ghurye's Ideology of Normative Hinduism: An Appraisal', *Contributions to Indian Sociology*, n.s., 20: 305–14.

VISWANATHAN, GAURI. 1989. *Masks of Conquest: Literary Study and British Rule in India*. New York: Columbia University Press.

WALZER, MICHAEL. 1984. *Spheres of Justice: A Defence of Pluralism and Equality*. New York: Basic Books.

———. 1994. *Thick and Thin: Moral Argument at Home and Abroad*. Notre Dame: University of Notre Dame Press.

Webster's Ninth New Collegiate Dictionary. 1985. Springfield: Merriam–Webster.

WEINER, ANNETTE B. 1995. 'Culture and Our Discontents', *American Anthropologist*, 97: 14–20.

WHITE, HAYDEN. 1973. *Metahistory: The Historical Imagination in Nineteenth-Century Europe.* Baltimore: Johns Hopkins University.
———. 1978. *Tropics of Discourse: Essays in Cultural Criticism.* Baltimore: Johns Hopkins University Press.
WHITTEN, NORMAN E., JR. 1988. 'Toward a Critical Anthropology', *American Ethnologist,* 15: 732–42.
WISDOM, JOHN. 1956. *Other Minds.* Oxford: Oxford University Press.
WRIGHT, R.M. 1988. 'Anthropological Presuppositions of Indigenous Advocacy', *Annual Reviews in Anthropology,* 17: 365–90.
ZELLIOT, ELEANOR. 1996. *From Untouchable to Dalit: Essays on the Ambedkar Movement* (Second Revised Edition). New Delhi: Manohar.
ZELLIOT, ELEANOR and MAXINE BERNTSEN (eds). 1988. *The Experience of Hinduism: Essays on Religion in Maharashtra.* Albany, N.Y.: State University Press of New York.
ZIMMERMANN, FRANCIS. 1987. *The Jungle and the Aroma of Meats: An Ecological Theme in Hindu Medicine.* Berkeley: University of California Press.

About the Author

R.S. Khare, a renowned scholar, is Professor of Anthropology at the University of Virginia, USA, and was recently a Fellow of the Wissenschaftskolleg zu Berlin (1996–97). Professor Khare is the author of numerous publications on India, including *The Changing Brahmans*, *The Hindu Hearth and Home*, and *The Untouchable as Himself*.

Index

Social Structure and Change
edited by
A.M. Shah ■ B.S. Baviskar ■ E.A. Ramaswamy

Volume 1: Theory and Method: An Evaluation of the Work of M.N. Srinivas

Srinivas' diversified angles of vision have been appreciated here with a deep sense of gratitude...but, at the same time, the present status of his findings and analysis have been critically evaluated without any sort of bias.

Man in India

Contributors: J.A. Barnes/I.P. Desai/J.V. Ferreira/M.S. Gore/P.C. Joshi/R.S. Khare/ T.N. Madan/A.M. Shah/Milton Singer
220 mm x 140 mm/1996/234pp/hb/pb

Volume 2: Women in Indian Society

An empirical study which provides rich material both for policy-framers in the government and social reformers outside, to facilitate their task of devising an appropriate strategy for the upliftment of women in Indian society.

The Tribune

Contributors: Karuna Chanana/Neera Desai/T. Scarlett Epstein/Aneeta A. Minocha/ Joan P. Mencher/Uma Ramaswamy/L.S. Vishwanath
220 mm x 140 mm/1996/214pp/hb/pb

Volume 3: Complex Organizations and Urban Communities

A very comprehensive account of the social undercurrents of India's urban–industrial centres and their impact.

Business Standard

Contributors: F.G. Bailey/A.P. Barnabas/Y.B. Damle/Victor D'Souza/Rajesh Gill/ Khadija Gupta/William H. Newell/M.N. Panini/E.A. Ramaswamy/N.R. Sheth/Harshad R. Trivedi
220 mm x 140 mm/1996/286pp/hb/pb

Volume 4: Development and Ethnicity

This volume has to be treated as an additional contribution to South Asian sociology. Each essay in it is the brain child of great social scientists.

The Hindu

Contributors: G.S. Arora/B.S. Baviskar/S.C. Dube/Pauline Kolenda/David G. Mandelbaum/T.K. Oommen/B.K. Roy Burman/Sachchidananda/V. Selvaratnam/ Chitra Sivakumar/S.S. Sivakumar
220 mm x 140 mm/1997/261pp/hb/pb

Volume 5: Religion and Kinship

Contributors: Veena Das/Mary Douglas/Leela Dube/K.D. Gangrade/Paul Hockings/ Raja Jayaraman/W.D. Merchant/Emrys L. Peters/J.P.S. Uberoi
220mm x 140mm/1998/220pp/hb/pb   Forthcoming